W9-BFK-025

taste of home MOST requested RECIPES

p. 199

350+ RECIPES READERS LOVE MOST!

At Taste of Home, we're proud to be the connection to personal recipes that bring family and friends together. You see, inspired cooks just like you send us their best-loved creations—the must-have dishes folks request time and again. This friendly exchange of favorite recipes, time-honored traditions, clever kitchen secrets and heartwarming personal stories is what the Taste of Home experience is all about.

With all this sharing going on, it seemed only natural to offer our readers a one-stop-shop for all of those tried-and-true, can't-live-without recipes. So we sifted through countless letters and online comments posted on TasteofHome.com to collect these treasured standbys, and we featured them in a brand-new annual cookbook, *Most Requested Recipes 2013.*

Now you, too, can enjoy a delicious sampling of these all-time favorites. Inside you'll find over 350 top-rated recipes our readers have proclaimed the best of the best—the Taste of Home dishes they tried and couldn't get enough of! Find delectable fare ranging from munchable appetizers and hearty main entrees to sensational sides, salads and sandwiches. We have also included our most popular breakfast delights to start the day off right, and showstopping desserts that put an extra special touch on any meal.

You will also find unique chapters such as Editors' Favorites that showcase the recipes readers wrote about or requested most often, as well as a few cherished selections taken directly from our editors' personal recipe boxes. Seasonal Specialties features the perfect foods for festive celebrations of all kinds. And our Casseroles & One-Pot Wonders section offers a lineup of fuss-free, meal-in-one favorites.

What sets these gems apart from the rest? Each item in this collection is shared from the recipe files of real family cooks just like you. So you can trust they're easy to prepare and made with the right combination of wholesome ingredients and affordable, everyday items. They also feature handy kitchen tips, easy-to-follow instructions, convenient prep/cook times and helpful Reader Rave comments from TasteofHome.com community members.

It's never been easier to set a hearty meal on the table that will have everyone's taste buds reeling. With this collection of cream-of-the-crop specialties at your fingertips, *Most Requested Recipes* is sure to become the most-used cookbook in your kitchen for years to come!

taste of home MOST requested RECIPES

EDITORIAL

Editor-in-Chief	Catherine Cassidy
Executive Editor/Print & Digital Books	Stephen C. George
Creative Director	Howard Greenberg
Editorial Services Manager	Kerri Balliet
Senior Editor/Print & Digital Books	Mark Hagen
Editors	Amy Glander, Krista Lanphier
Associate Creative Director	Edwin Robles Jr.
Art Director	Raeann Sundholm
Content Production Manager	Julie Wagner
Layout Designer	Nancy Novak
Copy Chief	Deb Warlaumont Mulvey
Copy Editor	Mary C. Hanson
Recipe Editor	Mary King
Recipe Content Manager	Colleen King
Assistant Photo Coordinator	Mary Ann Koebernik
Recipe Testing	Taste of Home Test Kitchen
Food Photography	Taste of Home Photo Studio
Editorial Assistant	Marilyn Iczkowski

BUSINESS

Vice President, Publisher	Jan Studin, jan_studin@rd.com
Regional Account Director	Donna Lindskog, donna_lindskog@rd.com
Eastern Account Director	Joanne Carrara
Eastern Account Manager	Kari Nestor
Account Manager	Gina Minerbi
Midwest & Western Account Director	Jackie Fallon
Midwest Account Manager	Lorna Phillips
Michigan Sales Representative	Linda C. Donaldson
Southwestern Account Representative	Summer Nilsson
Corporate Integrated Sales Director, N.A.	Steve Sottile
Associate Marketing Director, Integrated Solutions	Katie Gaon Wilson
Digital Sales Planner	Tim Baarda
General Manager, Taste of Home Cooking Schools	Erin Puariea
Direct Response Advertising	Katherine Zito, David Geller Associates
Vice President, Creative Director	Paul Livornese
Executive Director, Brand Marketing	Leah West
Senior Marketing Manager	Vanessa Bailey
Associate Marketing Manager	Betsy Connors
Vice President, Magazine Marketing	Dave Fiegel

READER'S DIGEST NORTH AMERICA

Vice President, Business Development	Jonathan Bigham
President, Books and Home Entertaining	Harold Clarke
Chief Financial Officer	Howard Halligan
Vice President, General Manager, Reader's Digest Media	Marilynn Jacobs
Chief Content Officer, Milwaukee	Mark Jannot
Chief Marketing Officer	Renee Jordan
Vice President, Chief Sales Officer	Mark Josephson
General Manager, Milwaukee	Frank Quigley
Vice President, Chief Content Officer	Liz Vaccariello

THE READER'S DIGEST ASSOCIATION, INC.

President and Chief Executive Officer	Robert E. Guth

©2012 Reiman Media Group, LLC
5400 S. 60th St., Greendale WI 53129

International Standard Book Number (13): 978-1-61765-109-0

International Standard Serial Number: 2166-0522

All rights reserved.

Taste of Home is a registered trademark of The Reader's Digest Association, Inc.

Printed in U.S.A.

1 3 5 7 9 10 8 6 4 2

Cover Photography: Taste of Home Photo Studio
Pictured on the front cover: Chili Mac Casserole (p. 118); Strawberry Romaine Salad (p. 77); Hungarian Nut Rolls (p. 136); Roasted Turkey a L'Orange (p. 92)

Pictured on the back cover: Sweet & Spicy Jalapeno Poppers (p. 9); Marshmallow-Almond Key Lime Pie (p. 186)

TABLE OF CONTENTS

37

95

214

COCONUT BERRY PIZZA, PAGE 19

12

11

8

APPETIZERS, SNACKS & BEVERAGES

Whether you're creating a mouthwatering holiday buffet, need an extra-special finger food for the big game-day party or simply want something sweet to sip on a lazy afternoon, you'll be happy you started here! Turn the page for the best in hot bites, meal starters, dips and spreads, munchies and snacks, refreshing beverages and more. Shared by other family cooks, these recipes are quick, versatile and guaranteed to be the hit of your party!

MEXICAN CORN DIP

For a tasty dip you can make in advance, try this chunky hot blend. It's mildly spicy but easy to alter if you want more or less kick. Make sure your tortilla chips are large enough to scoop up hearty helpings!

—Laura Cameron *Delaware, Ohio*

PREP: 15 MIN. + CHILLING

2	cups (8 ounces) shredded cheddar cheese
1	can (11 ounces) yellow and white whole kernel corn, drained
1	can (11 ounces) Mexicorn, drained
4	ounces pepper jack cheese, shredded
¼	cup chopped green onions
1	can (4 ounces) chopped green chilies
1	jalapeno pepper, seeded and chopped
¾	cup mayonnaise
¾	cup sour cream
⅛	teaspoon sugar

Additional chopped green onions, optional

Tortilla *or* corn chips

◉ In a large bowl, combine the first seven ingredients. In a small bowl, combine the mayonnaise, sour cream and sugar; stir into corn mixture. Cover and refrigerate overnight. Sprinkle with additional green onions. Serve with chips.

EDITOR'S NOTE: Wear disposable gloves when cutting hot peppers; the oils can burn skin. Avoid touching your face.

Yield: 8-10 servings.

> ❝Delicious! At every party I've brought this to, people have raved about it. It is easy to make, and my whole family loves it.❞

—SISSABOO FROM TASTEOFHOME.COM

BAKED POTATO SKINS

Be sure to make enough of these loaded spuds because they will absolutely disappear! You can use any leftover potato pulp to make a batch of mashed potatoes the next night.

—Terry Hill *Hairy Hill, Alberta*

PREP: 10 MIN. **BAKE:** 70 MIN. + COOLING

8	large baking potatoes
½	cup butter, melted
½	teaspoon salt
½	teaspoon paprika
½	cup finely chopped green onions
½	cup crumbled cooked bacon
½	cup chopped cooked shrimp *or* fully cooked ham, optional
½	cup chopped green peppers
1	cup (4 ounces) shredded cheddar cheese
1	cup (8 ounces) sour cream

◉ Bake potatoes at 400° for 1 hour or until tender. Cool slightly; cut in half lengthwise and scoop out pulp, leaving a ¼-in. shell. (Save removed potato pulp for another use.)

◉ Cut skins into strips or halves; brush skin sides with butter and place on a baking sheet. Sprinkle pulp sides with salt and paprika; top each with the green onions, bacon, ham or shrimp, chopped peppers and cheese.

◉ Bake at 450° for 10-15 minutes or until cheese is melted and skins are crisp. Serve with sour cream.

Yield: 6-10 servings.

HAM & CHEESE SANDWICH LOAF

This grilled, stacked wonder is one big bite of superior sandwichery. Crusty bread is filled with melted cheese, crisp veggies and tender ham. I guarantee this will be a favorite!
—**Pat Stevens** *Granbury, Texas*

PREP: 35 MIN. **BAKE:** 30 MIN.

- 1 loaf sourdough bread (1 pound)
- 1 cup sliced fresh mushrooms
- 1 medium green pepper, cut into strips
- 1 medium sweet red pepper, cut into strips
- 1 celery rib, sliced
- 3 green onions, sliced
- 2 tablespoons olive oil
- ½ cup mayonnaise
- 2 teaspoons Italian seasoning
- ½ teaspoon pepper
- 1 pound shaved deli ham
- 1 cup (4 ounces) shredded Colby cheese
- ½ cup shredded part-skim mozzarella cheese

○ Cut bread in half horizontally. Hollow out top and bottom halves, leaving ½-in. shells. (Discard removed bread or save for another use.)

○ In a large skillet, saute the mushrooms, peppers, celery and onions in oil until tender. Remove from the heat; set aside.

○ Combine the mayonnaise, Italian seasoning and pepper; spread over bread. On the bread bottom, layer half of the ham, vegetable mixture and cheeses. Repeat layers, gently pressing down if needed. Replace bread top.

○ Wrap tightly in heavy-duty foil. Bake at 400° or grill, covered, over medium heat for 30-35 minutes or until heated through. Cut into wedges with a serrated knife.

Yield: 8 servings.

BAKED CRAB DIP

Busy party givers will love the convenience of my bread bowl filled with a melty warm crab dip. It may look fancy, but I promise it's so easy to make! You can fill the bread ahead of time and let it chill until serving. Then, just remove from the fridge 30 minutes before baking.
—**Marie Shelley** *Exeter, Missouri*

PREP: 15 MIN. **BAKE:** 45 MIN.

- 1 package (8 ounces) cream cheese, softened
- 2 cups (16 ounces) sour cream
- 2 cans (6 ounces *each*) crabmeat, drained, flaked and cartilage removed *or* 2 cups flaked imitation crabmeat
- 2 cups (8 ounces) shredded cheddar cheese
- 4 green onions, thinly sliced
- 2 round loaves (1 pound *each*) unsliced sourdough *or* Italian bread

Additional sliced green onions, optional

Assorted crackers

○ In a bowl, beat cream cheese until smooth. Add sour cream; mix well. Fold in crab, cheese and onions. Cut the top third off each loaf of bread; carefully hollow out bottoms, leaving 1-in. shells. Cube removed bread and tops; set aside. Spoon crab mixture into bread bowls. Place on baking sheets. Place reserved bread cubes in a single layer around bread bowls.

○ Bake, uncovered, at 350° for 45-50 minutes or until the dip is heated through. Garnish with green onions if desired. Serve with toasted bread cubes and crackers.

Yield: 5 cups.

KITCHEN TIP

Bread-bowl dips are great for potlucks. To warm the filled bowl, put it in a floured oven cooking bag, seal and place in the oven. After baking, you can easily transport it in the bag, and it will still be warm upon arrival.

ROUND LOAF: RDA-GID

GARLIC CHEESE SPREAD

Here's a cheese spread that will please a hungry crowd with its bold flavor. It tastes great on flatbread, focaccia or crackers.
—**Taste of Home Test Kitchen** *Greendale, Wisconsin*

PREP: 10 MIN. + CHILLING

- 1 package (8 ounces) cream cheese, softened
- 1 tablespoon olive oil
- 3 tablespoons grated Parmesan cheese
- 2 tablespoons minced green onion
- 1 garlic clove, minced
- ¼ teaspoon pepper

Flatbread, focaccia bread *or* assorted crackers

● In a small bowl, beat the cream cheese and oil until fluffy. Add the Parmesan cheese, onion, garlic and pepper; beat mixture until well blended.

● Spoon into a small container. Cover and refrigerate for at least 1 hour. Serve with flatbread, focaccia or crackers. Store spread in the refrigerator.

Yield: 1 cup.

KITCHEN TIP

Store olive oil in a tightly capped bottle at room temperature or in the refrigerator for up to one year. When chilled, the oil turns cloudy and thick. Chilled olive oil will return to its original consistency when left at room temperature for a short time. Virgin olive oil is a good all-purpose oil, especially if you plan to keep only one type of olive oil on hand.

PARTY NACHOS

Put a new spin on nachos with tantalizing barbecued pork! Simple to make, this heaping stack of goodness makes ideal poker-night or game-day food. Consider a build-your-own nacho bar so guests can choose their toppings.
—**Mike Tchou** *Pepper Pike, Ohio*

PREP/TOTAL TIME: 20 MIN.

QUICK & EASY

- 1 carton (18 ounces) refrigerated fully cooked barbecued shredded pork
- 1 package (12½ ounces) nacho tortilla chips
- 2 cups (8 ounces) shredded Mexican cheese blend
- ½ cup sour cream
- ½ cup salsa
- ½ cup shredded lettuce
- ¼ cup thinly sliced green onions
- ¼ cup sliced ripe olives, optional
- ¼ cup pickled pepper rings, optional

● Heat pork according to the package directions. Place tortilla chips on a large microwave-safe serving plate. Layer with pork and cheese.

● Microwave, uncovered, on high for 1-2 minutes or until cheese is melted. Top with sour cream, salsa, lettuce and onions. Sprinkle with olives and pepper rings if desired.

EDITOR'S NOTE: This recipe was tested in a 1,100-watt microwave.

Yield: 12 servings.

OLIVE OIL: BRAND X PICTURES/PUNCHSTOCK

SOUTHWEST PRETZELS

Have you ever walked by one of those pretzel stands at the mall and come home with a sudden, serious hankering? Go ahead and satisfy your deepest craving with these soft bites that feature a mild Southwestern kick.
—**Cathy Tang** *Redmond, Washington*

PREP: 30 MIN. + STANDING **BAKE:** 25 MIN.

```
  4   cups all-purpose flour
  1   tablespoon sugar
  1   package (¼ ounce) quick-rise yeast
1½   teaspoons salt
  1   teaspoon dried minced onion
  ½   teaspoon chili powder
  ¼   teaspoon ground cumin
  ¼   teaspoon cayenne pepper
1½   cups warm water (120° to 130°)
  1   egg, lightly beaten
```
Coarse salt

Salsa con queso dip

◉ In a large bowl, combine 2 cups flour, sugar, yeast, salt, minced onion and spices. Add water. Beat just until moistened. Stir in enough remaining flour to form a soft dough.

◉ Turn onto a floured surface; knead until smooth and elastic, about 4-6 minutes. Cover and let rest for 10 minutes. Divide dough into 16 equal portions; roll each into a 15-in. rope and taper the ends. Cover and let rest 10 minutes longer.

◉ Shape each rope into a circle with about 2 in. of each end overlapping. Twist the ends where they overlap. Flip the twisted ends over the circle; place ends over the edge and pinch under.

◉ Place on greased baking sheets; brush with egg. Bake at 350° for 15 minutes. Brush again with egg; sprinkle with coarse salt. Bake 10-13 minutes longer or until golden brown. Remove to wire racks. Serve pretzels warm with dip.

Yield: 16 pretzels.

SWEET & SPICY JALAPENO POPPERS

Let's face it—bacon just makes everything better! And there's no faster way to get your party started than with these hot poppers that feature a perfect balance of flavors. To keep prep simple, make them in advance and bake just before serving.
—**Dawn Onuffer** *Crestview, Florida*

QUICK & EASY

PREP/TOTAL TIME: 30 MIN.

```
  6   jalapeno peppers
  4   ounces cream cheese, softened
  2   tablespoons shredded cheddar cheese
  6   bacon strips, halved widthwise
  ¼   cup packed brown sugar
  1   tablespoon chili seasoning
```

◉ Cut jalapenos in half lengthwise and remove seeds; set aside. In a small bowl, beat cheeses until blended. Spoon into pepper halves. Wrap a half-strip of bacon around each pepper half.

◉ Combine brown sugar and chili seasoning; coat peppers with sugar mixture. Place in a greased 15-in. x 10-in. x 1-in. baking pan.

◉ Bake at 350° for 18-20 minutes or until bacon is firm.

EDITOR'S NOTE: Wear disposable gloves when cutting hot peppers; the oils can burn skin. Avoid touching your face.

Yield: 1 dozen.

BEEF-STUFFED CRESCENTS

Easy-to-make, easy-to-take. That's the best way to describe my scrumptious hand-held bundles. Everybody loves 'em!
—**Jennifer Bumgarner** *Topeka, Kansas*

PREP: 25 MIN. **BAKE:** 15 MIN.

- 1 pound lean ground beef (90% lean)
- 1 can (4 ounces) chopped green chilies
- 1 package (8 ounces) cream cheese, cubed
- ¼ teaspoon ground cumin
- ¼ teaspoon chili powder
- 3 tubes (8 ounces *each*) refrigerated crescent rolls

● In a large skillet, cook beef and chilies over medium heat until meat is no longer pink; drain. Add the cream cheese, cumin and chili powder. Cool slightly.

● Separate crescent dough into 24 triangles. Place 1 tablespoon of beef mixture along the short end of each triangle; carefully roll up.

● Place point side down 2 in. apart on ungreased baking sheets. Bake at 375° for 11-14 minutes or until golden brown. Serve crescents warm.

Yield: 2 dozen.

CRANBERRY FIZZ

With just five basic ingredients, this tart and tangy party punch couldn't be much easier to stir together—or more refreshing!
—**Suzette Jury** *Keene, California*

PREP: 5 MIN. + CHILLING

QUICK & EASY

- 1 bottle (32 ounces) cranberry juice
- 1 cup orange juice

- 1 cup ruby red grapefruit juice
- ½ cup sugar
- 2 cups ginger ale, chilled

● In a pitcher, combine the cranberry, orange, grapefruit juices and sugar. Refrigerate until chilled. Just before serving, stir in the ginger ale.

Yield: 2 quarts.

CHEESE MEATBALLS

I often rely on these rich, cheesy meatballs for party appetizers, but sometimes on busy weeknights, I also serve them alongside a tossed salad and rolls for a quick family meal in minutes.
—**Rachel Frost** *Tallula, Illinois*

PREP: 20 MIN. **BAKE:** 15 MIN.

- 3 cups (12 ounces) finely shredded cheddar cheese
- 1 cup biscuit/baking mix
- ½ teaspoon salt
- ¼ teaspoon pepper
- ¼ teaspoon garlic powder
- 1 pound lean ground beef (90% lean)

● In a large bowl, combine the first five ingredients. Crumble beef over mixture and mix well. Shape into 1-in. balls. Place meatballs on a greased rack in a shallow baking pan.

● Bake at 400° for 12-15 minutes or until the meat is no longer pink; drain.

Yield: about 4 dozen.

SWEET 'N' TANGY CHICKEN WINGS

Smothered in a tongue-tingling sauce, these fall-off-the-bone wings slow cook to utterly messy, lick-your-lips perfection! If you like, temper the heat with a little cool bleu cheese salad dressing.
—*Ida Tuey* *South Lyon, Michigan*

PREP: 20 MIN. **COOK:** 3¼ HOURS

3 pounds chicken wingettes (about 30)	2 tablespoons Worcestershire sauce
½ teaspoon salt, *divided*	1 tablespoon Dijon mustard
Dash pepper	1 teaspoon minced garlic
1½ cups ketchup	1 teaspoon Liquid Smoke, optional
¼ cup packed brown sugar	Sesame seeds, optional
¼ cup red wine vinegar	

● Sprinkle chicken wings with a dash of salt and pepper. Broil 4-6 in. from the heat for 5-10 minutes on each side or until golden brown. Transfer to a greased 5-qt. slow cooker.

● Combine the ketchup, brown sugar, vinegar, Worcestershire sauce, mustard, garlic, Liquid Smoke if desired and remaining salt; pour over wings. Toss to coat.

● Cover and cook on low for 3¼ to 3¾ hours or until chicken juices run clear. Sprinkle wings with sesame seeds if desired.

Yield: about 2½ dozen.

GORGONZOLA & CRANBERRY CHEESE BALL

A cheese ball is a classic appetizer to take to any gathering. Studded with tangy dried cranberries, this one is as wonderful to eat as it is beautiful to serve!
—**Kathy Hahn** *Pollock Pines, California*

PREP: 15 MIN. + CHILLING

- 1 package (8 ounces) cream cheese, softened
- 1 cup (4 ounces) crumbled Gorgonzola cheese
- 1 cup dried cranberries
- 2 tablespoons *each* finely chopped onion, celery, green pepper and sweet red pepper
- ¼ teaspoon hot pepper sauce
- ¾ cup chopped pecans

Assorted crackers

- In a small bowl, combine cheeses. Stir in the cranberries, vegetables and pepper sauce. Shape into a ball; wrap in plastic wrap. Refrigerate for 1 hour or until firm. Roll cheese ball in pecans. Serve with crackers.

Yield: 2 cups.

KITCHEN TIP

It's easy to shape a round cheese ball without creating a mess. Keep your hands and the countertop clean by spooning the cheese mixture onto a piece of plastic wrap. Working from the underside of the wrap, pat the mixture into a ball. Complete recipe as directed.

CHAI TEA LATTE

My family loves to sip this comforting spiced tea instead of cocoa on cold nights. I simplified the original recipe by using the filter basket of my coffeepot.
—**Julie Plummer** *Sykesville, Maryland*

PREP/TOTAL TIME: 15 MIN.

QUICK & EASY

- 2 individual tea bags
- 1 teaspoon ground cinnamon
- ½ teaspoon ground ginger
- ¼ teaspoon ground allspice
- 1 cup water
- 1 cup milk
- ¼ cup packed brown sugar
- 2 tablespoons refrigerated French vanilla nondairy creamer

Whipped topping and ground nutmeg, optional

- Place the tea bags, cinnamon, ginger and allspice in the coffee filter of a drip coffeemaker. Add water; brew according to manufacturer's directions.

- Meanwhile, in a small saucepan, combine the milk, brown sugar and creamer. Cook and stir over medium heat until heated through and sugar is dissolved. Pour milk mixture into mugs; stir in tea. Dollop with whipped topping and sprinkle with nutmeg if desired.

Yield: 2 servings.

PLASTIC WRAP: RDA-GID

CHEDDAR-VEGGIE APPETIZER TORTE

Set this quiche-like torte oozing with cheese on the buffet table and just watch your guests gather around! The wedges are easy to eat as finger food, and it's delicious served hot or cold.
—**Barbara Estabrook** *Rhinelander, Wisconsin*

PREP: 25 MIN. **BAKE:** 30 MIN. + COOLING

1⅓ cups finely crushed multigrain crackers	¼ cup finely chopped sweet red pepper
¼ cup butter, melted	1 tablespoon olive oil
2 cups (8 ounces) shredded sharp cheddar cheese	1 carton (8 ounces) spreadable garlic and herb cream cheese
1 small zucchini, finely chopped	4 eggs, lightly beaten
5 small fresh mushrooms, sliced	2 tablespoons crumbled cooked bacon
⅓ cup finely chopped red onion	2 tablespoons grated Parmesan cheese

◉ In a small bowl, combine cracker crumbs and butter. Press onto the bottom of a greased 9-in. springform pan. Sprinkle with cheddar cheese. In a large skillet, saute the zucchini, mushrooms, onion and red pepper in oil until tender. Spoon over cheese.

◉ In a large bowl, beat cream cheese until smooth. Add eggs; beat on low speed just until combined. Stir in bacon. Pour over vegetable mixture. Sprinkle with Parmesan cheese.

◉ Place pan on a baking sheet. Bake at 375° for 30-35 minutes or until center is almost set. Cool on a wire rack for 10 minutes. Carefully run a knife around edge of pan to loosen; remove sides of pan. Serve warm or chilled. Refrigerate leftovers.

Yield: 16 servings.

HOMEMADE LEMONADE

Who doesn't love chilled lemonade on a hot, sticky day? Made with club soda, my homemade version is sparkling and bursting with a delicious sweet-tart citrus flavor.
—**Rebecca Baird** *Salt Lake City, Utah*

PREP: 15 MIN. + CHILLING

QUICK & EASY

> ¾ cup sugar
> ½ cup water
> ¼ cup lemon peel strips (about 1½ lemons)
> ¾ cup lemon juice (about 3 lemons)
> 1 cup club soda, chilled

◦ In a small saucepan, heat sugar and water over medium heat until sugar is dissolved, stirring frequently. Stir in lemon strips. Bring to a boil. Reduce heat; simmer, uncovered, for 5 minutes. Cool slightly.

◦ Transfer to a pitcher. Stir in lemon juice; cover and refrigerate until chilled. Discard lemon strips. Stir in club soda. Serve over ice.

Yield: 2½ cups.

"My friends and I loved this! I have to make a huge batch though because two servings isn't enough!"

—JULES.I.M FROM TASTEOF HOME.COM

LUSCIOUS LEMON FRUIT DIP

This creamy dip is a sweet change of pace from the usual savory dips. It was one of the treats served at my bridal shower, and it received such raves that I asked for the recipe. Now I'm proud to bring it to showers and other gatherings I attend.
—**Deb Ceman** *Wauwatosa, Wisconsin*

PREP/TOTAL TIME: 20 MIN.

QUICK & EASY

> 2 cups sugar
> ⅔ cup cornstarch
> 1 cup cold water
> 4 eggs, lightly beaten
> ⅔ cup lemon juice
> 2 teaspoons vanilla extract
> 2 cups heavy whipping cream, whipped

Assorted fresh fruit

◦ In a large heavy saucepan, combine the sugar and cornstarch. Gradually whisk in water until smooth. Cook and stir over medium-high heat until thickened and bubbly. Reduce heat; cook and stir 2 minutes longer. Remove from the heat.

◦ Stir a small amount of hot mixture into eggs; return all to the pan, stirring constantly. Bring to a gentle boil; cook and stir 2 minutes longer. Remove from the heat. Gently stir in lemon juice and vanilla.

◦ Transfer to a large bowl. Cool to room temperature without stirring. Cover surface of mixture with waxed paper; refrigerate until cooled. Fold in whipped cream. Serve with fresh fruit.

Yield: 5 cups.

MAKEOVER NUTTY MONKEY MALTS

Everyone will go bananas for this classic diner milkshake. With only a fraction of the fat and calories loaded up in regular malts, you can sip without guilt!
—*Taste of Home Test Kitchen*

PREP/TOTAL TIME: 5 MIN.

QUICK & EASY

- ¼ cup fat-free milk
- 1 small banana, cut into chunks
- ¼ cup chocolate malted milk powder
- 2 tablespoons reduced-fat creamy peanut butter
- 2 cups fat-free frozen chocolate yogurt

Whipped cream, optional

- In a blender, combine the milk, banana, malted milk powder and peanut butter. Cover and process for 10 seconds or until smooth. Add frozen yogurt. Cover and process 10 seconds longer or until blended. Stir if necessary. Pour into chilled glasses; garnish with whipped cream if desired. Serve immediately.

Yield: 5 servings.

KITCHEN TIP

Look for plump bananas that are evenly yellow-colored. Green bananas are under-ripe, while a flecking of brown flecks indicates ripeness. If bananas are too green, place in a paper bag until ripe.

HAM AND SWISS DIP

I've been making my creamy ham and Swiss dip for years, and I can't think of a single time I haven't received multiple requests for this recipe! It's wonderful for holiday celebrations, sports parties and brunch buffets.
—*Laurie LaClair* North Richland Hills, Texas

PREP/TOTAL TIME: 30 MIN.

QUICK & EASY

- 1 package (8 ounces) cream cheese, softened
- ⅔ cup mayonnaise
- 1½ cups diced fully cooked ham
- 1 cup (4 ounces) shredded Swiss cheese
- 1 tablespoon finely chopped green pepper
- 1 tablespoon spicy brown mustard
- ¾ cup rye cracker crumbs
- 2 tablespoons butter, melted

Rye crackers

- In a small bowl, beat cream cheese and mayonnaise until smooth. Stir in the ham, cheese, green pepper and mustard. Spread into an ungreased 9-in. pie plate.
- Toss the cracker crumbs and butter; sprinkle over cream cheese mixture. Bake, uncovered, at 400° for 12-15 minutes or until heated through. Serve with crackers.

Yield: about 3 cups.

BANANA: BRAND X PICTURES

SPINACH CHEESE TRIANGLES

Filled with three kinds of cheese and lots of spinach, these light little pockets pack a delectable punch. Friends and family will think you fussed, but these starters come together quickly.
—**Sherri Melotik** *Oak Creek, Wisconsin*

PREP: 40 MIN. **BAKE:** 10 MIN.

⅓ cup finely chopped onion	2 eggs, lightly beaten
1 tablespoon butter	2 tablespoons soft bread crumbs
1 package (10 ounces) frozen chopped spinach, thawed and squeezed dry	¼ teaspoon salt
1 cup grated Parmesan cheese	¼ teaspoon pepper
¾ cup shredded part-skim mozzarella cheese	12 sheets phyllo dough (14 inches x 9 inches)
3 tablespoons crumbled feta cheese	Butter-flavored cooking spray

○ In a large skillet, saute onion in butter until tender. Stir in spinach; cook over medium-low heat just until spinach is wilted. Transfer to a large bowl; add the cheeses, eggs, bread crumbs, salt and pepper. Set aside.

○ Place one sheet of phyllo dough on a work surface with a long side facing you. (Keep remaining phyllo covered with plastic wrap to prevent it from drying out.) Spray sheet with butter-flavored spray; cut into four 9-in. x 3½-in. strips.

○ Place 1 tablespoon of filling on the lower corner of each strip. Fold dough over filling, forming a triangle. Fold triangle up, then fold triangle over, forming another triangle. Continue folding, like a flag, until you come to the end of the strip.

○ Spritz end of dough with spray and press onto triangle to seal. Turn triangle and spritz top with cooking spray. Repeat with remaining phyllo and filling.

○ Place triangles on baking sheets coated with cooking spray. Bake at 375° for 10-12 minutes or until triangles are golden brown.

Yield: 4 dozen.

ASPARAGUS APPETIZER ROLL-UPS

Take advantage of spring's bounty of fresh, green spears of asparagus with my quick and easy roll-ups.
—**Howard Lansinger** *Pineola, North Carolina*

PREP/TOTAL TIME: 25 MIN.

QUICK & EASY

- 12 slices white bread, crusts removed
- 1 container (8 ounces) spreadable cream cheese
- 2 tablespoons chopped green onions
- 8 bacon strips, cooked and crumbled
- 24 fresh asparagus spears, trimmed
- ¼ cup butter, melted
- 3 tablespoons grated Parmesan cheese

● Flatten bread with a rolling pin. In a small bowl, combine the cream cheese, onions and bacon. Spread mixture over bread slices. Cut asparagus to fit bread; place two spears on each bread slice. Roll up bread and place, seam side down, on a greased baking sheet. Brush with butter; sprinkle roll-ups with Parmesan cheese.

● Bake at 400° for 10-12 minutes or until lightly browned. Serve immediately.

Yield: 1 dozen.

BACON CHEESEBURGER BUNS

Looking for a fun way to serve up the same great flavor of a bacon cheeseburger but in a bite-sized bundle? Give these hot, tasty nibblers a try. They're even better when dipped in your favorite sauce or salad dressing.
—**Marjorie Miller** *Haven, Kansas*

PREP: 1 HOUR + RISING **BAKE:** 10 MIN.

- 2 packages (¼ ounce *each*) active dry yeast
- ⅔ cup warm water (110° to 115°)
- ⅔ cup warm milk (110° to 115°)

- ¼ cup sugar
- ¼ cup shortening
- 2 eggs
- 2 teaspoons salt
- 4½ to 5 cups all-purpose flour

FILLING:
- 1 pound sliced bacon, diced
- 2 pounds ground beef
- 1 small onion, chopped
- 1½ teaspoons salt
- ½ teaspoon pepper
- 1 pound process cheese (Velveeta), cubed
- 3 to 4 tablespoons butter, melted

Ketchup *or* barbecue sauce, optional

● In a large bowl, dissolve yeast in warm water. Add the milk, sugar, shortening, eggs, salt and 3½ cups flour; beat until smooth. Stir in enough remaining flour to form a soft dough.

● Turn onto a floured surface; knead until smooth and elastic, about 6-8 minutes. Place in a greased bowl, turning once to grease top. Cover and let rise in a warm place until doubled, about 1 hour.

● Meanwhile, in a large skillet, cook bacon over medium heat until crisp. Using a slotted spoon, remove to paper towels. In a Dutch oven, cook the beef, onion, salt and pepper over medium heat until meat is no longer pink; drain. Add bacon and cheese; cook and stir until cheese is melted. Remove from the heat.

● Punch dough down. Turn onto a lightly floured surface; divide into fourths. Roll each portion into an 12-in. x 8-in. rectangle; cut each into six squares. Place ¼ cup of the meat mixture in the center of each square. Bring corners together in the center and pinch to seal.

● Place 2 in. apart on greased baking sheets. Bake at 400° for 9-11 minutes or until lightly browned. Brush with butter. Serve warm with ketchup if desired.

Yield: 2 dozen.

WATERMELON SHERBET SMOOTHIES

These fast-to-fix smoothies have become a summertime staple for my kids. There's nothing quite as refreshing as these chilled drinks to beat the heat.
—*Jamie Cockerel* *Kalamazoo, Michigan*

PREP/TOTAL TIME: 10 MIN.

QUICK & EASY

- 3 cups cubed seedless watermelon
- 1 cup crushed ice
- 1 cup watermelon, raspberry *or* lime sherbet
- 4 teaspoons lime juice
- 2 teaspoons miniature semisweet chocolate chips

◎ In a blender, combine the watermelon, ice, sherbet and lime juice; cover and process for 30 seconds or until smooth. Stir if necessary. Pour into chilled glasses; sprinkle with chocolate chips. Serve immediately.

Yield: 4 servings.

❝ I served this on a 100-degree day. We all really enjoyed it. It was fresh and surprisingly light.❞

—**HYDEE SHRADER** FROM TASTEOFHOME.COM

NEW ENGLAND ICED TEA

I was fortunate to spend my childhood summers vacationing at our family's beach cottage in Massachusetts. I recall this popular beverage always making an appearance at the many oceanside clam bakes. Now that I'm all grown up, I happily carry on the tradition!
—*Ann Liebergen* *Brookfield, Wisconsin*

PREP/TOTAL TIME: 10 MIN.

QUICK & EASY

- 2 tablespoons sugar
- 1 ounce vodka
- 1 ounce light rum
- 1 ounce gin
- 1 ounce Triple Sec
- 1 ounce lime juice
- 1 ounce tequila
- 1 to 1½ cups ice cubes
- 2 ounces cranberry juice

Lemon slice, optional

◎ In a mixing glass or tumbler, combine the sugar, vodka, rum, gin, Triple Sec, lime juice and tequila; stir until sugar is dissolved.

◎ Place ice in a highball glass; pour in the sugar mixture. Top with cranberry juice. Garnish with lemon if desired.

EDITOR'S NOTE: To make Long Island Iced Tea, substitute cola for the cranberry juice.

Yield: 1 serving.

COCONUT BERRY PIZZA

Berry lovers rejoice! This colorful appetizer pizza lightly dusted with coconut is a feast for the mouth *and* the eyes. It's great for any warm-weather party or gathering, especially a tropical-inspired luau.
—**Joan Warner Carr** *Kingwood, West Virginia*

PREP: 10 MIN. + CHILLING **BAKE:** 15 MIN.

2 tubes (8 ounces *each*) refrigerated crescent rolls	4 medium kiwifruit, peeled and sliced
1 package (8 ounces) cream cheese, softened	1⅓ cups sliced fresh strawberries
1 cup confectioners' sugar	1⅓ cups *each* fresh raspberries, blueberries and blackberries
2 tablespoons seedless raspberry jam	½ cup flaked coconut, toasted
1 carton (8 ounces) frozen whipped topping, thawed	

● Unroll crescent dough and place in a greased 15-in. x 10-in. x 1-in. baking pan. Press onto the bottom and up the sides of pan; seal seams. Bake at 375° for 15-20 minutes or until golden brown. Cool on a wire rack.

● Meanwhile, in a small bowl, beat the cream cheese, confectioners' sugar and jam until smooth. Fold in whipped topping. Spread over crust. Arrange fruit over top. Sprinkle with coconut. Chill until serving.

Yield: 16 servings.

ZESTY MARINATED SHRIMP

These easy shrimp look impressive on any buffet table and taste even better! The zesty marinade gives them a wonderfully spicy citrus flavor.
—Mary Jane Guest *Alamosa, Colorado*

PREP: 5 MIN. + CHILLING

- ½ cup canola oil
- ½ cup lime juice
- ½ cup thinly sliced red onion
- 12 lemon slices
- 1 tablespoon minced fresh parsley
- ½ teaspoon salt
- ½ teaspoon dill weed
- ⅛ teaspoon hot pepper sauce
- 2 pounds medium shrimp, cooked, peeled and deveined

● In a large bowl, combine the first eight ingredients. Stir in shrimp. Cover and refrigerate for 4 hours, stirring occasionally. Drain before serving.

Yield: 12 servings.

HERB-CRUSTED SWEET ONION RINGS

Looking for the ultimate in onion rings? Lightly battered and seasoned to perfection with herbs and Dijon mustard, these cook up crisp and golden brown.
—Denise Patterson *Bainbridge, Ohio*

PREP/TOTAL TIME: 30 MIN.

QUICK & EASY

- 1 cup all-purpose flour
- 1 cup beer *or* nonalcoholic beer
- 2 tablespoons Dijon mustard
- 2 teaspoons salt-free Italian herb seasoning
- 1 teaspoon salt

- ¼ teaspoon cayenne pepper
- 2 large sweet onions

Oil for deep-fat frying

● In a shallow bowl, whisk the first six ingredients. Cut onions into ¼-in. slices and separate into rings. Dip in flour mixture.

● In an electric skillet or deep-fat fryer, heat 1 in. of oil to 375°. Fry onion rings, a few at a time, for 1-2 minutes on each side or until golden brown. Drain on paper towels. Serve immediately.

Yield: 8 servings.

RED SANGRIA

Filled with frozen fruit, this refreshing blend is a snap to put together. It makes an elegant, thirst-quenching beverage for summer parties. Serve over ice if desired.
—Taste of Home Test Kitchen

PREP/TOTAL TIME: 10 MIN.

QUICK & EASY

- 1 bottle (750 milliliters) red Zinfandel *or* other dry red wine
- 2 cups diet lemon-lime soda
- ½ cup orange juice
- 4½ teaspoons sugar
- 1 cup *each* frozen unsweetened blueberries, raspberries and sliced peaches

Ice cubes, optional

● In a pitcher, stir the wine, soda, orange juice and sugar until sugar is dissolved. Add the frozen fruit. Serve over ice if desired.

Yield: 9 servings.

MUSHROOM CHEESE BREAD

Here's a savory grilled bread that makes a great appetizer and is also delightful served alongside your favorite soup or entree and vegetable. To shake things up, I sometimes use half cheddar cheese and half mozzarella.
—**Dolly McDonald** *Edmonton, Alberta*

QUICK & EASY

PREP/TOTAL TIME: 15 MIN.

- 1 cup (4 ounces) shredded part-skim mozzarella cheese
- 1 can (4 ounces) mushroom stems and pieces, drained
- ⅓ cup mayonnaise
- 2 tablespoons shredded Parmesan cheese
- 2 tablespoons chopped green onion
- 1 loaf (1 pound) unsliced French bread

● In a small bowl, combine the mozzarella cheese, mushrooms, mayonnaise, Parmesan cheese and onion. Cut bread in half lengthwise; spread cheese mixture over cut sides.

● Grill, covered, over indirect heat or broil 4 in. from the heat for 5-10 minutes or until lightly browned. Slice and serve warm.

Yield: 10-12 servings.

CINNAMON TOASTED ALMONDS

Crunchy, cinnamon-glazed almonds are an easy and welcome treat to bring to a party or other gathering. We think these taste just like the ones sold at carnivals and fairs.
—**Janice Thompson** *Stacy, Minnesota*

PREP: 15 MIN. **BAKE:** 25 MIN. + COOLING

- 2 egg whites
- 6 teaspoons vanilla extract
- 4 cups unblanched almonds
- ⅓ cup sugar
- ⅓ cup packed brown sugar
- 1 teaspoon salt
- ½ teaspoon ground cinnamon

● In a large bowl, beat egg whites until frothy; beat in vanilla. Add almonds; stir gently to coat. Combine the sugars, salt and cinnamon; add to nut mixture and stir gently to coat.

● Spread evenly into two greased 15-in. x 10-in. x 1-in. baking pans. Bake at 300° for 25-30 minutes or until almonds are crisp, stirring once. Cool. Store in an airtight container.

Yield: about 4 cups.

ALMOND-BACON CHEESE CROSTINI

Try these savory noshes for a change from the usual toasted tomato appetizers. For a unique presentation, slice the baguette at an angle instead of making a straight cut.
—**Leondre Hermann** *Stuart, Florida*

PREP: 30 MIN. **BAKE:** 15 MIN.

- 1 French bread baguette (1 pound), cut into 36 slices
- 2 cups (8 ounces) shredded Monterey Jack cheese
- ⅔ cup mayonnaise
- ½ cup sliced almonds, toasted
- 6 bacon strips, cooked and crumbled
- 1 green onion, chopped

Dash salt

Additional toasted almonds, optional

● Place bread slices on an ungreased baking sheet. Bake at 400° for 8-9 minutes or until lightly browned.

● Meanwhile, in a large bowl, combine the cheese, mayonnaise, almonds, bacon, onion and salt. Spread over bread. Bake for 7-8 minutes or until cheese is melted. Sprinkle with additional almonds if desired. Serve warm.

Yield: 3 dozen.

BEER DIP

Beer. Cheese. Pretzels. What's not to love? Take one bite, and I guarantee my hall-of-fame-bound dip will become your new trusted standby anytime you need a dish to pass.
—**Michelle Long** *New Castle, Colorado*

PREP/TOTAL TIME: 5 MIN.

QUICK & EASY

- 2 packages (8 ounces *each*) cream cheese, softened
- ⅓ cup beer *or* nonalcoholic beer
- 1 envelope ranch salad dressing mix
- 2 cups (8 ounces) shredded cheddar cheese

Pretzels

- In a large bowl, beat the cream cheese, beer and dressing until smooth. Stir in cheddar cheese. Serve with pretzels. Refrigerate leftovers.

Yield: 3½ cups.

CHICKEN AND PORK EGG ROLLS

I take these crispy sensations packed with meat and veggies to every family event. Their sweet-sour flavors are always a hit!
—**Bruce Beaver** *Florissant, Missouri*

PREP: 2½ HOURS **COOK:** 30 MIN.

- 1 medium head cabbage, shredded
- 3 celery ribs, chopped
- 1 can (8 ounces) bamboo shoots, drained and chopped
- 1 can (8 ounces) sliced water chestnuts, drained and chopped
- 5 green onions, chopped
- 2 tablespoons canola oil
- 1 to 2 garlic cloves, minced
- 2¼ cups diced cooked chicken breasts
- 2 cups diced cooked pork

- ¼ cup chicken broth
- ¼ cup soy sauce
- ¼ teaspoon salt
- ¼ teaspoon pepper
- 2 packages (16 ounces *each*) egg roll wrappers
- 1 egg, lightly beaten

Additional oil for deep-fat frying

SAUCE:

- 1½ cups unsweetened pineapple juice
- ¾ cup cider vinegar
- ½ cup packed brown sugar
- 1 tablespoon soy sauce
- ⅛ to ¼ teaspoon white pepper
- 3 tablespoons cornstarch
- 2 tablespoons cold water

- In a large nonstick wok, stir-fry the cabbage, celery, bamboo shoots, water chestnuts and onions in oil until crisp-tender. Add garlic; cook 1 minute longer. Stir in the chicken, pork, broth, soy sauce, salt and pepper. Cook and stir for 1 minute or until heated through.

- Position an egg roll wrapper with one point toward you. Place about ¼ cup of meat mixture in the center. Fold bottom corner over filling; fold sides toward center over filling. Roll toward the remaining point. Moisten top corner with beaten egg; press to seal. Repeat with remaining wrappers and filling.

- In an electric skillet or deep-fat fryer, heat oil to 375°. Fry egg rolls, a few at a time, for 1-2 minutes on each side or until golden brown. Drain on paper towels.

- In a saucepan, combine the first five sauce ingredients. Bring to a boil. Combine the cornstarch and cold water until smooth; stir into boiling mixture. Cook and stir for 2 minutes or until thickened. Serve warm with egg rolls.

Yield: about 3 dozen.

CHOCOLATE-COVERED BACON

Chocolate-covered bacon has become a smokin' hot trend at state fairs everywhere, and now you can wow guests by making this salty-sweet concoction at home. May the best appetizer win! (That would be this one.)

—**Taste of Home Test Kitchen**

PREP: 20 MIN. **BAKE:** 20 MIN.

- 12 thick-sliced bacon strips (about 1 pound)
- 12 wooden skewers (12 inches)
- 6 ounces white candy coating, chopped
- 1 cup semisweet chocolate chips
- 1 tablespoon shortening

Optional toppings: chopped dried apple chips, apricots and crystallized ginger, finely chopped pecans and pistachios, toasted coconut, kosher salt, brown sugar, cayenne pepper and coarsely ground black pepper

● Thread each bacon strip onto a wooden skewer. Place on a rack in a large baking pan. Bake at 400° for 20-25 minutes or until crisp. Cool completely.

● In a microwave, melt candy coating; stir until smooth. Combine chocolate chips and shortening; melt in a microwave and stir until smooth.

● With pastry brushes, coat bacon on both sides with melted coatings. Top each strip as desired. Place on waxed paper-lined baking sheets. Refrigerate until firm. Store in the refrigerator.

Yield: 1 dozen.

KITCHEN TIP

Use shortening (not margarine) when melting chocolate that will be used to coat candy or other foods. Margarine contains some water, which will cause the chocolate to seize or curdle.

CLAM-STUFFED MUSHROOMS

Those who love seafood and mushrooms can now enjoy the best of both worlds with these bite-sized wonders. I fill mushroom caps with a savory combo of minced clams, seasonings and cheese for an appetizer that's out of this world!

—**Maria Regakis** *Somerville, Massachusetts*

PREP: 20 MIN. **BAKE:** 20 MIN.

- 24 large fresh mushrooms
- 2 cans (6½ ounces *each*) minced clams, drained
- ¾ cup dry bread crumbs
- ½ cup grated Parmesan cheese
- ½ cup finely chopped green pepper
- 1 small onion, finely chopped
- 2 garlic cloves, minced
- 2 tablespoons Italian seasoning
- 2 tablespoons dried parsley flakes
- ⅛ teaspoon pepper
- 1½ cups butter, melted, *divided*
- ½ cup shredded part-skim mozzarella cheese

● Remove mushroom stems (discard or save for another use); set caps aside. In a large bowl, combine the clams, bread crumbs, Parmesan cheese, green pepper, onion, garlic, Italian seasoning, parsley and pepper. Stir in ¾ cup butter. Fill each mushroom cap with about 1 tablespoon of the clam mixture.

● Place in an ungreased 15-in. x 10-in. x 1-in. baking pan. Sprinkle with mozzarella cheese; drizzle with remaining butter. Bake, uncovered, at 350° for 20-25 minutes or until lightly browned. Serve warm.

Yield: 2 dozen.

CHOCOLATE: COMSTOCK

- In a small bowl, combine the cream cheese, hot pepper sauce and salad dressing. Stir in chicken.

- Spread into an ungreased 11-in. x 7-in. baking dish. Sprinkle with cheddar cheese. Bake, uncovered, at 350° for 20-22 minutes or until heated through. Sprinkle with green onions if desired. Serve with chips.

Yield: 5 cups.

APPETIZER TORTILLA PINWHEELS

A friend gave me the recipe for this attractive and tasty appetizer. I like to prepare the pinwheels in advance and then slice them just before serving. That gives me plenty of time for other last-minute party preparations.

—*Pat Waymire* Yellow Springs, Ohio

PREP: 20 MIN. + CHILLING

- 1 cup (8 ounces) sour cream
- 1 package (8 ounces) cream cheese, softened
- 1 can (4¼ ounces) chopped ripe olives
- 1 can (4 ounces) chopped green chilies, well drained
- 1 cup (4 ounces) shredded cheddar cheese
- ½ cup chopped green onions

Garlic powder to taste

Seasoned salt to taste

- 5 flour tortillas (10 inches), room temperature

Fresh parsley for garnish

Salsa

- In a large bowl, beat the first eight ingredients until blended. Spread over the tortillas; roll up tightly. Wrap each with plastic wrap, twisting ends; refrigerate for several hours.

- Unwrap; cut into ½-in. to ¾-in. slices. (An electric knife works best.) Discard ends. Garnish with parsley. Serve pinwheels with salsa if desired.

Yield: about 4 dozen.

BAKED ASPARAGUS DIP

I'm from Wisconsin, so I add cheese to just about everything. This creamy dip studded with fresh asparagus is always a party favorite. It's also great scooped up with chips or fresh veggies.

—*Sandra Baratka* Phillips, Wisconsin

PREP/TOTAL TIME: 30 MIN.

QUICK & EASY

- 1 pound diced cooked fresh asparagus, drained
- 1 cup grated Parmesan cheese
- 1 cup mayonnaise

Snack rye bread

- In a large bowl, combine the asparagus, cheese and mayonnaise. Place in a 2-cup ovenproof bowl. Bake at 375° for 20 minutes or until heated through. Serve warm with bread.

Yield: about 2 cups.

CREAMY BUFFALO CHICKEN DIP

This slightly spicy dip cleverly captures the flavor of buffalo wings. Using canned chicken makes for easy preparation.

—*Allyson DiLascio* Saltsburg, Pennsylvania

PREP/TOTAL TIME: 30 MIN.

QUICK & EASY

- 1 package (8 ounces) cream cheese, softened
- 1 cup Louisiana-style hot sauce
- 1 cup ranch salad dressing
- 3 cans (4½ ounces *each*) chunk white chicken, drained and shredded
- 1 cup (4 ounces) shredded cheddar cheese

Thinly sliced green onions, optional

Corn *or* tortilla chips

ROASTED RED PEPPER HUMMUS

My son taught me how to make hummus, which is a great alternative to the typical calorie-loaded dips. Fresh roasted red bell peppers make this recipe extra-special.
—Nancy Watson-Pistole *Shawnee, Kansas*

PREP: 30 MIN. + STANDING

- 2 large sweet red peppers
- 2 cans (15 ounces *each*) garbanzo beans *or* chickpeas, rinsed and drained
- ⅓ cup lemon juice
- 3 tablespoons tahini
- 1 tablespoon olive oil
- 2 garlic cloves, peeled
- 1¼ teaspoons salt
- 1 teaspoon curry powder
- ½ teaspoon ground coriander
- ½ teaspoon ground cumin
- ½ teaspoon pepper

Pita bread, warmed and cut into wedges, and reduced-fat wheat snack crackers

Additional garbanzo beans *or* chickpeas, optional

● Broil red peppers 4 in. from the heat until skins blister, about 5 minutes. With tongs, rotate peppers a quarter turn. Broil and rotate until all sides are blistered and blackened. Immediately place peppers in a bowl; cover and let stand for 15-20 minutes.

● Peel off and discard charred skin. Remove the stems and seeds. Place the peppers in a food processor. Add the beans, lemon juice, tahini, oil, garlic and seasonings; cover and process until blended.

● Transfer to a serving bowl. Serve with pita bread and assorted crackers. Garnish with additional beans if desired.

Yield: 3 cups.

GRILLED BACON-ONION APPETIZERS

I'm the proud father of three girls, but that doesn't stop me from whipping up authentically awesome dude food. You wouldn't think grilled onions would be a top pick in a house full of ladies, but they can't get enough of my signature appetizers!
—Dayton Hulst *Moorhead, Minnesota*

PREP: 20 MIN. + MARINATING **GRILL:** 10 MIN.

- 2 large sweet onions
- 12 hickory-smoked bacon strips
- ½ cup packed brown sugar
- ½ cup balsamic vinegar
- ¼ cup molasses
- 2 tablespoons barbecue sauce

● Cut each onion into 12 wedges. Cut bacon strips in half widthwise; wrap a piece of bacon around each onion wedge and secure with toothpicks. Place in an ungreased 13-in. x 9-in. dish.

● In a small bowl, combine the brown sugar, vinegar, molasses and barbecue sauce; pour ½ cup over onions. Cover and refrigerate for 1 hour, turning once. Cover and refrigerate remaining marinade for basting.

● Drain and discard marinade. Grill onions, covered, over medium heat for 10-15 minutes, turning and basting frequently with the reserved marinade.

Yield: 2 dozen.

OMELET CROISSANTS, PAGE 33

28

31

38

BREAKFAST & BRUNCH

You're sure to start the day off right when you're greeted with any one of the delicious sunrise specialties in this chapter. Whether you're feeding just a few or an entire crowd, you can't go wrong with these scrumptious, quick-to-fix breakfast delights, make-ahead marvels, oven-baked sensations and handheld foods to grab as you dash out the door. With this selection of hearty, home-cooked morning fare, the most important meal of the day will soon become your *favorite* meal of the day!

BREAKFAST CASSEROLE

This cheesy sausage casserole is perfect for a family breakfast or brunch. Assemble the night before, then just pop the pan in the oven in the morning for a no-fuss meal.
—**Mary Stoddard** *Fountain Inn, South Carolina*

PREP: 20 MIN. + CHILLING **BAKE:** 35 MIN. + STANDING

- 12 ounces reduced-fat bulk pork sausage
- 1 medium onion, chopped
- 2 eggs
- 4 egg whites
- 2 cups fat-free milk
- 1½ teaspoons ground mustard
- 1 teaspoon salt
- ¼ teaspoon pepper
- 8 slices firm white bread, cubed
- 2 cups (8 ounces) shredded reduced-fat cheddar cheese

● In a nonstick skillet, cook sausage and onion over medium heat until sausage is no longer pink; drain and cool.

● In a large bowl, beat the eggs, egg whites, milk, mustard, salt and pepper. Stir in the bread cubes, cheese and sausage mixture. Pour into a 13-in. x 9-in. baking dish coated with cooking spray. Cover and refrigerate overnight.

● Remove from the refrigerator 30 minutes before baking. Bake, uncovered, at 350° for 35-40 minutes or until a knife inserted near the center comes out clean. Let stand for 5 minutes before cutting.

Yield: 12 servings.

FRENCH TOAST CASSEROLE

I sprinkle a cinnamon-sugar topping on my easy oven version of French toast. I love the fact that I can assemble it the previous night and save time in the morning.
—**Sharyn Adams** *Crawfordsville, Indiana*

PREP: 15 MIN. + CHILLING **BAKE:** 45 MIN. + STANDING

- 1 loaf (1 pound) French bread, cut into 1-inch cubes
- 8 eggs, lightly beaten
- 3 cups 2% milk
- 4 teaspoons sugar
- 1 teaspoon vanilla extract
- ¾ teaspoon salt

TOPPING:

- 2 tablespoons butter
- 3 tablespoons sugar
- 2 teaspoons ground cinnamon

Maple syrup, optional

● Place bread cubes in a greased 13-in. x 9-in. baking dish. In a large bowl, whisk the eggs, milk, sugar, vanilla and salt. Pour over bread. Cover and refrigerate for 8 hours or overnight.

● Remove from refrigerator 30 minutes before baking. Dot with butter. Combine sugar and cinnamon; sprinkle over the top.

● Cover and bake at 350° for 45-50 minutes or until a knife inserted near the center comes out clean. Let stand for 5 minutes. Serve with maple syrup if desired.

Yield: 12 servings.

KITCHEN TIP

When I take a stick of butter out of its carton, I cut slits completely through the butter and its wrapping at each tablespoon mark. When a recipe calls for butter, I just break off the number of tablespoons needed and remove the wrapping. It's fast, and I don't have to dirty a knife every time I measure butter.

—**LAURA DOTSON,** COATSBURG, ILLINOIS

BUTTER: RDA-GID

ICED COFFEE LATTE

Here's a great alternative to that regular cup of joe and it's much more economical than those fancy store-bought blends. A hint of chocolate lends a special touch.

—*Heather Nandell* Johnston, Iowa

QUICK & EASY

PREP/TOTAL TIME: 10 MIN.

- ½ cup instant coffee granules
- ½ cup boiling water
- 4 cups chocolate milk
- 2 cups cold water
- 1 can (14 ounces) sweetened condensed milk

Ice cubes

- In a large bowl, dissolve coffee in boiling water. Stir in the chocolate milk, cold water and condensed milk. Serve over ice.

Yield: 8 servings.

SAUSAGE & EGG BREAKFAST PIZZA

Pizza for breakfast? Yes, please! This hearty morning meal keeps prep simple with convenient crescent rolls. Try it for brunch, camping, sleepovers or anytime you have to feed a crowd.

—*Julie Tucker* Columbus, Nebraska

PREP: 30 MIN. **BAKE:** 5 MIN.

- 2 packages (8 ounces *each*) refrigerated crescent rolls
- 1 pound bulk pork sausage
- ⅓ cup chopped onion
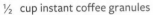
- 1 small green pepper, chopped
- 1 envelope country gravy mix
- 6 eggs
- 2 tablespoons milk
- ½ teaspoon salt
- ¼ teaspoon pepper
- 1 tablespoon butter
- 1¼ cups sliced fresh mushrooms
- 2 cups (8 ounces) shredded cheddar cheese
- 1 cup (4 ounces) shredded pepper jack cheese

- Separate crescent dough into 16 triangles and place on a greased 14-in. round pizza pan with points toward the center. Press onto the bottom and up the sides of pan to form a crust; seal seams. Bake the pizza crust at 375° for 11-13 minutes or until golden brown.

- Meanwhile, in a large skillet, cook the sausage, onion and green pepper over medium heat until sausage is no longer pink; drain. Prepare gravy according to package directions. Stir into sausage mixture; set aside.

- In a small bowl, whisk the eggs, milk, salt and pepper. In a large skillet, heat butter over medium heat. Add egg mixture; cook and stir until almost set. Spread gravy mixture over crust. Top with eggs, mushrooms and cheeses. Bake 5-10 minutes longer or until the eggs are set and the cheese is melted. Cut pizza into wedges.

Yield: 8 servings.

> **Awesome. That's almost all you have to say. My family loves this breakfast pizza, and I have passed out the recipe many times.**

—**NESTING IN ILLINOIS** FROM TASTEOFHOME.COM

WAFFLES WITH PEACH-BERRY COMPOTE

I created this compote one summer morning when I was looking for a lighter alternative to butter and maple syrup to top my waffles. I was amazed at the results!
—**Brandi Waters** *Fayetteville, Arkansas*

PREP: 25 MIN. **COOK:** 5 MIN./BATCH

1 cup chopped peeled fresh peaches *or* frozen unsweetened sliced peaches, thawed and chopped
½ cup orange juice
2 tablespoons brown sugar
¼ teaspoon ground cinnamon
1 cup fresh *or* frozen blueberries
½ cup sliced fresh *or* frozen strawberries

BATTER:
1¼ cups all-purpose flour
½ cup whole wheat flour
2 tablespoons flaxseed
1 teaspoon baking powder
1 teaspoon baking soda
½ teaspoon ground cinnamon
1 cup buttermilk
¾ cup orange juice
1 tablespoon canola oil
1 teaspoon vanilla extract

● In a small saucepan, combine the peaches, orange juice, brown sugar and cinnamon; bring to a boil over medium heat. Add berries; cook and stir for 8-10 minutes or until thickened.

● In a large bowl, combine the flours, flaxseed, baking powder, baking soda and cinnamon. Combine the buttermilk, orange juice, oil and vanilla; stir into dry ingredients just until moistened.

● Bake in a preheated waffle iron according to manufacturer's directions until golden brown. Serve waffles with compote.

Yield: 12 waffles (1½ cups compote).

FLAXSEED OATMEAL PANCAKES

My husband and I love pancakes and maple syrup, but all the sugar and carbs can easily add up. So I came up with this lighter, healthier version that we both really enjoy. These flapjacks have great texture and a delightful cinnamon taste.

—*Sharon Hansen* *Pontiac, Illinois*

PREP/TOTAL TIME: 20 MIN.

- ⅓ cup whole wheat flour
- 3 tablespoons quick-cooking oats
- 1 tablespoon flaxseed
- ½ teaspoon baking powder
- ¼ teaspoon ground cinnamon
- ⅛ teaspoon baking soda

Dash salt

- 1 egg, *separated*
- ½ cup buttermilk
- 1 tablespoon brown sugar
- 1 tablespoon canola oil
- ½ teaspoon vanilla extract

- In a large bowl, combine the first seven ingredients. In a small bowl, whisk the egg yolk, buttermilk, brown sugar, oil and vanilla; stir into dry ingredients just until moistened.

- In a small bowl, beat egg white on medium speed until stiff peaks form. Fold into batter.

- Pour batter by ¼ cupfuls onto a hot griddle coated with cooking spray; turn when bubbles form on top. Cook until the second side is golden brown.

Yield: 4 pancakes.

FRUIT-FILLED FRENCH TOAST WRAPS

What a pretty way to add a little fiber boost to your diet! With all the classic ingredients of a yogurt parfait, these luscious wraps are as easy to make as they are delicious and different.

—*Dawn Jarvis* *Breckenridge, Minnesota*

PREP/TOTAL TIME: 25 MIN.

- 1 egg
- ¼ cup 2% milk
- 1 teaspoon ground cinnamon
- ½ teaspoon ground nutmeg
- 2 whole wheat tortillas (8 inches)
- 2 teaspoons butter
- ⅔ cup sliced fresh strawberries
- ⅔ cup fresh blueberries
- ⅔ cup sliced ripe banana
- ¾ cup (6 ounces) vanilla yogurt
- ¼ cup granola
- 1 teaspoon confectioners' sugar

- In a shallow bowl, whisk the egg, milk, cinnamon and nutmeg. Dip both sides of tortillas in egg mixture. In a nonstick skillet, cook tortillas in butter over medium-high heat for 2 minutes on each side or until golden brown.

- In a small bowl, combine the berries, banana, yogurt and granola. Spoon down the center of tortillas. Roll up; sprinkle with confectioners' sugar. Serve immediately.

Yield: 2 servings.

BREAKFAST RICE PUDDING

This yummy rice pudding is one of my husband's specialties. It's equally good with fresh blueberries substituted for the cherries.
—*Sue Draheim* Waterford, Wisconsin

PREP: 15 MIN. **BAKE:** 25 MIN.

> 1⅓ cups uncooked long grain *or* basmati rice
> 1 can (15¼ ounces) peach halves, drained
> 1 cup canned *or* frozen pitted tart cherries, drained
> 1 cup heavy whipping cream
> ½ cup packed brown sugar, *divided*
> ¼ cup old-fashioned oats
> ¼ cup flaked coconut
> ¼ cup chopped pecans
> ¼ cup butter, melted

● Cook rice according to package directions. In a large bowl, combine the rice, peaches, cherries, cream and ¼ cup brown sugar. Transfer to a greased 1½ quart baking dish.

● Combine the oats, coconut, pecans, butter and remaining brown sugar; sprinkle over rice. Bake, uncovered, at 375° for 25-30 minutes or until golden brown.

Yield: 8 servings.

BREAKFAST BURRITOS

Here's my strategy for steering clear of hunger in the morning without slowing down—just zap one of these burritos in the microwave. This is my family's favorite combination, but it's also scrumptious made with cooked breakfast sausage.
—*Audra Niederman* Aberdeen, South Dakota

PREP: 20 MIN. + FREEZING

> 12 bacon strips, diced
> 12 eggs, lightly beaten
>
> Salt and pepper to taste
> 10 flour tortillas (8 inches)
> 1½ cups (6 ounces) shredded cheddar cheese
> ½ cup thinly sliced green onions

● In a large skillet, cook bacon until crisp; remove to paper towels. Drain, reserving 1-2 tablespoons drippings. Add eggs, salt and pepper to drippings; cook and stir over medium heat until the eggs are completely set.

● Spoon about ¼ cup of egg mixture down the center of each tortilla; sprinkle with cheese, onions and reserved bacon. Fold bottom and sides of each tortilla over filling. Wrap each in waxed paper and aluminum foil. Freeze for up to 1 month.

TO USE FROZEN BURRITOS: Remove foil. Place waxed paper-wrapped burritos on a microwave-safe plate. Microwave at 60% power for 1 to 1½ minutes or until heated through. Let stand for 20 seconds.

EDITOR'S NOTE: This recipe was tested in a 1,100-watt microwave.

Yield: 10 burritos.

OMELET CROISSANTS

Bacon and eggs never tasted so good! Stacked with cheese, greens, tomato and more, this dish is sized just right for two.
—**Edna Coburn** *Tucson, Arizona*

PREP/TOTAL TIME: 30 MIN.

QUICK & EASY

- 3 eggs
- 1 tablespoon water
- 1 teaspoon chicken bouillon granules
- 1 green onion, finely chopped
- 2 tablespoons finely chopped sweet red pepper
- ¼ teaspoon lemon-pepper seasoning
- ½ teaspoon butter
- 2 croissants, split
- 4½ teaspoons ranch salad dressing
- 4 slices Canadian bacon
- 4 slices Muenster cheese
- ½ cup fresh arugula
- 4 thin slices tomato

◉ In a small bowl, whisk the eggs, water and bouillon; set aside.

◉ In a small nonstick skillet over medium heat, cook the onion, red pepper and lemon-pepper in butter until tender.

◉ Add egg mixture. As eggs set, push cooked edges toward the center, letting uncooked portion flow underneath. When eggs are completely set, fold omelet in half and cut into two wedges.

◉ Spread croissants with salad dressing. On croissant bottoms, layer the bacon, omelet, cheese, arugula and tomato. Replace croissant tops.

◉ Cook on a panini maker or indoor grill for 2-4 minutes or until cheese is melted.

Yield: 2 servings.

HOLIDAY BRUNCH CASSEROLE

Consider this colorful casserole the next time you're hosting overnight company. Guests will be impressed with the hearty, wonderful flavors; you'll love the make-ahead convenience.
—**Nelda Cronbaugh** *Belle Plaine, Iowa*

PREP: 15 MIN. + CHILLING **BAKE:** 30 MIN. + STANDING

- 4 cups frozen shredded hash brown potatoes
- 1 pound bulk pork sausage, cooked and drained
- ½ pound bacon strips, cooked and crumbled
- 1 medium green pepper, chopped
- 2 cups (8 ounces) shredded cheddar cheese, *divided*
- 1 green onion, chopped
- 1 cup reduced-fat biscuit/baking mix
- ½ teaspoon salt
- 4 eggs
- 3 cups 2% milk

◉ In a large bowl, combine the hash browns, sausage, bacon, green pepper, 1 cup cheese and onion. Transfer to a greased 13-in. x 9-in. baking dish.

◉ In another bowl, whisk the biscuit mix, salt, eggs and milk; pour over the top. Sprinkle with remaining cheese. Cover and refrigerate overnight.

◉ Remove from the refrigerator 30 minutes before baking. Bake, uncovered, at 375° for 30-35 minutes or until a knife inserted near the center comes out clean. Let stand for 10 minutes before cutting.

Yield: 12 servings.

for 2 minutes or until thickened. Strain and discard the seeds; cool slightly.

○ Gently stir the remaining berries into syrup. Sprinkle French toast cups with cinnamon if desired; serve with syrup.

Yield: 2 servings.

SWEDISH PANCAKES

When we spend the night at my mother-in-law's house, our kids beg her to make these crepe-like sensations for breakfast. We enjoy them most with fresh berries and jam, but cream cheese and Nutella also make great toppings.

—**Susan Johnson** *Lyons, Kansas*

PREP/TOTAL TIME: 20 MIN.

2	cups milk
4	eggs
1	tablespoon canola oil
1½	cups all-purpose flour
3	tablespoons sugar
¼	teaspoon salt

Lingonberries *or* raspberries

Seedless raspberry jam *or* fruit spread, warmed

Whipped topping

○ In a blender, combine the first six ingredients. Cover and process until blended. Heat a lightly greased 8-in. nonstick skillet; pour ¼ cup batter into center of pan. Lift and tilt pan to evenly coat bottom. Cook until top appears dry; turn and cook 15-20 seconds longer.

○ Repeat with remaining batter, adding oil to skillet as needed. Stack pancakes with waxed paper or paper towels in between. Reheat in the microwave if desired.

○ Fold pancakes into quarters; serve with berries, raspberry jam and whipped topping.

Yield: 20 pancakes.

RASPBERRY FRENCH TOAST CUPS

These individual treats are a delightful twist on French toast. I made this recipe for my mom as a special treat on Mother's Day, and it was so good, it's now one of our family favorites.

—**Sandi Tuttle** *Hayward, Wisconsin*

PREP: 20 MIN. + CHILLING **BAKE:** 25 MIN.

2	slices Italian bread, cut into ½-inch cubes
½	cup fresh *or* frozen raspberries
2	ounces cream cheese, cut into ½-inch cubes
2	eggs
½	cup milk
1	tablespoon maple syrup

RASPBERRY SYRUP:

2	teaspoons cornstarch
⅓	cup water
2	cups fresh *or* frozen raspberries, *divided*
1	tablespoon lemon juice
1	tablespoon maple syrup
½	teaspoon grated lemon peel

Ground cinnamon, optional

○ Divide half of the bread cubes between two greased 8-oz. custard cups. Sprinkle with raspberries and cream cheese. Top with remaining bread. In a small bowl, whisk the eggs, milk and syrup; pour over the bread cubes. Cover and refrigerate for at least 1 hour.

○ Remove custard cups from the refrigerator 30 minutes before baking. Bake, uncovered, at 350° for 25-30 minutes or until golden brown.

○ Meanwhile, in a small saucepan, combine cornstarch and water until smooth. Add 1½ cups raspberries, lemon juice, syrup and lemon peel. Bring to a boil; reduce heat. Cook and stir

OVERNIGHT CHERRY DANISH ROLLS

With their cherry-filled centers and sweet icing, these rolls are melt-in-your-mouth good! They'll add a touch of color to your table, and also store well, unfrosted, in the freezer.
—**Leann Sauder** *Tremont, Illinois*

PREP: 1½ HOURS + RISING **BAKE:** 15 MIN. + COOLING

2 packages (¼ ounce *each*) active dry yeast	6 egg yolks, lightly beaten
½ cup warm 2% milk (110° to 115°)	1 can (21 ounces) cherry pie filling
6 cups all-purpose flour	ICING:
⅓ cup sugar	2 tablespoons butter, softened
2 teaspoons salt	3 cups confectioners' sugar
1 cup cold butter, cubed	¼ teaspoon vanilla extract
1½ cups warm half-and-half cream	Dash salt
(110° to 115°)	4 to 5 tablespoons half-and-half cream

● In a small bowl, dissolve yeast in warm milk. In a large bowl, combine the flour, sugar and salt. Cut in butter until crumbly. Add the yeast mixture, cream and egg yolks; stir until mixture forms a soft dough (dough will be sticky). Cover and refrigerate overnight.

● Punch down dough; divide into quarters. Roll each portion into an 18-in. x 4-in. rectangle; cut into 1-in. x 4-in. strips.

● Place two strips side by side; twist together. Shape into a ring; pinch ends together. Repeat with remaining strips. Place 2 in. apart on greased baking sheets. Cover and let rise in a warm place until doubled, about 45 minutes.

● Using the end of a wooden spoon handle, make a ½-in.-deep indentation in the center of each roll. Fill each with about 1 tablespoon pie filling.

● Bake at 350° for 14-16 minutes or until lightly browned. Remove from pans to wire racks to cool.

● For icing, in a large bowl, beat butter until fluffy. Gradually beat in the confectioners' sugar, vanilla, salt and enough cream to achieve a drizzling consistency. Drizzle over warm rolls.

Yield: 3 dozen.

BACON VEGETABLE QUICHE

You'll love this recipe and its versatility. Change it up with Vidalia onions, green onions or leeks. Asparagus can take the place of broccoli, and you can use whatever fresh herbs or cheese you have on hand.
—**Shannon Koene** *Blacksburg, Virginia*

PREP: 25 MIN. **BAKE:** 35 MIN.

1 unbaked pastry shell (9 inches)	1 tablespoon minced fresh rosemary *or*
2 cups fresh baby spinach	1 teaspoon dried rosemary, crushed
1 cup sliced fresh mushrooms	¼ teaspoon salt
1 cup chopped fresh broccoli	¼ teaspoon pepper
¾ cup chopped sweet onion	1 cup (4 ounces) shredded cheddar cheese
2½ teaspoons olive oil	6 bacon strips, cooked and crumbled
3 eggs, lightly beaten	½ cup crumbled tomato and basil feta cheese
1 can (5 ounces) evaporated milk	

● Line unpricked pastry shell with a double thickness of heavy-duty foil. Bake at 450° for 8 minutes. Remove foil; bake 5 minutes longer.

● Meanwhile, in a large skillet, saute the spinach, mushrooms, broccoli and onion in oil until tender. In a large bowl, whisk the eggs, milk, rosemary, salt and pepper.

● Using a slotted spoon, transfer vegetables to egg mixture. Stir in cheddar cheese and bacon. Pour into crust. Sprinkle with feta cheese.

● Cover edges loosely with foil. Bake at 375° for 30-35 minutes or until a knife inserted near the center comes out clean. Let stand for 5 minutes before cutting.

Yield: 6 servings.

FOUR-BERRY SMOOTHIES

My breakfast smoothies taste even more scrumptious and refreshing when I think of how much money I save by whipping up my own at home. They're filled with a powerhouse of antioxidants from all the berries, so I know I'm treating myself to something delicious *and* good for me.

—**Krista Johnson** *Crosslake, Minnesota*

PREP/TOTAL TIME: 10 MIN.

QUICK & EASY

- 1½ cups fat-free milk
- ½ cup frozen blackberries
- ½ cup frozen blueberries
- ½ cup frozen unsweetened raspberries
- ½ cup frozen unsweetened strawberries
- 2 tablespoons lemonade concentrate
- 1 tablespoon sugar
- ½ teaspoon vanilla extract

● In a blender, combine all the ingredients. Cover and process until smooth. Pour into chilled glasses; serve immediately.

Yield: 2 servings.

> **"**This egg scramble was fantastic! It made for a nice hearty breakfast. My husband and I both thoroughly enjoyed it.**"**
>
> —**STEPH BROWN** FROM TASTEOFHOME.COM

EGG SCRAMBLE

Perfect for that special-occasion breakfast or brunch, this easy egg scramble ensures that everyone gets their ham and eggs hot and at the same time! It's always a crowd-pleaser.

—**Vicki Holloway** *Joelton, Tennessee*

PREP: 15 MIN. **COOK:** 20 MIN.

- 1½ cups diced peeled potatoes
- ½ cup chopped sweet red pepper
- ½ cup chopped green pepper
- ½ cup chopped onion
- 2 teaspoons canola oil, *divided*
- 2 cups cubed fully cooked ham
- 16 eggs
- ⅔ cup sour cream
- ½ cup 2% milk
- 1 teaspoon onion salt
- ½ teaspoon garlic salt
- ¼ teaspoon pepper
- 2 cups (8 ounces) shredded cheddar cheese, *divided*

● Place potatoes in a small saucepan and cover with water. Bring to a boil. Reduce heat; cover and simmer for 10-15 minutes or until tender. Drain.

● In a large skillet, saute half of the peppers and onion in 1 teaspoon of oil until tender. Add half of the ham and potatoes; saute 2-3 minutes longer.

● Meanwhile, in a blender, combine the eggs, sour cream, milk, onion salt, garlic salt and pepper. Cover and process until mixture is smooth.

● Pour half over vegetable mixture; cook and stir over medium heat until eggs are completely set. Sprinkle with 1 cup cheese. Repeat with remaining ingredients.

Yield: 10 servings.

SUNNY MORNING DOUGHNUTS

I love, love, love doughnuts! But making a stop at my local bakery every Saturday morning can get expensive. This recipe is economical and delicious. It beats any store-bought variety.
—*Sherry Flaquel* Cutler Bay, Florida

PREP: 30 MIN. + CHILLING **COOK:** 5 MIN./BATCH

- 4½ to 5 cups all-purpose flour
- 1¼ cups sugar
- 4 teaspoons baking powder
- 1 teaspoon salt
- 3 eggs, lightly beaten
- 1 cup 2% milk
- ¼ cup canola oil
- 2 tablespoons orange juice
- 4 teaspoons grated orange peel

Oil for deep-fat frying

Confectioners' sugar

- In a large bowl, combine 4½ cups flour, sugar, baking powder and salt.

- Combine the eggs, milk, oil, orange juice and peel; stir into dry ingredients just until moistened. Stir in enough remaining flour to form a soft dough. Cover dough and refrigerate for at least 1 hour.

- Turn onto a floured surface; roll to ½-in. thickness. Cut with a floured 2½-in. doughnut cutter.

- In an electric skillet or deep-fat fryer, heat oil to 375°. Fry doughnuts, a few at a time, until golden brown on both sides. Drain on paper towels. Dust warm doughnuts with confectioners' sugar.

Yield: 20 doughnuts.

ITALIAN MINI-FRITTATAS

These adorable mini-frittatas bake in under 15 minutes. They're great for special events or for a nutritious breakfast on the run.
—*Taste of Home Cooking School*

PREP: 20 MIN. **BAKE:** 15 MIN.

- 1 cup coarsely shredded yellow summer squash
- 1 cup coarsely shredded zucchini
- 1 cup chopped fresh mushrooms
- 2 tablespoons butter
- ½ teaspoon salt
- ¼ teaspoon pepper
- ½ cup all-purpose flour
- 4 eggs, beaten
- 5 tablespoons chopped ripe olives, *divided*
- 2 tablespoons grated Parmesan cheese
- 1 teaspoon dried basil
- ½ teaspoon garlic salt
- 1 small onion, thinly sliced
- ½ cup diced grape tomatoes
- ½ cup shredded Monterey Jack cheese

English muffins, split and toasted, optional

- In a large nonstick skillet, saute squash and mushrooms in butter until tender. Season with salt and pepper; set aside.

- In a bowl, whisk the flour and eggs until smooth. Stir in reserved vegetables and ¼ cup olives. Coat 12 muffin cups with cooking spray; fill half full with egg mixture. Bake at 450° for 6-8 minutes or until set.

- Combine the Parmesan cheese, basil and garlic salt; sprinkle over egg mixture. Combine the onion, tomatoes and remaining olives; spoon over the top. Sprinkle with Monterey Jack cheese. Bake for 5 minutes or until cheese is melted. Serve on English muffins if desired.

Yield: 6 servings.

BLUEBERRY-POPPY SEED BRUNCH CAKE

In summer, I freeze fresh-picked blueberries to keep on hand all year long for desserts, breads and muffins. This heavenly glazed cake studded with poppy seeds is a family favorite.
—**Ruth Gruchow** *Yorba Linda, California*

PREP: 15 MIN. **BAKE:** 50 MIN. + COOLING

½ cup butter, softened
⅔ cup sugar
1 egg
1½ cups all-purpose flour
2 tablespoons poppy seeds
½ teaspoon baking powder
¼ teaspoon baking soda
¼ teaspoon salt
½ cup sour cream
2 teaspoons grated lemon peel

TOPPING:
⅓ cup sugar
2 teaspoons all-purpose flour
¼ teaspoon ground nutmeg
2 cups fresh *or* frozen unsweetened blueberries

GLAZE:
½ cup confectioners' sugar
1 tablespoon milk

● In a small bowl, cream butter and sugar until light and fluffy. Beat in egg. Combine the flour, poppy seeds, baking powder, baking soda and salt; add to the creamed mixture alternately with sour cream. Beat just until combined. Stir in lemon peel. Spread into a greased 9-in. springform pan.

● For topping, in a small bowl, combine the sugar, flour and nutmeg; gently stir in blueberries until coated. Sprinkle over batter.

● Bake at 350° for 50-55 minutes or until a toothpick inserted near the center comes out clean. Cool for 10 minutes on a wire rack; remove sides of pan.

● Meanwhile, in a small bowl, whisk confectioners' sugar and milk until smooth; drizzle over cake. Refrigerate leftovers.

EDITOR'S NOTE: If using frozen blueberries, use without thawing to avoid discoloring the batter.

Yield: 8 servings.

GREATEST GRANOLA

After clipping granola recipes for years, I chose my favorite ingredients from each one, tossed in a few of my own and came up with this unique creation. My family can't get enough!
—**Jonie Daigle** *Greensburg, Pennsylvania*

PREP: 15 MIN. **BAKE:** 25 MIN. + COOLING

2 cups old-fashioned oats	¼ teaspoon ground cinnamon
1 cup Grape-Nuts	1 cup crisp rice cereal
½ cup sliced almonds	½ cup toasted wheat germ
½ cup honey	½ cup chopped dried apricots
⅓ cup canola oil	½ cup dried cranberries, chopped
¼ cup packed brown sugar	Yogurt flavor of your choice, optional
1½ teaspoons vanilla extract	

● In a large bowl, combine the oats, Grape-Nuts and almonds. Spread mixture onto a greased, foil-lined 15-in. x 10-in. x 1-in. baking pan. Coat mixture with cooking spray. Bake, uncovered, at 300° for 20 minutes, stirring once.

● Meanwhile, in a small saucepan, combine the honey, oil and brown sugar. Cook and stir over low heat until heated through. Remove from the heat; stir in vanilla and cinnamon.

● Stir cereal and wheat germ into oat mixture. Drizzle with honey mixture; stir to coat. Bake 5-10 minutes longer or until golden brown. Cool on a wire rack.

● Break granola into pieces. Sprinkle with apricots and cranberries and mix well. Store in an airtight container. Serve with yogurt if desired.

Yield: about 8 cups.

HAM & CHEESE BREAKFAST STRUDELS

These savory little beauties will get any morning off to a great start. You can assemble them in advance and freeze individually, then bake as needed.

—Jo Groth *Plainfield, Iowa*

PREP: 25 MIN. **BAKE:** 15 MIN.

- 3 tablespoons butter, *divided*
- 2 tablespoons all-purpose flour
- 1 cup milk
- ⅓ cup shredded Swiss cheese
- 2 tablespoons grated Parmesan cheese
- ¼ teaspoon salt
- 5 eggs, lightly beaten
- ¼ pound ground fully cooked ham (about ¾ cup)
- 6 sheets phyllo dough
- ½ cup butter, melted
- ¼ cup dry bread crumbs

TOPPING:

- 2 tablespoons grated Parmesan cheese
- 2 tablespoons minced fresh parsley

● In a small saucepan, melt 2 tablespoons of butter. Stir in flour until smooth; gradually add milk. Bring to a boil; cook and stir for 2 minutes or until thickened. Stir in cheeses and salt. Set mixture aside.

● In a large nonstick skillet, melt remaining butter over medium heat. Add eggs to the pan; cook and stir until almost set. Stir in ham and the reserved cheese sauce; heat through. Remove from the heat.

● Place one sheet of phyllo dough on a work surface. (Keep remaining phyllo covered with plastic wrap and a damp towel to prevent it from drying out.) Brush with melted butter. Sprinkle with 2 teaspoons bread crumbs. Fold in half lengthwise; brush again with butter. Spoon ½ cup filling onto phyllo about 2 in. from a short side. Fold side and edges over filling and roll up.

● Brush with butter. Repeat. Place desired number of strudels on a greased baking sheet; sprinkle each with 1 teaspoon cheese and 1 teaspoon parsley. Bake at 375° for 10-15 minutes or until golden brown. Serve immediately.

● To freeze and bake strudels: Individually wrap uncooked strudels in waxed paper and foil. Freeze for up to 1 month.

● Place 2 in. apart on a greased baking sheet; sprinkle with cheese and parsley. Bake at 375° for 30-35 minutes or until golden brown.

Yield: 6 servings.

PECAN FRENCH TOAST

A touch of grated orange peel and crunchy pecans make this oven-baked French toast extra special.

—Allan Whytock *Lebanon, Oregon*

PREP: 10 MIN. + CHILLING **BAKE:** 20 MIN.

- 4 eggs
- ⅔ cup orange juice
- ⅓ cup 2% milk
- ¼ cup sugar
- 1 tablespoon grated orange peel
- ½ teaspoon vanilla extract
- ¼ teaspoon ground nutmeg
- 6 slices Italian bread (1 inch thick)
- ⅓ cup butter, melted
- ¾ cup chopped pecans

Maple syrup

● In a small bowl, whisk the first seven ingredients. Place bread in a 13-in. x 9-in. dish; pour egg mixture over the top. Cover and refrigerate overnight, turning slices once.

● Pour butter into a 15-in. x 10-in. x 1-in. baking pan; top with bread. Sprinkle with pecans. Bake at 400° for 20-25 minutes or until golden brown. Serve with syrup.

Yield: 6 servings.

FLAVORFUL TOMATO JUICE

Jalapenos, spicy pepper sauce and horseradish are a few of my favorite cooking ingredients. I knew they'd make the perfect spicy blend to amp up homemade tomato juice!
—**Jeannie Linsavage** *Albuquerque, New Mexico*

PREP: 20 MIN. **COOK:** 45 MIN. + CHILLING

    8   medium tomatoes, chopped
 1½   cups water
    1   small onion, chopped
    3   garlic cloves, minced
    1   jalapeno pepper, seeded and chopped
    3   tablespoons sugar
    3   tablespoons lime juice
    2   teaspoons celery seed
    1   teaspoon salt
    1   teaspoon ground mustard
    1   teaspoon prepared horseradish
 ⅛   teaspoon dried basil
 ⅛   teaspoon dried parsley flakes
Dash hot pepper sauce

● In a large saucepan, combine all ingredients. Bring to a boil. Reduce heat; simmer, uncovered, for 30 minutes or until tomatoes are tender. Cool to room temperature.

● Transfer mixture to a blender; cover and process until blended. Strain and discard seeds. Return tomato juice to saucepan. Bring to a boil. Reduce heat; simmer, uncovered, for 12-18 minutes or until juice measures 3 cups. Cool. Transfer to a pitcher; cover and refrigerate until chilled.

EDITOR'S NOTE: Wear disposable gloves when cutting hot peppers; the oils can burn skin. Avoid touching your face.

Yield: 4 servings.

WAFFLES FROM SCRATCH

Every Saturday morning my mom would make my favorite homemade waffles before we'd set off on a fun-filled day of shopping. They're wonderful topped with fruit or maple syrup.
—**Florence Dean** *Towson, Maryland*

PREP/TOTAL TIME: 20 MIN.

QUICK & EASY

 1½   cups all-purpose flour
    1   teaspoon baking powder
 ½   teaspoon salt
    2   eggs, *separated*
    1   cup 2% milk
 ¼   cup butter, melted
Confectioners' sugar and fresh fruit *or* maple syrup

● In a large bowl, combine the flour, baking powder and salt. In a small bowl, whisk egg yolks, milk and butter. Stir into dry ingredients just until moistened.

● In a small bowl, beat egg whites on medium speed until soft peaks form. Fold into batter.

● Bake in a preheated waffle iron according to manufacturer's directions until golden brown. Top with confectioners' sugar and fruit or serve with syrup.

TO MAKE OAT WAFFLES: Add ¼ cup old-fashioned oats to flour mixture. Add an extra tablespoon of milk. Stir ½ teaspoon vanilla extract into egg yolk mixture.

TO MAKE SPICED WAFFLES: Stir ½ teaspoon ground cinnamon and ⅛ teaspoon each ground nutmeg and cloves into flour mixture. Fold ⅓ cup grated carrot, apple or zucchini into batter.

Yield: 8 waffles (about 4 inches).

QUICHE: RDA-GID

GOLDEN CORN QUICHE

This comforting quiche makes a great meatless entree for breakfast or dinner. I like to serve it alongside fresh fruit for a complete meal. You can also pair it with a slice or two of ham or Canadian bacon.
—**Donna Gonda** *North Canton, Ohio*

PREP: 20 MIN. **BAKE:** 35 MIN. + STANDING

1 unbaked pastry shell (9 inches)	1 tablespoon all-purpose flour
1⅓ cups half-and-half cream	1 tablespoon sugar
3 eggs	1 teaspoon salt
3 tablespoons butter, melted	2 cups frozen corn, thawed
½ small onion, cut into wedges	

⦿ Let pastry shell stand at room temperature for 10 minutes. Line unpricked pastry shell with a double thickness of heavy-duty foil. Bake at 375° for 5 minutes. Remove foil; bake 5 minutes longer.

⦿ In a blender, combine the cream, eggs, butter, onion, flour, sugar and salt; cover and process until blended. Stir in corn; pour into crust.

⦿ Bake for 35-40 minutes or until a knife inserted near the center comes out clean. Let stand for 10 minutes before cutting.

Yield: 8 servings.

KITCHEN TIP

To avoid water at the bottom of the pie crust when making a quiche, use an oven thermometer to check your oven's temperature first. Then, to avoid overbaking the item, simply do the "knife test." When the quiche appears to have set around the edges but still seems a little soft in the very center, carefully insert a knife near the center of the quiche. You know that the quiche is done baking if the knife comes out clean.

CAPPUCCINO CINNAMON ROLLS

A rich coffee flavor and sweet drizzled icing make these morning delights over-the-top indulgent. You may want to make a double batch because they won't last long!

—**Sherri Cox** *Lucasville, Ohio*

PREP: 45 MIN. + RISING **BAKE:** 25 MIN.

- 1 package (¼ ounce) active dry yeast
- 1 cup warm water (110° to 115°)
- ¾ cup warm milk (110° to 115°)
- ½ cup buttermilk
- 3 tablespoons sugar
- 2 tablespoons butter, softened
- 1¼ teaspoons salt
- 5½ to 6 cups all-purpose flour

FILLING:
- ¼ cup butter, melted
- 1 cup packed brown sugar
- 4 teaspoons instant coffee granules
- 2 teaspoons ground cinnamon

ICING:
- 1½ cups confectioners' sugar
- 2 tablespoons butter, softened
- 1 to 2 tablespoons milk
- 2 teaspoons cappuccino mix
- ½ teaspoon vanilla extract

- In a large bowl, dissolve yeast in warm water. Add the warm milk, buttermilk, sugar, butter, salt and 4 cups flour. Beat on medium speed until smooth. Stir in enough remaining flour to form a soft dough (dough will be sticky).

- Turn onto a floured surface; knead until smooth and elastic, about 6-8 minutes. Place in a greased bowl, turning once to grease the top. Cover and let rise in a warm place until doubled, about 1 hour.

- Punch dough down; turn onto a floured surface. Roll into an 18-in. x 12-in. rectangle; brush with butter. Combine the brown sugar, coffee granules and cinnamon; sprinkle over dough to within ½ in. of edges.

- Roll up jelly-roll style, starting with a long side; pinch seam to seal. Cut into 12 slices. Place rolls, cut side down, in a greased 13-in. x 9-in. baking pan. Cover and let rise until doubled, about 30 minutes.

- Bake at 350° for 22-28 minutes or until golden brown. Place pan on a wire rack. In a small bowl, beat the icing ingredients until smooth. Spread over warm rolls. Serve warm.

Yield: 1 dozen.

HEARTY SCRAMBLED EGGS

My hefty and satisfying breakfast dish includes traditional omelet ingredients in a fun egg scramble that's quick to fix. You'll never go back to plain scrambled eggs, I guarantee it!

—**Carole Anhalt** *Manitowoc, Wisconsin*

PREP/TOTAL TIME: 20 MIN.

QUICK & EASY

- 8 eggs
- 1-1/4 cups diced fully cooked ham
- 3/4 cup diced cheddar cheese
- 1/2 cup chopped fresh mushrooms
- 1/4 cup chopped onion
- 2 to 3 tablespoons butter

- In a bowl, beat eggs. Add ham, cheese, mushrooms and onion. Melt butter in a skillet; add egg mixture. Cook and stir over medium heat until eggs are completely set and the cheese is melted.

Yield: 4 servings.

> 66 Excellent! I sauteed the mushrooms and onions first then added them to the ham, eggs and cheese. The flavors worked so well together. A very filling breakfast. 99

— **HBCOOK** FROM TASTEOFHOME.COM

RASPBERRY KEY LIME CREPES

Key lime juice turns plain cream cheese into a refreshing filling for these raspberry crepes. Strawberries also pair well with the tangy lime flavor. Another fun variation is chop the berries into small pieces and pipe the sweet filling into phyllo-dough cones.
—**Wolfgang Hanau** *West Palm Beach, Florida*

PREP: 20 MIN. + CHILLING

- 3 tablespoons key lime juice
- 1 package (12.3 ounces) silken firm tofu, crumbled
- 6 ounces reduced-fat cream cheese, cubed
- ⅔ cup confectioners' sugar, *divided*
- 2½ teaspoons grated lime peel

Dash salt

Dash ground nutmeg

- 6 prepared crepes (9 inches)
- 1½ cups fresh raspberries

○ In a blender, combine the lime juice, tofu and cream cheese; cover and process until smooth. Set aside 1 teaspoon confectioners' sugar. Add the lime peel, salt, nutmeg and remaining confectioners' sugar; cover and process until blended. Cover and refrigerate for at least 1 hour.

○ Spread cream cheese mixture over crepes. Sprinkle with raspberries; roll up. Dust with reserved confectioners' sugar.

Yield: 6 servings.

EGGS BENEDICT WITH JALAPENO HOLLANDAISE

Try my zesty take on classic eggs Benedict. Cool and creamy avocado tames the jalapeno perfectly.
—**Laura Denney** *Redondo Beach, California*

QUICK & EASY

PREP/TOTAL TIME: 20 MIN.

- 1 tablespoon white vinegar
- 4 eggs
- ¼ cup butter, cubed
- 1 cup milk
- 1 package hollandaise sauce mix
- 2 tablespoons chopped seeded jalapeno pepper
- 2 English muffins, split and toasted
- 4 slices Canadian bacon, warmed
- 4 slices tomato
- 1 medium ripe avocado, peeled and sliced

○ Place 2-3 in. of water in a large skillet with high sides; add vinegar. Bring to a boil; reduce heat and simmer gently. Break cold eggs, one at a time, into a custard cup or saucer. Holding the cup close to the surface of the water, slip each egg into the water. Cook, uncovered, until whites are completely set and yolks begin to thicken (but are not hard), about 4-5 minutes.

○ Meanwhile, in a small saucepan, melt butter over medium heat; whisk in milk and sauce mix. Bring to a boil. Reduce heat; simmer, uncovered, for 1 minute or until thickened. Stir in jalapeno. Set aside and keep warm.

○ With a slotted spoon, lift each egg out of the water. On each muffin half, layer the Canadian bacon, tomato, avocado and an egg; spoon sauce over tops. Serve immediately.

EDITOR'S NOTE: Wear disposable gloves when cutting hot peppers; the oils can burn skin. Avoid touching your face.

Yield: 4 servings.

CHICKEN LETTUCE WRAPS, PAGE 65

64

57

61

SOUPS & SANDWICHES

If you love the classic pairing of a soup and sandwich, start here for an assortment of fresh, good-for-you recipes that are guaranteed to satisfy your deepest comfort food craving. When soup calls, warm up with steamy spoonfuls of everything from timeless favorites to unique change-of-pace stockpot specialties. And when only a flavorful creation stacked high with meat, cheese and veggies will hit the spot, be sure to turn here for an endless variety of hunger-pleasing sandwiches.

BART'S BLACK BEAN SOUP

You can whip up my friend Bart's famous soup in mere minutes. We enjoy it with rolls and a salad for a complete meal that's both tasty and easy.
—*Sharon Ullyot* London, Ontario

PREP/TOTAL TIME: 10 MIN.

QUICK & EASY

    1 can (15 ounces) black beans, rinsed and drained
  1½ cups chicken broth
    ¾ cup chunky salsa
    ½ cup canned whole kernel corn, drained
Dash hot pepper sauce
    2 teaspoons lime juice
    1 cup (4 ounces) shredded cheddar cheese
    2 tablespoons chopped green onions

• In a microwave-safe bowl, combine the first five ingredients. Cover and microwave on high for 2 minutes or until heated through. Pour into four serving bowls; drizzle each with lime juice. Sprinkle with cheese and green onions.

EDITOR'S NOTE: This recipe was tested in a 1,100-watt microwave.

Yield: 4 servings.

EGG SALAD SANDWICHES

The ingredients in this sandwich are simple, yet each one contributes a special flavor, making it hard to stop with just one bite!
—*Anna Jean Allen* West Liberty, Kentucky

PREP/TOTAL TIME: 15 MIN.

QUICK & EASY

    1 cup (4 ounces) shredded cheddar cheese
    ½ cup chopped green pepper
    ½ cup sweet pickles, chopped
    ¼ cup mayonnaise
    2 tablespoons horseradish sauce
    1 tablespoon sweet pickle juice
    ¼ teaspoon salt
    6 hard-cooked eggs, chopped
  12 slices white bread
Lettuce leaves and tomato slices, optional

• In a small bowl, combine the first seven ingredients; stir in eggs.

• On six slices of bread, layer with ½ cup egg salad, lettuce and tomato slices if desired. Top with remaining bread slices.

Yield: 6 servings.

SOUPS & SANDWICHES

WHITE CHILI

My friend and I created this succulent slow-cooked chicken chili. The Alfredo sauce base makes it stand apart from other white chilis. Reduce the amount of cayenne pepper if you'd like a little less heat.
—**Cindi Mitchell** *St. Marys, Kansas*

PREP: 30 MIN. **COOK:** 3 HOURS

3 cans (15½ ounces each) great northern beans, rinsed and drained

3 cups cubed cooked chicken breast

1 jar (15 ounces) Alfredo sauce

2 cups chicken broth

1 to 2 cans (4 ounces each) chopped green chilies

1½ cups frozen gold and white corn

1 cup (4 ounces) shredded Monterey Jack cheese

1 cup (4 ounces) shredded pepper jack cheese

1 cup sour cream

1 small sweet yellow pepper, chopped

1 small onion, chopped

3 garlic cloves, minced

1 tablespoon ground cumin

1½ teaspoons white pepper

1 to 1½ teaspoons cayenne pepper

Salsa verde and chopped fresh cilantro, optional

• In a 5- or 6-qt. slow cooker, combine the first 15 ingredients. Cover and cook on low for 3-4 hours or until heated through, stirring once. Serve with salsa verde and cilantro if desired.

Yield: 12 servings (1 cup each).

PESTO-TURKEY LAYERED LOAF

Best. Sandwich. Ever. I guarantee this masterpiece will go over big when you're catering to a huddle of hungry football fans. Change up the meat and cheese to keep things interesting.
—**Marion Sundberg** *Yorba Linda, California*

PREP: 20 MIN. **COOK:** 25 MIN. + STANDING

- 1 loaf (1 pound) French bread
- 1 cup prepared pesto
- 1 pound thinly sliced deli turkey
- ½ pound provolone cheese, thinly sliced
- 2 small zucchini, thinly sliced
- 2 medium tomatoes, thinly sliced
- 1 medium red onion, thinly sliced

○ Cut the top fourth off a loaf of bread. Carefully hollow out the bottom, leaving a ½-in. shell. (Discard removed bread or save for another use.) Spread pesto on the inside of top and bottom of bread. Set top aside.

○ In bottom of bread, layer with turkey, cheese, zucchini, tomatoes and onion. Gently press the layers together. Replace bread top and wrap tightly in foil.

○ Place on a baking sheet. Bake at 350° for 25-30 minutes or until heated through. Let stand for 10 minutes before cutting.

Yield: 6 servings.

KITCHEN TIP

The best way to cut through the skin of a tomato is with a serrated, not straight-edged, knife. Cut a tomato vertically, from stem end to blossom end, for slices that will be less juicy and hold their shape better.

HOMEMADE TURKEY SOUP

With this recipe, you can make the most of even the smallest pieces of leftover meat on a turkey. This comforting soup balances its wonderful rich flavor with a creamy broth full of tender rice and vegetables.
—**June Sangrey** *Manheim, Pennsylvania*

PREP: 30 MIN. **COOK:** 2 HOURS 35 MIN.

- 1 leftover turkey carcass (from a 10- to 12-pound turkey)
- 2 quarts water
- 1 medium onion, halved
- ½ teaspoon salt
- 2 bay leaves
- 1 cup chopped carrots
- 1 cup uncooked long grain rice
- ⅓ cup chopped celery
- ¼ cup chopped onion
- 1 can (10¾ ounces) condensed cream of chicken *or* cream of mushroom soup, undiluted

○ Place the turkey carcass in a stockpot; add the water, onion, salt and bay leaves. Slowly bring to a boil over low heat; cover and simmer for 2 hours.

○ Remove carcass; cool. Strain broth and skim off fat. Discard onion and bay leaves. Return broth to the pan. Add the carrots, rice, celery and chopped onion; cover and simmer until rice and vegetables are tender.

○ Remove the turkey from bones; discard bones and cut turkey into bite-size pieces. Add the turkey and cream soup to broth; heat through.

Yield: 8-10 servings (about 2 quarts).

TOMATOES: BRAND X PICTURES

MOO SHU SLOPPY JOES

Say sayonara to ordinary sloppy joes and hello to these Asian-infused wraps boasting a unique blend of hoisin sauce, barbecue sauce and coleslaw mix.
—**Mike Tchou** *Pepper Pike, Ohio*

PREP/TOTAL TIME: 30 MIN.

QUICK & EASY

- 2 teaspoons cornstarch
- ½ cup cold water
- ¼ cup barbecue sauce
- ¼ cup hoisin sauce
- 2 tablespoons reduced-sodium soy sauce
- 2 teaspoons minced fresh gingerroot
- 1 teaspoon minced garlic
- ¼ teaspoon salt
- 1 small onion, sliced
- 1 small sweet red pepper, sliced
- 2 teaspoons canola oil
- 1 pound lean ground beef (90% lean)
- 3 cups coleslaw mix
- 8 flour tortillas (6 inches), warmed

In a small bowl, combine the cornstarch, water, barbecue sauce, hoisin sauce, soy sauce, ginger, garlic and salt until blended; set aside.

In a large skillet, saute onion and red pepper in oil until crisp-tender; remove and set aside. In the same skillet, cook beef over medium heat until meat is no longer pink; drain.

Stir cornstarch mixture and add to the skillet. Bring to a boil; cook and stir for 1-2 minutes or until thickened. Add coleslaw mix; stir to coat. Spoon meat mixture into the center of each tortilla; top with onion mixture. Roll up tightly.

Yield: 4 servings.

GOLDEN POTATO SOUP

Looking for pure comfort food to warm you up on a cold night? Give my chunky potato soup a try. Pair it with warm, tender biscuits or garlic toast, and mmm, dinner's served!
—**Sheila Harms** *Battle Lake, Minnesota*

PREP/TOTAL TIME: 30 MIN.

QUICK & EASY

- 1 tablespoon butter
- 1 tablespoon canola oil
- 3 medium potatoes, peeled and cubed
- ½ teaspoon garlic salt
- ⅛ teaspoon pepper
- 1 can (14½ ounces) reduced-sodium chicken broth
- 1 small onion, chopped
- ¼ cup crumbled cooked bacon
- 1 garlic clove, minced
- 1 teaspoon dried rosemary, crushed
- 1 teaspoon dried thyme
- 1 cup hot water
- 2 teaspoons chicken bouillon granules
- 1 cup heavy whipping cream
- ½ cup shredded cheddar cheese

In a large saucepan, heat the butter and oil until butter is melted. Add the potatoes, garlic salt and pepper. Cook over medium heat for 4-6 minutes or until potatoes are tender and lightly browned.

Stir in the broth, onion, bacon, garlic, rosemary and thyme. Bring to a boil. Reduce heat; cover and simmer for 15 minutes. Stir in water and bouillon. Gradually stir in cream; heat through. Add cheese, stirring until melted.

Yield: 4½ cups.

CHILI CONEY DOGS

Long live summertime favorites! But there's no need to wait for warm weather to enjoy these jazzed-up dogs. The convenience of your slow cooker means you can relish them any time a craving calls.
—**Michele Harris** *Vicksburg, Michigan*

PREP: 15 MIN. **COOK:** 4 HOURS

- 1 pound lean ground beef (90% lean)
- 1 can (15 ounces) tomato sauce
- ½ cup water
- 2 tablespoons Worcestershire sauce
- 1 tablespoon dried minced onion
- ½ teaspoon garlic powder
- ½ teaspoon ground mustard
- ½ teaspoon chili powder
- ½ teaspoon pepper

Dash cayenne pepper

- 8 hot dogs
- 8 hot dog buns, split

Shredded cheddar cheese, relish and chopped onion, optional

- In a large skillet, cook beef over medium heat until meat is no longer pink; drain. Stir in the tomato sauce, water, Worcestershire sauce, onion and spices.

- Place hot dogs in a 3-qt. slow cooker; top with beef mixture. Cover and cook on low for 4-5 hours or until heated through. Serve on buns with cheese, relish and onion if desired.

Yield: 8 servings.

HAM & CORN CHOWDER

Generous amounts of corn, ham and potato turn this chowder into a fast favorite. No one will know it came together in a mere 25 minutes, especially if you add the pretty garnishes on top.
—**Marion St. Jean** *Homosassa, Florida*

PREP/TOTAL TIME: 25 MIN.

QUICK & EASY

- 1 can (10¾ ounces) reduced-fat reduced-sodium condensed cream of celery soup, undiluted
- 1½ cups fat-free milk
- 1 can (15¼ ounces) whole kernel corn, drained
- 1 can (14¾ ounces) cream-style corn
- ½ cup cubed fully cooked ham
- 2 tablespoons dried minced onion
- 2 tablespoons minced fresh parsley
- 1 can (14½ ounces) diced potatoes, drained

Sour cream, shredded cheddar cheese *and/or* paprika, optional

- In a large saucepan, combine soup and milk. Heat through, stirring frequently. Stir in the corn, ham, onion and parsley. Bring to a boil. Reduce heat; cover and simmer for 5 minutes. Stir in potatoes; heat through. Garnish with sour cream, cheese and/or paprika if desired.

Yield: 6 servings.

BAKED LASAGNA IN A BUN

Lasagna...oh, how I love thee! But sometimes I like to shake things up by tucking my favorite ingredients for this classic inside hollowed-out sandwich buns. This is one open-faced wonder that never disappoints.
—**Cindy Morelock** Afton, Tennessee

PREP: 20 MIN. **BAKE:** 25 MIN.

8 submarine *or* hoagie buns (8 inches)	¼ cup grated Parmesan cheese
1 pound lean ground beef (90% lean)	1 cup (4 ounces) shredded cheddar cheese, *divided*
1 cup spaghetti sauce	
1 tablespoon garlic powder	1 cup (4 ounces) shredded part-skim mozzarella cheese, *divided*
1 tablespoon Italian seasoning	
1 cup ricotta cheese	

● Make a 2-in.-wide V-shaped cut in the center of each bun to within 1 inch of the bottom. Remove cut portion and save for another use; set aside.

● In a large skillet, cook beef over medium heat until no longer pink; drain. Add the spaghetti sauce, garlic powder and Italian seasoning. Cook 4-5 minutes or until heated through.

● Meanwhile, combine the ricotta, Parmesan cheese and half of cheddar and mozzarella cheeses. Spoon meat sauce into buns; top with cheese mixture. Place on a baking sheet. Cover loosely with foil.

● Bake at 350° for 20-25 minutes. Uncover; sprinkle with remaining cheddar and mozzarella. Return to the oven for 2-3 minutes or until the cheese is melted.

Yield: 8 servings.

CHICKEN WILD RICE SOUP

Wild rice has an intense, nutty flavor that's delicious in this savory soup, along with tender cubes of chicken and fresh vegetables. The down-home appeal will satisfy the deepest comfort food craving.
—**Virginia Montmarquet** *Riverside, California*

PREP: 10 MIN. **COOK:** 40 MIN.

2 quarts chicken broth
½ pound fresh mushrooms, chopped
1 cup finely chopped celery
1 cup shredded carrots
½ cup finely chopped onion
1 teaspoon chicken bouillon granules
1 teaspoon dried parsley flakes
¼ teaspoon garlic powder
¼ teaspoon dried thyme

¼ cup butter, cubed
¼ cup all-purpose flour
1 can (10¾ ounces) condensed cream of mushroom soup, undiluted
½ cup dry white wine *or* additional chicken broth
3 cups cooked wild rice
2 cups cubed cooked chicken

● In a large saucepan, combine the first nine ingredients. Bring to a boil. Reduce heat; cover and simmer for 30 minutes.

● In Dutch oven, melt butter; stir in flour until smooth. Gradually whisk in broth mixture. Bring to a boil; cook and stir for 2 minutes or until thickened. Whisk in soup and wine. Add rice and chicken; heat through.

Yield: 14 servings (3½ quarts).

CHUNKY CHIPOTLE PORK CHILI

My chili is the best way to make use of leftover pork roast. I like to make it a day in advance and let it sit overnight so the flavors fully blend. That's *if* I have enough resistance to wait!
—**Peter Halferty** *Corpus Christi, Texas*

PREP: 15 MIN. **COOK:** 20 MIN.

- 1   medium green pepper, chopped
- 1   small onion, chopped
- 1   chipotle pepper in adobo sauce, finely chopped
- 1   tablespoon canola oil
- 3   garlic cloves, minced
- 1   can (16 ounces) red beans, rinsed and drained
- 1   cup beef broth
- ½   cup salsa
- 2   teaspoons ground cumin
- 2   teaspoons chili powder
- 2   cups cubed cooked pork
- ¼   cup sour cream

○ In a large saucepan, saute green pepper, onion and chipotle pepper in oil until tender. Add the garlic; cook 1 minute longer.

○ Add the beans, broth, salsa, cumin and chili powder. Bring to a boil. Reduce heat; simmer, uncovered, for 10 minutes or until thickened. Add pork; heat through. Serve with sour cream.

Yield: 4 servings.

MONTEREY ARTICHOKE PANINI

Looking for a unique sandwich idea? This tasty combination of cheese, artichokes, spinach and tomatoes layered between classic panini bread is something straight out of a bistro!
—**Jean Ecos** *Hartland, Wisconsin*

QUICK & EASY

PREP/TOTAL TIME: 25 MIN.

- 4   slices sourdough *or* multigrain bread
- 4   slices Monterey Jack cheese (¾ ounce *each*)
- ½   cup water-packed artichoke hearts, rinsed, drained and halved
- ½   cup fresh baby spinach
- 4   slices tomato
- 1   tablespoon butter, softened

○ On two slices of bread, layer a slice of cheese, artichokes, spinach, two slices of tomato and remaining cheese. Top with remaining bread. Spread butter on outsides of sandwiches.

○ Cook on a panini maker or indoor grill until bread is toasted and cheese is melted.

Yield: 2 servings.

❝ We love Monterey Artichoke Paninis. Most times we add a dash of Italian dressing on the artichokes, but the recipe is great on its own! ❞

—**KITCHENSWEEP** FROM TASTEOFHOME.COM

MEXICAN CHICKEN SOUP

This zesty dish is loaded with chicken, corn and black beans in a mildly spicy red broth. You can also use cubed rotisserie chicken and cook on the stovetop on those nights when you have to get dinner on the table in a hurry.
—**Marlene Kane** *Lainesburg, Michigan*

PREP: 10 MIN. **COOK:** 3 HOURS

- 1½ pounds boneless skinless chicken breasts, cubed
- 2 teaspoons canola oil
- ½ cup water
- 1 envelope reduced-sodium taco seasoning
- 1 can (32 ounces) V8 juice
- 1 jar (16 ounces) salsa
- 1 can (15 ounces) black beans, rinsed and drained
- 1 package (10 ounces) frozen corn, thawed
- 6 tablespoons reduced-fat cheddar cheese
- 6 tablespoons reduced-fat sour cream
- 2 tablespoons minced fresh cilantro

⊚ In a large nonstick skillet, saute chicken in oil until no longer pink. Add water and taco seasoning; simmer, uncovered, until chicken is well coated.

⊚ Transfer to a 5-qt. slow cooker. Stir in the V8 juice, salsa, beans and corn. Cover and cook on low for 3-4 hours or until heated through. Serve with cheese, sour cream and cilantro.

Yield: 6 servings.

AUTUMN CHOWDER

I like to whip up this hearty chowder as soon as the temperature takes a tumble. Brimming with veggies and topped with bacon, it actually gets mouths watering with sweet anticipation.
—**Sheena Hoffman** *North Vancouver, British Columbia*

PREP: 10 MIN. **COOK:** 35 MIN.

- 2 bacon strips, diced
- ¼ cup chopped onion
- 1 medium red potato, cubed
- 1 small carrot, halved lengthwise and thinly sliced
- ½ cup water
- ¾ teaspoon chicken bouillon granules
- 1 cup milk
- ⅔ cup frozen corn
- ⅛ teaspoon pepper
- 2½ teaspoons all-purpose flour
- 2 tablespoons cold water
- ¾ cup shredded cheddar cheese

⊚ In a large saucepan, cook bacon over medium heat until crisp; remove to paper towels. Drain, reserving 1 teaspoon drippings. In the drippings, saute onion until tender. Add the potato, carrot, water and bouillon. Bring to a boil. Reduce the heat; cover and simmer for 15-20 minutes or until the vegetables are almost tender.

⊚ Stir in the milk, corn and pepper. Cook 5 minutes longer. Combine the flour and cold water until smooth; gradually whisk into soup. Bring to a boil; cook and stir for 1-2 minutes or until thickened. Remove from the heat; stir in cheese until melted. Sprinkle with bacon.

Yield: 2 servings.

KITCHEN TIP

Try Mexican Chicken Soup with homemade tortilla dumplings. Cut a stack of tortillas into strips. Then add the strips to the simmering mixture and let them thicken up.

—**AL PEOPLES,** LOUISBURG, NORTH CAROLINA

TORTILLA: RD-MKE

SOUPS & SANDWICHES

CHIPOTLE PULLED PORK SANDWICHES

One day I was making my famous pulled pork and decided to kick up the flavor a notch. Red current jelly was the perfect addition to the tender, slow-cooked sensation.
—**Tatiana Kushnir** *Montara, California*

PREP: 10 MIN. **COOK:** 8½ HOURS

1 boneless pork shoulder butt roast
   (3 pounds)
2 tablespoons steak seasoning
½ cup water

1 cup red currant jelly
3 tablespoons minced chipotle peppers in adobo sauce
10 kaiser rolls, split

○ Cut roast in half. Place in a 5-qt. slow cooker; sprinkle with steak seasoning. Add water. Cover and cook on low for 8-10 hours or until meat is tender.

○ In a small saucepan, combine jelly and peppers. Cook over medium heat for 5 minutes or until heated through. Remove meat from slow cooker; discard cooking liquid. Shred pork with two forks. Return to the slow cooker; top with jelly mixture. Cover and cook on low for 30 minutes or until heated through. Spoon about ⅔ cup meat onto each roll.

EDITOR'S NOTE: This recipe was tested with McCormick's Montreal Steak Seasoning. Look for it in the spice aisle of your local grocery.

Yield: 10 servings.

❝I loved this! I used the red currant jelly but would love to try it with homemade pomegranate jelly. It has a nice kick to it.❞

— **S_PANTS** FROM TASTEOFHOME.COM

SOUTHWESTERN TURKEY SOUP

This spicy soup is loaded with turkey, beans, corn and tomatoes. We like it really hot, so we tend to use all three tablespoons of jalapenos...and then some. It's sure to warm you up on a cold, wintry day.
—**Brenda Kruse** *Ames, Iowa*

PREP: 20 MIN. **COOK:** 30 MIN.

1 medium onion, chopped
1 tablespoon olive oil
1 can (14½ ounces) chicken broth
2 to 3 tablespoons diced jalapeno pepper
3 teaspoons ground cumin
1½ teaspoons chili powder
¼ teaspoon salt
¼ teaspoon cayenne pepper

3 cups cubed cooked turkey
1 can (15 ounces) black beans, rinsed and drained
1 can (10 ounces) diced tomatoes and green chilies, undrained
1½ cups frozen corn

Sour cream, coarsely crushed tortilla chips, shredded cheddar cheese and sliced ripe olives, optional

◉ In a large saucepan, saute onion in oil until tender. Stir in the broth, jalapeno, cumin, chili powder, salt and cayenne. Add the turkey, beans, tomatoes and corn.

◉ Bring to a boil. Reduce heat; cover and simmer for 20-30 minutes to allow flavors to blend. Garnish with sour cream, chips, cheese and olives if desired.

EDITOR'S NOTE: Always wear disposable gloves when cutting hot peppers; the oils can burn skin. Avoid touching your face.

Yield: 7 servings.

SUNNY BLT SANDWICHES

Yes, you can have the best of both worlds. I dress up my BLTs with creamy homemade egg salad. Smoky bacon, ripe tomatoes and crisp lettuce make them visually appealing *and* delicious.
—**Kelly McDonald** *Edinburg, Texas*

PREP/TOTAL TIME: 20 MIN.

QUICK & EASY

- 4 bacon strips
- 4 hard-cooked eggs, chopped
- 2 tablespoons 4% cottage cheese
- 1 tablespoon cream cheese, softened
- 2 teaspoons sweet pickle juice
- ½ teaspoon prepared mustard
- ¼ teaspoon onion powder
- ⅛ teaspoon salt
- ⅛ teaspoon pepper
- ⅛ teaspoon Worcestershire sauce
- 4 slices whole wheat bread, toasted
- 2 lettuce leaves
- 2 slices tomato
- 2 slices Swiss cheese (¾ ounce each)

● In a large skillet, cook bacon over medium heat until crisp. Remove to paper towels to drain.

● In a large bowl, combine the eggs, cottage cheese, cream cheese, pickle juice, mustard, onion powder, salt, pepper and Worcestershire sauce. On two slices of toast, layer the lettuce, tomato, cheese slices and bacon. Top with egg salad and remaining toast.

Yield: 2 servings.

BROCCOLI CHEESE SOUP

Frozen broccoli-cheese sauce makes this hearty soup a speedy addition to a lunchtime or evening meal. The recipe can easily be doubled to serve a larger group.
—**Laura Mihalenko-DeVoe** *Charlotte, North Carolina*

PREP/TOTAL TIME: 25 MIN.

QUICK & EASY

- 2 tablespoons chopped onion
- 1 tablespoon butter
- 1 cup chicken broth
- 1 package (10 ounces) frozen broccoli and cheese sauce, thawed
- ½ cup cooked long grain rice
- ¼ cup heavy whipping cream

● In a small saucepan, cook onion in butter until tender. Stir in broth and broccoli with sauce. Bring to a boil. Reduce heat; simmer, uncovered, for 4 minutes.

● Add rice and cream. Cook 3-4 minutes longer or until heated through and broccoli is tender (do not boil).

Yield: 2 servings.

"My family loves broccoli and definitely loves this soup. I am keeping the recipe and will be making it many more times.**"**

—**TKARINAS** FROM TASTEOFHOME.COM

HOT ITALIAN SAUSAGE SOUP

I'm part owner of a small tavern, and on Saturdays we provide deli sandwiches and soups free of charge. Our patrons love this one loaded with zesty sausage and an array of veggies. A hint of brown sugar balances the heat with a little sweetness, making it a real crowd-pleaser!
—**Dan Bute** *Ottawa, Illinois*

PREP/TOTAL TIME: 25 MIN.

- 1 pound bulk hot Italian sausage
- 1 can (14½ ounces) Italian stewed tomatoes
- 1 can (8 ounces) tomato sauce
- 1 cup frozen Italian vegetables
- ¾ cup julienned green, sweet red *and/or* yellow pepper
- ¼ cup chopped onion
- ¼ cup white wine *or* chicken broth
- 1 teaspoon brown sugar
- 1 teaspoon minced fresh parsley
- ½ teaspoon Italian seasoning
- ⅛ teaspoon salt
- ⅛ teaspoon pepper

● In a large skillet, cook sausage over medium heat until no longer pink.

● Meanwhile, in a large saucepan, combine the remaining ingredients. Bring to a boil. Reduce heat; cover and simmer for 10 minutes or until vegetables are tender.

● Drain sausage; add to soup and heat through. Serve immediately or cool and transfer to freezer containers. May be frozen for up to 3 months.

TO USE FROZEN SOUP: Thaw in the refrigerator overnight. Transfer to a saucepan. Cover and cook over medium heat until heated through.

Yield: 4 servings.

TOMATO TORTELLINI SOUP

This flavorful and filling pasta soup tastes homemade all the way. No one will guess you "cheated" by using convenience items! Feel free to toss in extra tortellini to make it extra hearty.
—**Sandra Fick** *Lincoln, Nebraska*

PREP/TOTAL TIME: 25 MIN.

- 1 package (9 ounces) refrigerated cheese tortellini
- 2 cans (10¾ ounces *each*) reduced-sodium condensed tomato soup, undiluted
- 2 cups vegetable broth
- 2 cups 2% milk
- 2 cups half-and-half cream
- ½ cup chopped oil-packed sun-dried tomatoes
- 1 teaspoon onion powder
- 1 teaspoon garlic powder
- 1 teaspoon dried basil
- ½ teaspoon salt
- ½ cup shredded Parmesan cheese

Additional shredded Parmesan cheese, optional

● Cook tortellini according to package directions.

● Meanwhile, in a Dutch oven, combine the soup, broth, milk, cream, tomatoes and seasonings. Heat through, stirring frequently. Drain tortellini; carefully add to soup. Stir in cheese. Sprinkle each serving with additional cheese if desired.

Yield: 10 servings (2½ quarts).

KITCHEN TIP

Use the finest section of your grating tool when grating Parmesan cheese. You can also use a blender. Simply cut the cheese into 1-inch cubes and process 1 cup of cubes at a time on high until finely grated.

PARMESAN: RDA-GID

SOUPS & SANDWICHES

BAKED POTATO SOUP

My thick and heartwarming soup brings a little zip with each delicious spoonful. I add hot pepper sauce and basil to make this version stand out from the rest.

—Kristi Teague *Southside, Tennessee*

PREP: 30 MIN. **COOK:** 10 MIN.

1 large potato	¼ teaspoon pepper
1 bacon strip, diced	1½ cups chicken broth
2 tablespoons chopped onion	½ cup half-and-half cream
1 small garlic clove, minced	6 to 8 drops hot pepper sauce, optional
5 teaspoons all-purpose flour	2 tablespoons shredded cheddar cheese
½ teaspoon dried basil	2 teaspoons minced fresh parsley

⊙ Scrub and pierce potato. Microwave on high for 4-6 minutes or bake at 400° for 50-75 minutes or until tender, turning once. When cool enough to handle, peel and cube potato; set aside.

⊙ In a small saucepan, cook the bacon over medium heat until crisp. Using a slotted spoon, remove bacon to a paper towel.

⊙ In the drippings, saute onion and garlic until tender. Stir in the flour, basil and pepper until blended. Gradually add broth. Bring to a boil; cook and stir for 2 minutes.

⊙ Add the cream, cubed potato and hot pepper sauce if desired; heat through (do not boil). Top each serving with bacon, cheese and parsley.

EDITOR'S NOTE: This recipe was tested in a 1,100-watt microwave.

Yield: 2 servings.

HAMBURGER MINESTRONE

This hearty minestrone will chase away chills on a cold day. Use frozen mixed vegetables or any combination that suits your taste. You can also use any type of pasta.
—*Taste of Home Test Kitchen*

QUICK & EASY

PREP/TOTAL TIME: 30 MIN.

- ½ cup small uncooked pasta shells
- 1 pound lean ground beef (90% lean)
- ½ cup chopped onion
- 3 cans (14½ ounces *each*) beef broth
- 1 package (16 ounces) frozen mixed vegetables
- 1 can (16 ounces) kidney beans, rinsed and drained
- 1 can (14½ ounces) diced tomatoes, undrained
- 1 can (6 ounces) tomato paste
- 3 teaspoons Italian seasoning
- 1 teaspoon salt
- ¼ teaspoon dried thyme
- ¼ teaspoon dried basil
- ¼ teaspoon pepper

● Cook pasta according to package directions. Meanwhile, in a large saucepan, cook beef and onion over medium heat until meat is no longer pink; drain.

● Stir in the remaining ingredients. Bring to a boil. Reduce heat; simmer, uncovered, for 15 minutes. Drain pasta and add to the pan. Cook 5 minutes longer or until heated through.

Yield: 6 servings.

KITCHEN TIP

Italian seasoning can be found in the spice aisle of most grocery stores. A basic blend might contain marjoram, thyme, rosemary, savory, sage, oregano and basil.

ONE-POT CHILI

Here's a hearty low-fat entree that doesn't skimp on flavor or fulfillment. It's quick, easy and, because the dried pasta cooks right in the chili, there's one less pot to wash!
—*Dawn Forsberg* Saint Joseph, Missouri

PREP: 25 MIN. **COOK:** 15 MIN.

- 1 pound lean ground turkey
- 1 small onion, chopped
- ¼ cup chopped green pepper
- 1 teaspoon olive oil
- 2 cups water
- 1 can (15 ounces) pinto beans, rinsed and drained
- 1 can (14½ ounces) reduced-sodium beef broth
- 1 can (14½ ounces) diced tomatoes with mild green chilies, undrained
- 1 can (8 ounces) no-salt-added tomato sauce
- 2 teaspoons chili powder
- 1 teaspoon ground cumin
- ½ teaspoon dried oregano
- 2 cups uncooked multigrain penne pasta
- ¼ cup reduced-fat sour cream
- ¼ cup minced fresh cilantro

● In a large saucepan coated with cooking spray, cook the turkey, onion and pepper in oil over medium heat until meat is no longer pink; drain.

● Stir in the water, beans, broth, tomatoes, tomato sauce, chili powder, cumin and oregano. Bring to a boil. Add pasta; cook for 15-20 minutes or until tender, stirring occasionally. Serve with sour cream; sprinkle with cilantro.

Yield: 6 servings (2 quarts).

HERB: BRANDX PICTURES

SOUPS & SANDWICHES

CARAMELIZED FRENCH ONION SOUP

Caramelized onions give a touch of sweetness to this traditional soup topped with toasted cheese bread. It's such a simple version of a timeless classic.
—*Pat Stevens* *Granbury, Texas*

PREP: 10 MIN. **COOK:** 40 MIN.

1	medium onion, sliced
1	tablespoon butter
1	to 2 teaspoons sugar
1	teaspoon Worcestershire sauce
1⅓	cups beef broth
1	tablespoon white wine *or* water

Coarsely ground pepper to taste

2	slices French bread (1 inch thick)
⅓	cup shredded Swiss cheese
3	tablespoons grated Parmesan cheese

◉ In a saucepan, saute onion in butter until tender. Sprinkle with sugar and Worcestershire sauce; cook and stir for 13-15 minutes or until onion is caramelized.

◉ Add the broth, wine or water and pepper. Bring to a boil. Reduce heat; cover and simmer for 15 minutes.

◉ Place bread on an ungreased baking sheet. Broil 4 in. from the heat until toasted. Turn; sprinkle with cheeses. Broil until cheese is melted and bubbly. Ladle soup into bowls; top with toast.

Yield: 2 servings.

“**This recipe is really good—and quick! I added a bay leaf, a clove of garlic and a dash of nutmeg for an even richer flavor.**”

—SETHBOOKERT FROM TASTEOFHOME.COM

BEEF VEGETABLE SOUP

There's nothing better than coming home after a long, hard day to the glorious aroma of a simmering, ready-to-eat meal. This slow-cooked wonder goes well with a salad and breadsticks.
—*Jean Hutzell* *Dubuque, Iowa*

PREP: 15 MIN. **COOK:** 9 HOURS

1	pound lean ground beef (90% lean)
1	medium onion, chopped
½	teaspoon salt
¼	teaspoon pepper
3	cups water
3	medium potatoes, peeled and cut into ¾-inch cubes
1	can (14½ ounces) Italian diced tomatoes, undrained
1	can (11½ ounces) V8 juice
1	cup chopped celery
1	cup sliced carrots
2	tablespoons sugar
1	tablespoon dried parsley flakes
2	teaspoons dried basil
1	bay leaf

◉ In a nonstick skillet, cook beef and onion over medium heat until meat is no longer pink; drain. Stir in salt and pepper.

◉ Transfer to a 5-qt. slow cooker. Add the remaining ingredients. Cover and cook on low for 9-11 hours or until vegetables are tender. Discard bay leaf before serving.

Yield: 7 servings.

ITALIAN CHICKEN WRAPS

These tasty, make-ahead wraps are wonderfully portable for a picnic or tailgate party. Try a blend of assorted peppers and zucchini if you prefer fresh vegetables instead of frozen.
—**Cathy Hofflander** *Adrian, Michigan*

PREP/TOTAL TIME: 25 MIN.

QUICK & EASY

- 1 package (16 ounces) frozen stir-fry vegetable blend
- 2 packages (6 ounces *each*) ready-to-use grilled chicken breast strips
- ½ cup fat-free Italian salad dressing
- 3 tablespoons shredded Parmesan cheese
- 6 flour tortillas (8 inches), room temperature

● In a large saucepan, cook vegetables according to package directions; drain. Stir in the chicken, salad dressing and cheese. Simmer, uncovered, for 3-4 minutes or until heated through. Spoon about ¾ cup of mixture down the center of each tortilla; roll up tightly.

Yield: 6 servings.

CUCUMBER SANDWICHES

Cool, crisp cucumbers make this light sandwich a pleasant change of pace. I sometimes add bacon and thinly sliced onions on top for a little extra vigor.
—**Karen Schriefer** *Stevensville, Maryland*

PREP/TOTAL TIME: 15 MIN.

QUICK & EASY

- 1 carton (8 ounces) spreadable cream cheese
- 2 teaspoons ranch salad dressing mix
- 12 slices pumpernickel rye bread
- 2 to 3 medium cucumbers

● In a large bowl, combine cream cheese and dressing mix. Spread on one side of each slice of bread. Peel cucumbers if desired; thinly slice and place on six slices of bread. Top with remaining bread. Serve immediately.

Yield: 6 servings.

SWISS TUNA MELTS

Your family will love these hot sandwiches that brown to a melty perfection. The celery lends a nice crunch to the creamy tuna filling. If you'd like to kick up the flavor a notch, simply add a pinch of garlic powder and dill relish.
—**Karen Owen** *Rising Sun, Indiana*

PREP/TOTAL TIME: 20 MIN.

QUICK & EASY

- 1 can (6 ounces) light water-packed tuna, drained and flaked
- ¾ cup shredded Swiss cheese
- ¼ cup chopped onion
- ¼ cup chopped celery
- ½ cup sour cream
- ½ cup mayonnaise

Pepper to taste

- 8 slices bread
- 2 to 3 tablespoons butter, softened

● In a large bowl, combine the tuna, cheese, onion and celery. In a small bowl, combine sour cream and mayonnaise. Pour over tuna mixture and toss to coat. Spread about ½ cup over four slices of bread; top with remaining bread. Butter the outside of the sandwiches.

● On a griddle or in a large skillet over medium heat, toast the sandwiches for 4-5 minutes on each side or until lightly browned.

Yield: 4 servings.

CHICKEN LETTUCE WRAPS

This is one of my go-to recipes when I want a sassy hand-held meal. I love the spicy Asian flavors against the cool lettuce and the added crunch of almonds and water chestnuts.
—**Kendra Doss** *Kansas City, Missouri*

QUICK & EASY

PREP/TOTAL TIME: 25 MIN.

1½ pounds boneless skinless chicken breasts, cubed
1 tablespoon plus 1½ teaspoons peanut oil, *divided*
¾ cup chopped fresh mushrooms
1 can (8 ounces) water chestnuts, drained and diced
1 tablespoon minced fresh gingerroot
2 tablespoons rice vinegar

2 tablespoons reduced-sodium teriyaki sauce
1 tablespoon reduced-sodium soy sauce
½ teaspoon garlic powder
¼ teaspoon crushed red pepper flakes
1½ cups shredded carrots
½ cup julienned green onions
12 Bibb *or* Boston lettuce leaves
⅓ cup sliced almonds, toasted

● In a large nonstick skillet coated with cooking spray, cook chicken in 1 tablespoon oil for 3 minutes; drain. Add the mushrooms, water chestnuts and ginger; cook 4-6 minutes longer or until chicken is no longer pink. Drain and set aside.

● In a small bowl, whisk the vinegar, teriyaki sauce, soy sauce, garlic powder, red pepper flakes and remaining oil. Stir in the carrots, onions and chicken mixture.

● Spoon onto lettuce leaves; sprinkle with almonds. If desired, fold sides of lettuce over filling and roll up.

Yield: 6 servings.

CHEESY CORN CHOWDER

I've been making this cheesy corn chowder for, well, let's just say a long time. A few decades later, and my large, hungry brood *still* can't get enough. Thank goodness it makes a big pot!
—Lola Comer *Marysville, Washington*

PREP: 30 MIN. **COOK:** 30 MIN.

- 6 bacon strips, chopped
- ¾ cup chopped sweet onion
- 2½ cups water
- 2½ cups cubed peeled potatoes
- 2 cups sliced fresh carrots
- 2 teaspoons chicken bouillon granules
- 3 cans (11 ounces *each*) gold and white corn, drained
- ½ teaspoon pepper
- 7 tablespoons all-purpose flour
- 5 cups 2% milk
- 3 cups (12 ounces) shredded cheddar cheese
- 1 cup cubed process cheese (Velveeta)

● In a Dutch oven, cook bacon and onion over medium heat until onion is tender. Add the water, potatoes, carrots and bouillon; bring to a boil. Reduce heat; cover and simmer for 15-20 minutes or until potatoes are tender.

● Stir in corn and pepper. In a large bowl, whisk flour and milk until smooth; add to soup. Bring to a boil; cook and stir for 2 minutes or until thickened. Reduce heat. Add the cheeses; cook and stir until melted.

Yield: 15 servings (3¾ quarts).

> ❝Very good chowder that features bacon and cheese with a touch of sweetness from the corn. Makes a complete meal when you pair it with hot rolls.❞

—TEXASCOOKIE FROM TASTEOFHOME.COM

HAM 'N' SAUSAGE STROMBOLI

I guarantee your guests will go crazy for this heavyweight champ of a sandwich. One bite and you'll know why...gooey cheese, warm bread and savory deli meats...what's not to love?
—Lee Gregory *Ashland, Ohio*

PREP: 25 MIN. **BAKE:** 35 MIN. + COOLING

- 1 package (16 ounces) hot roll mix
- 1¼ cups warm water (120° to 130°)
- 3 tablespoons olive oil, *divided*
- ⅓ pound sliced deli ham
- ⅓ pound sliced salami
- 4 slices process American cheese, cut into thin strips
- 1 cup (4 ounces) shredded part-skim mozzarella *or* provolone cheese
- ¼ pound bulk Italian sausage, cooked and crumbled
- 2 tablespoons grated Parmesan cheese
- 1 teaspoon dried oregano
- ½ teaspoon garlic powder
- ¼ teaspoon coarsely ground pepper

● In a large bowl, combine the contents of the roll mix and yeast packets. Stir in warm water and 2 tablespoons oil until dough pulls away from sides of bowl.

● Turn onto a floured surface; knead until smooth and elastic, about 5 minutes. Cover and let rest for 5 minutes. Press into a lightly greased 15-in. x 10-in. x 1-in. baking pan.

● Layer with ham, salami, American cheese, mozzarella cheese and Italian sausage over dough. Roll up jelly-roll style, starting with a long side; pinch seam to seal. Place diagonally in pan. Brush dough with remaining oil; sprinkle with Parmesan cheese, oregano, garlic powder and pepper.

● Bake at 375° for 35-40 minutes or until golden brown. Let stand for 10 minutes before slicing.

Yield: 18 servings.

GNOCCHI CHICKEN MINESTRONE

My Italian heritage—and my mother, who was a wizard with soup—inspired my take on minestrone. Using frozen gnocchi saves time and adds extra heftiness to this chunky version.
—**Barbara Estabrook** *Rhinelander, Wisconsin*

PREP: 30 MIN. **COOK:** 30 MIN.

- 1¼ pounds chicken tenderloins, cut into ½-inch pieces
- ¾ teaspoon dried oregano
- ¼ teaspoon salt
- ¼ teaspoon pepper
- 2 tablespoons olive oil, *divided*
- 1 *each* small green, sweet red and yellow peppers, finely chopped
- 1 medium zucchini, finely chopped
- 1 cup chopped fresh baby portobello mushrooms
- ⅓ cup chopped red onion
- ⅓ cup chopped prosciutto *or* deli ham
- 4 garlic cloves, minced
- 2 cans (14½ ounces *each*) chicken broth
- 1 can (14½ ounces) Italian diced tomatoes, undrained
- ¾ cup canned white kidney *or* cannellini beans, rinsed and drained
- ½ cup frozen peas
- 3 tablespoons tomato paste
- 1 package (16 ounces) potato gnocchi
- ½ cup shredded Asiago cheese
- 8 fresh basil leaves, thinly sliced

● Sprinkle chicken with oregano, salt and pepper. In a Dutch oven, saute chicken in 1 tablespoon oil until no longer pink. Remove from the pan and set aside.

● In the same pan, cook the peppers, zucchini, mushrooms and onion in remaining oil until tender. Add prosciutto and garlic; cook 1 minute longer. Add the broth, tomatoes, beans, peas,

tomato paste and chicken. Bring to a boil. Reduce heat; simmer, uncovered, for 20 minutes, stirring occasionally.

● Meanwhile, cook gnocchi according to package directions. Drain; stir into soup. Garnish each serving with cheese and basil.

EDITOR'S NOTE: Look for potato gnocchi in the pasta or frozen foods section.

Yield: 8 servings (2¾ quarts).

ALL-AMERICAN HAMBURGERS

We're the family that lives for the great outdoors. Whether we're camping in the woods, lounging at the beach or just chilling in our own backyard, this classic burger is our top choice when dining alfresco.
—**Diane Hixon** *Niceville, Florida*

PREP/TOTAL TIME: 20 MIN.

- 2 tablespoons finely chopped onion
- 2 tablespoons chili sauce
- 2 teaspoons Worcestershire sauce
- 2 teaspoons prepared mustard
- 1 pound lean ground beef (90% lean)
- 4 slices American *or* cheddar cheese, halved diagonally
- 2 slices Swiss cheese, halved diagonally
- 4 hamburger buns, split and toasted
  Lettuce leaves, sliced tomato and onion, cooked bacon, ketchup and mustard, optional

● In a large bowl, combine the first four ingredients. Crumble beef over mixture and mix well. Shape into four patties.

● Grill, covered, over medium heat for 6 minutes on each side or until a meat thermometer reads 160° and juices run clear.

● During the last minute of cooking, top each patty with two triangles of American cheese and one triangle of Swiss cheese. Serve on buns with additional condiments if desired.

Yield: 4 servings.

SUMMER VEGETABLE SALAD, PAGE 82

70

80

77

SALADS, SIDES & MORE!

A memorable menu just isn't complete without on-the-side sensations that perfectly complement the main course. From picnic crowd-pleasers to speedy weeknight favorites, you'll find all the best in salads, fruit and vegetable medleys, classic side dish casseroles, relishes, condiments and more right here. Flip through the pages that follow, and you'll see just how easy it is to mix together the right ingredients for fresh and tasty toss-ups that are ripe for the picking!

CREAMY GRAPE SALAD

Everyone raves when I bring this refreshing, creamy salad to family gatherings. For a special finishing touch, I sprinkle it with brown sugar and pecans.
—**Marge Elling** *Jenison, Michigan*

PREP/TOTAL TIME: 20 MIN.

QUICK & EASY

- 1 package (8 ounces) cream cheese, softened
- 1 cup (8 ounces) sour cream
- ⅓ cup sugar
- 2 teaspoons vanilla extract
- 2 pounds seedless red grapes
- 2 pounds seedless green grapes
- 3 tablespoons brown sugar
- 3 tablespoons chopped pecans

- In a large bowl, beat the cream cheese, sour cream, sugar and vanilla until blended. Add grapes and toss to coat.

- Transfer to a serving bowl. Cover and refrigerate until serving. Sprinkle with brown sugar and pecans just before serving.

Yield: 21-24 servings.

SUMMER SQUASH CASSEROLE

With its crunchy topping, this rich side is a wonderful dish to take to potlucks and picnics or to pair up with a wide variety of entrees.
—**Jennifer Wallace** *Canal Winchester, Ohio*

PREP: 20 MIN. **BAKE:** 25 MIN.

- 2 medium yellow summer squash, diced
- 1 large zucchini, diced
- ½ pound sliced fresh mushrooms
- 1 cup chopped onion
- 2 tablespoons olive oil
- 2 cups (8 ounces) shredded cheddar cheese
- 1 can (10¾ ounces) condensed cream of mushroom soup, undiluted
- ½ cup sour cream
- ½ teaspoon salt
- 1 cup crushed butter-flavored crackers (about 25 crackers)
- 1 tablespoon butter, melted

- In a large skillet, saute the summer squash, zucchini, mushrooms and onion in oil until tender; drain.

- In a large bowl, combine the vegetable mixture, cheese, soup, sour cream and salt. Transfer to a greased 11-in. x 7-in. baking dish. Combine cracker crumbs and butter. Sprinkle over vegetable mixture.

- Bake, uncovered, at 350° for 25-30 minutes or until bubbly.

Yield: 10 servings.

SALADS, SIDES & MORE

GRILLED VEGETABLE PLATTER

Brightly colored and packed with flavor, these no-fuss veggies are perfect for entertaining or even as a light snack. Grilling brings out their natural sweetness, while the seasoning kicks them up a notch.
—Heidi Hall *North St. Paul, Minnesota*

PREP: 20 MIN. + MARINATING **GRILL:** 10 MIN.

¼ cup olive oil	3 small carrots, cut in half lengthwise
2 tablespoons honey	1 large sweet red pepper, cut into 1-inch strips
1 tablespoon plus ½ teaspoon balsamic vinegar, *divided*	1 medium yellow summer squash, cut into ½-inch slices
1 teaspoon dried oregano	1 medium red onion, cut into four wedges
½ teaspoon garlic powder	⅛ teaspoon pepper
1 pound fresh asparagus, trimmed	Dash salt

● In a small bowl, combine the oil, honey, 1 tablespoon vinegar, oregano and garlic powder. Pour 3 tablespoons marinade into a large resealable plastic bag; add the vegetables. Seal bag and turn to coat; refrigerate for 1½ hours. Cover and refrigerate remaining marinade.

● Place vegetables on a grilling grid. Transfer to grill rack. Grill, covered, over medium heat for 4-6 minutes on each side or until crisp-tender.

● Transfer to a large serving platter. Combine reserved marinade and remaining vinegar; drizzle over vegetables. Sprinkle with pepper and salt.

EDITOR'S NOTE: If you don't have a grilling grid, use a disposable foil pan. Poke holes in the bottom of the pan with a meat fork to allow liquid to drain.

Yield: 6 servings.

COUNTRY POTATO SALAD

I felt as though my usual potato salad recipe was missing something. So I experimented with some different ingredients, and the result was this tangy delight!
—**Ramona Hook Wysong** *Barlow, Kentucky*

PREP: 40 MIN. + CHILLING

    5 pounds potatoes, cooked, peeled and diced
    2 hard-cooked eggs, chopped
   ¼ cup thinly sliced green onions
   ¼ cup finely chopped green *or* sweet red pepper
   ¼ cup minced fresh parsley
    1 small garlic clove, minced
    6 slices bacon, cooked and crumbled
    1 teaspoon celery seed
    1 teaspoon dill weed
    1 teaspoon salt
   ½ teaspoon ground pepper

DRESSING:

   ¾ cup mayonnaise
    2 tablespoons sour cream
    1 teaspoon horseradish
    1 teaspoon Dijon mustard

Pinch oregano

Pinch chives

• In a large salad bowl, combine the first 11 ingredients. Set aside. Combine dressing ingredients; pour over potato mixture and toss to coat. Cover and refrigerate for up to 24 hours.

Yield: 20 servings.

CARROT RAISIN SALAD

This traditional salad is one of my mother-in-law's favorites. It's fun to eat because of its crunchy texture, and the raisins lend a slightly sweet flavor. It's also good with crushed pineapple.
—**Denise Baumert** *Dalhart, Texas*

QUICK & EASY

PREP/TOTAL TIME: 10 MIN.

    4 cups shredded carrots (about 4 large)
   ¾ to 1½ cups raisins
   ¼ cup mayonnaise
    2 tablespoons sugar
    2 to 3 tablespoons 2% milk

• Place carrots and raisins in a large bowl. In a small bowl, combine the mayonnaise, sugar and enough milk to achieve dressing consistency. Pour over carrot mixture; toss to coat.

Yield: 8 servings.

66 This salad brings back memories of my childhood in the '50s! It's sweet and crunchy and oh so good! 99

—CELINDA FROM TASTEOFHOME.COM

SALADS, SIDES & MORE

KITCHEN TIP

Instead of frying bacon, lay strips on a jelly roll pan and bake at 350° for 30 minutes. Prepared this way, bacon comes out crisp and flat. Plus, the pan cleans easily, and there's no stove-top spattering.

—**LOU H.**, MOBRIDGE, SOUTH DAKOTA

HEARTY BAKED BEANS

This saucy dish is flavorful and filling, and chock-full of ground beef, bacon and four varieties of beans. I've had the recipe for more than 10 years and often make it for big appetites at home and potlucks at work and church.
—*Cathy Swancutt* Junction City, Oregon

PREP: 15 MIN. **BAKE:** 1 HOUR

- 1 pound lean ground beef (90% lean)
- 2 large onions, chopped
- ¾ pound sliced bacon, cooked and crumbled
- 4 cans (15 ounces *each*) pork and beans
- 1 bottle (18 ounces) honey barbecue sauce
- 1 can (16 ounces) kidney beans, rinsed and drained
- 1 can (15¼ ounces) lima beans, rinsed and drained
- 1 can (15 ounces) black beans, rinsed and drained
- ½ cup packed brown sugar
- 3 tablespoons cider vinegar
- 1 tablespoon Liquid Smoke, optional
- 1 teaspoon salt
- ½ teaspoon pepper

- In a large skillet, cook beef and onions over medium heat until meat is no longer pink; drain. Transfer to a 5-qt. Dutch oven. Stir in the remaining ingredients.

- Cover and bake at 350° for 1 hour or until heated through.

Yield: 18 servings.

BACON CHEESEBURGER SALAD

Think kids don't eat salad? Serve up this burger-inspired creation and see what happens! Cooked ground beef is mixed with ketchup and mustard, then placed on lettuce and served with all your favorite burger toppings.
—*Taste of Home Test Kitchen*

PREP/TOTAL TIME: 30 MIN.

QUICK & EASY

- 2 hamburger buns, cut into 1-inch cubes
- 2 teaspoons olive oil
- ⅛ teaspoon garlic salt
- 1 pound ground beef
- ¾ cup chopped onion
- ¾ cup ketchup
- 1 tablespoon prepared mustard
- ⅛ teaspoon pepper
- 8 cups shredded lettuce
- 2 cups chopped tomatoes
- 4 slices process American cheese, cut into strips
- ½ cup crumbled cooked bacon
- 8 dill pickle slices

- For croutons, place bun cubes on a baking sheet. Drizzle with oil and sprinkle with garlic salt; toss to coat. Broil 4 in. from the heat for 4-6 minutes or until golden brown, turning once.

- In a large skillet, cook beef and onion over medium heat until meat is no longer pink; drain. Add the ketchup, mustard and pepper; heat through.

- Divide lettuce among four dinner plates; top each with tomatoes, meat mixture, cheese and bacon. Garnish with croutons and pickles.

Yield: 4 servings.

BACON: RDA-MKE

PINEAPPLE MANGO SALSA

This tangy, refreshing fruit salsa is great with your favorite tortilla chips. It can also be served over fish and even chicken entrees.

—Mary Gloede *Lakewood, Wisconsin*

PREP: 10 MIN. + CHILLING

1 cup chopped peeled mango	2 green onions, sliced
1 cup pineapple tidbits	2 tablespoons lime juice
½ cup diced sweet red pepper	1 tablespoon lemon juice
1 plum tomato, seeded and chopped	1 jalapeno pepper, finely chopped
3 tablespoons minced fresh cilantro	Tortilla chips

● In a large bowl, combine the first nine ingredients. Cover and refrigerate for 1 hour or until chilled. Serve with tortilla chips.

EDITOR'S NOTE: Wear disposable gloves when cutting hot peppers; the oils can burn skin. Avoid touching your face.

Yield: 2⅔ cups.

SOUR CREAM CUCUMBERS

My mom always served this sweet-tart cucumber medley at family picnics, and now it's one of my go-to dishes for parties. The sauce is creamy and the cucumbers have a nice crunch.
—**Pamela Eaton** *Monclova, Ohio*

PREP: 15 MIN. + CHILLING

- ½ cup sour cream
- 3 tablespoons white vinegar
- 1 tablespoon sugar

Pepper to taste

- 4 medium cucumbers, thinly sliced
- 1 small sweet onion, thinly sliced and separated into rings

◦ In a serving bowl, combine the sour cream, vinegar, sugar and pepper. Stir in cucumbers and onion. Cover and refrigerate for at least 4 hours. Serve with a slotted spoon.

Yield: 8 servings.

SEASONED RED POTATOES

I'm proud to serve these simple but tasty potatoes on the menu at my Side Track Cafe in Metamora, Indiana. The dressed-up spuds go well with just about any meaty entree.
—**Nancy Johnson** *Connersville, Indiana*

PREP: 10 MIN. **BAKE:** 50 MIN.

- 12 to 14 small red potatoes
- ¼ cup olive oil
- ¼ cup butter, melted
- 1 teaspoon salt
- 1 teaspoon garlic powder
- 1 teaspoon dried basil
- ½ teaspoon dried thyme
- ½ teaspoon pepper

◦ Peel a strip from around each potato. Place potatoes in an ungreased 3-qt. baking dish. In a small bowl, combine the oil, butter and seasonings; drizzle over potatoes.

◦ Bake, uncovered, at 350°, for 50-55 minutes or until tender, stirring every 15 minutes.

Yield: 6 servings.

SWEET POTATO CASSEROLE

I received this recipe from a friend, and it's won a special place in my recipe box. So many of my guests have enjoyed it that I've sent the recipe all over the country! It's a traditional staple for my Thanksgiving Day spread, and it's also delicious alongside chicken, ham or pork entrees.
—**Eleanor Sherry** *Highland Park, Illinois*

PREP: 10 MIN. **BAKE:** 25 MIN.

CASSEROLE:

- 2¼ to 2½ pounds (about 4 cups) sweet potatoes, cooked, peeled and mashed
- ⅓ cup butter, melted
- 2 eggs, lightly beaten
- ½ cup milk
- 1 teaspoon vanilla extract
- ½ cup sugar

TOPPING:

- ½ cup chopped nuts
- ½ cup flaked coconut
- ½ cup packed brown sugar
- 3 tablespoons butter, melted

◦ In a large bowl, combine the mashed potatoes, butter, eggs, milk, vanilla extract and sugar. Spread mixture into a greased 1½-qt. casserole.

◦ For topping, combine all the ingredients and sprinkle over potatoes. Bake at 375° for 25 minutes or until a thermometer reads 160°.

Yield: 6-8 servings.

MOCK APPLE BUTTER

Here, cinnamon, cloves and nutmeg combine to create a mouthwatering blend of spices in a sweet apple spread.
—**Nannette Sharon** *Tucson, Arizona*

PREP: 5 MIN. **COOK:** 30 MIN. + COOLING

2 cups unsweetened applesauce
¼ cup sugar
½ teaspoon ground cinnamon
¼ teaspoon ground allspice
⅛ teaspoon ground ginger
⅛ teaspoon ground cloves

○ In a small saucepan, combine all ingredients. Bring to a boil. Reduce heat; simmer, uncovered, for 30-35 minutes, stirring often. Remove from the heat; cool. Store in an airtight container in the refrigerator.

Yield: 1¼ cups.

KITCHEN TIP

Make your own homemade applesauce! Simply cut four red apples into fine slices (do not peel) and blend them in the blender. Chill and follow the recipe as directed.

—**SHEILA D.,** VICTORIA, BRITISH COLUMBIA

ANTIPASTO PICNIC SALAD

With a tempting blend of meats, veggies and pasta for your picnic, how can you go wrong? My recipe goes together in no time, serves a crowd and tastes as good at room temperature as it does cold. If you're expecting a smaller group, simply halve the ingredients to accommodate your number of guests.
—**Michele Larson** *Baden, Pennsylvania*

PREP: 30 MIN. **COOK:** 15 MIN.

1 package (16 ounces) medium pasta shells
2 jars (16 ounces *each*) giardiniera
1 pound fresh broccoli florets
½ pound cubed part-skim mozzarella cheese
½ pound hard salami, cubed
½ pound deli ham, cubed
2 packages (3½ ounces *each*) sliced pepperoni, halved
1 large green pepper, cut into chunks
1 can (6 ounces) pitted ripe olives, drained

DRESSING:

½ cup olive oil
¼ cup red wine vinegar
2 tablespoons lemon juice
1 teaspoon Italian seasoning
1 teaspoon coarsely ground pepper
½ teaspoon salt

○ Cook pasta according to package directions. Meanwhile, drain giardiniera, reserving ¾ cup liquid. In a large bowl, combine the giardiniera, broccoli, mozzarella, salami, ham, pepperoni, green pepper and olives. Drain pasta and rinse in cold water; stir into meat mixture.

○ For dressing, in a small bowl, whisk the oil, vinegar, lemon juice, Italian seasoning, pepper, salt and reserved giardiniera liquid. Pour over salad and toss to coat. Refrigerate until serving.

EDITOR'S NOTE: Giardiniera, a pickled vegetable mixture, is available in mild and hot varieties and can be found in the Italian or pickle section of your grocery store.

Yield: 25 servings (1 cup each).

APPLES: RDA-MKE

STRAWBERRY ROMAINE SALAD

My family is always happy to see this colorful salad on the table. If fresh strawberries aren't available, substitute mandarin oranges and dried cranberries.
—**Irene Keller** *Kalamazoo, Michigan*

PREP/TOTAL TIME: 30 MIN.

¼ cup sugar	CREAMY POPPY SEED DRESSING:
⅓ cup slivered almonds	¼ cup mayonnaise
1 bunch romaine, torn	2 tablespoons sugar
1 small onion, halved and thinly sliced	1 tablespoon sour cream
2 cups halved fresh strawberries	1 tablespoon milk
	2¼ teaspoons cider vinegar
	1½ teaspoons poppy seeds

● In a small heavy skillet over medium-low heat, cook and stir the sugar until melted and caramel in color, about 10 minutes. Stir in almonds until coated. Spread on foil to cool; break into small pieces.

● In a large bowl, combine the romaine, onion and strawberries. Combine the dressing ingredients; drizzle over salad and toss to coat. Sprinkle with coated almonds.

Yield: 10 servings.

GRILLED GARDEN VEGGIES

I've grown to rely on this recipe because I can use whatever vegetables I have on hand. It tastes great with any combination!
—**Holly Wilhelm** *Sioux Falls, South Dakota*

PREP/TOTAL TIME: 30 MIN.

- 2 tablespoons olive oil, *divided*
- 1 small onion, chopped
- 2 garlic cloves, minced
- 1 teaspoon dried rosemary, crushed, *divided*
- 2 small zucchini, sliced
- 2 small yellow summer squash, sliced
- ½ pound medium fresh mushrooms, quartered
- 1 large tomato, diced
- ¾ teaspoon salt
- ¼ teaspoon pepper

● Drizzle 1 tablespoon oil over a double thickness of heavy-duty foil (about 24 in. x 12 in.). Combine the onion, garlic and ½ teaspoon rosemary; spoon over foil. Top with zucchini, yellow squash, mushrooms and tomato; drizzle with the remaining oil. Sprinkle with salt, pepper and remaining rosemary.

● Fold foil around vegetables and seal tightly. Grill, covered, over medium heat for 15-20 minutes or until tender. Open foil carefully to allow steam to escape.

Yield: 8 servings.

HOMEMADE PIZZA SAUCE

Flavored with garlic, basil and Italian seasoning, here's a versatile sauce from our Test Kitchen staff that will add some Italian flair to all kinds of appetizing entrees.
—**Taste of Home Test Kitchen**

PREP: 10 MIN. **COOK:** 35 MIN.

- 3 garlic cloves, minced
- 3 tablespoons olive oil
- 1 can (29 ounces) tomato puree

- 1 can (28 ounces) crushed tomatoes
- 2 tablespoons brown sugar
- 1 tablespoon Italian seasoning
- 1 teaspoon dried basil
- ½ teaspoon salt
- ½ teaspoon crushed red pepper flakes

● In a large saucepan, saute garlic in oil until tender. Stir in the remaining ingredients. Bring to a boil. Reduce heat; simmer, uncovered, for 30 minutes or until sauce reaches desired thickness. Use in any recipe that calls for pizza sauce. Sauce may be refrigerated for up to 1 week.

Yield: 5½ cups.

HERB BUTTER

We love to use this savory butter on fresh corn on the cob, but it's also yummy on many fresh vegetables. It's a super way to make use of your summer herbs.
—**Donna Smith** *Victor, New York*

PREP/TOTAL TIME: 5 MIN.

- ½ cup butter, softened
- 1 tablespoon minced chives
- 1 tablespoon minced fresh dill
- 1 tablespoon minced fresh parsley
- ½ teaspoon dried thyme
- ¼ teaspoon salt

Dash garlic powder

Dash cayenne pepper

Hot cooked corn on the cob

● In a small bowl, combine the first eight ingredients. Serve with corn. Refrigerate leftovers.

Yield: ⅔ cup.

SALADS, SIDES & MORE

TWICE-BAKED POTATO CASSEROLE

My daughter gave me her casserole recipe because she knows I love potatoes. Her hearty dish is loaded with a crowd-pleasing combination of bacon, cheeses, green onions and sour cream.
—*Betty Miars* Anna, Ohio

PREP: 15 MIN. **BAKE:** 20 MIN.

- 1½ pounds red potatoes (about 6 medium), baked
- ¼ teaspoon salt
- ¼ teaspoon pepper
- 1 pound sliced bacon, cooked and crumbled
- 3 cups (24 ounces) sour cream
- 2 cups (8 ounces) shredded mozzarella cheese
- 2 cups (8 ounces) shredded cheddar cheese
- 2 green onions, sliced

○ Cut baked potatoes into 1-in. cubes. Place half in a greased 13-in. x 9-in. baking dish. Sprinkle potatoes with half of the salt, pepper and bacon. Top with half of the sour cream and cheeses. Repeat layers.

○ Bake, uncovered, at 350° for 20-25 minutes or until cheeses are melted. Sprinkle with onions.

Yield: 6-8 servings.

" This is my absolute favorite potato casserole recipe of all time! I've made it on many occasions with fabulous results."

—ROCKAMAMA FROM TASTEOFHOME.COM

FOUR-FRUIT COMPOTE

I'm always looking for new and creative ways to use fresh pears. Serve this compote over oatmeal for breakfast, alongside ham or chicken for dinner, or even alone for a sweet dessert.
—*Eileen Bishop* Vale, Oregon

PREP: 10 MIN. **COOK:** 35 MIN.

- 1 teaspoon aniseed
- 2 cups water
- ¼ cup sugar
- 2 medium pears, peeled and cubed
- ⅓ cup dried apricots, halved
- ¼ cup golden raisins
- ¼ cup dried cherries
- 1 tablespoon lemon juice

○ Place aniseed on a double thickness of cheesecloth; bring up corners of cloth and tie with kitchen string to form a bag. In a small saucepan, combine water and sugar. Add spice bag. Bring to a boil; boil for 5 minutes. Discard spice bag.

○ Add the pears, apricots, raisins and cherries to sugar syrup. Bring to a boil. Reduce heat; simmer, uncovered, for 20-25 minutes or until pears are tender. Stir in lemon juice. Serve warm or chilled.

Yield: 1½ cups.

GARDEN TOMATO RELISH

It's so easy to have a tasty relish on hand for hot dogs, hamburgers and other dishes. Why not share a jar with a friend or neighbor?
—**Kelly Martel** *Tillsonburg, Ontario*

PREP: 1½ HOURS + SIMMERING **PROCESS:** 20 MIN.

10 pounds tomatoes	2½ cups packed brown sugar
3 large sweet onions, finely chopped	3 tablespoons canning salt
2 medium sweet red peppers, finely chopped	2 teaspoons ground ginger
2 medium green peppers, finely chopped	2 teaspoons ground cinnamon
2 teaspoons mustard seed	1 teaspoon ground allspice
1 teaspoon celery seed	1 teaspoon ground cloves
4½ cups white vinegar	1 teaspoon ground nutmeg

○ In a large saucepan, bring 8 cups water to a boil. Add tomatoes, a few at a time; boil for 30 seconds. Drain and immediately place tomatoes in ice water. Drain and pat dry; peel and finely chop. Place in a stockpot. Add onions and peppers.

○ Place mustard and celery seed on a double thickness of cheesecloth; bring up corners of cloth and tie with string to form a bag. Add spice bag and the remaining ingredients to the pot. Bring to a boil. Reduce heat; cover and simmer for 60-70 minutes or until slightly thickened. Discard spice bag.

○ Carefully ladle relish into hot 1-pint jars, leaving ½-in. headspace. Remove air bubbles; wipe rims and adjust lids. Process in boiling-water canner for 20 minutes.

EDITOR'S NOTE: The processing time listed is for altitudes of 1,000 feet or less. For altitudes up to 3,000 feet, add 5 minutes; 6,000 feet, add 10 minutes; 8,000 feet, add 15 minutes; 10,000 feet, add 20 minutes.

Yield: 10 pints.

CHUNKY APPLESAUCE

There's just something extra-special about homemade applesauce. This simple recipe is tart and not too sweet. It makes the perfect side dish, especially with pork chops or a pork roast.
—**Deborah Amrine** *Fort Myers, Florida*

PREP: 15 MIN. **COOK:** 30 MIN.

    8 cups chopped peeled tart apples (about 3½ pounds)
    ½ cup packed brown sugar
    1 teaspoon ground cinnamon
    2 teaspoons vanilla extract

● In a Dutch oven, combine apples, brown sugar and cinnamon. Cover and cook over medium-low heat for 30-40 minutes or until apples are tender, stirring occasionally. Remove from the heat; stir in vanilla. Mash apples slightly if desired. Serve warm or cold.

SPICED APPLESAUCE: Reduce vanilla to ½ teaspoon. Add 1 tablespoon lemon juice, ½ teaspoon ground ginger, ¼ teaspoon each ground nutmeg and mace and ⅛ teaspoon ground cardamom to apples before cooking.

NEW ENGLAND APPLESAUCE: Use Rome Beauty or McIntosh apples. Omit brown sugar and vanilla. Reduce cinnamon to ¼ teaspoon. Add 1 cup each honey and water and ½ cup lemon juice to apples before cooking. If desired, stir 2 tablespoons grenadine syrup into mashed apples.

Yield: about 3½ cups.

AMBROSIA SALAD

This tropical medley is great as a last-minute menu addition because it's so easy to prepare. Even better, it requires only five basic ingredients. How easy is that?
—**Judi Bringegar** *Liberty, North Carolina*

PREP: 10 MIN. + CHILLING

    1 can (11 ounces) mandarin oranges, drained
    1 can (8 ounces) pineapple chunks, drained
    1 cup miniature marshmallows
    1 cup flaked coconut
    1 cup (8 ounces) sour cream

● In a large bowl, combine the oranges, pineapple, marshmallows and coconut. Add sour cream and toss to mix. Cover and refrigerate for several hours.

Yield: 4 servings.

> ❝I use flavored miniature marshmallows to add color to this dish. It has become a favorite.❞

—TTARK54 FROM TASTEOFHOME.COM

SUMMER VEGETABLE SALAD

We're always looking for ways to use our garden produce in the summer, and this salad is great because you can use whatever vegetables you have on hand. You'll love the dill dressing!
—**Mari Roseberry** *Dunning, Nebraska*

PREP: 15 MIN. + CHILLING

- 1 cup fresh cauliflowerets
- 1 cup fresh baby carrots
- 1 cup sliced red onion
- 1 cup halved grape tomatoes
- 1 cup chopped zucchini
- 3 tablespoons cider vinegar
- 2 tablespoons olive oil
- 1 teaspoon dill weed
- ½ teaspoon salt
- ½ teaspoon ground mustard
- ¼ to ½ teaspoon garlic powder
- ¼ teaspoon pepper

- In a large bowl, combine the cauliflower, carrots, onion, tomatoes and zucchini. In a small bowl, whisk the remaining ingredients. Pour over vegetables and toss to coat.

- Cover and refrigerate for at least 2 hours, stirring occasionally. Serve with a slotted spoon.

Yield: 6 servings.

SUSIE'S HOT MUSTARD

My husband enjoys spreading this bold, robust mustard on anything that needs an extra hit of flavor.
—**Susie Gibson** *Alta Loma, California*

PREP: 15 MIN. + STANDING **COOK:** 20 MIN. + COOLING

- 1 can (4 ounces) ground mustard
- 1 cup white wine vinegar
- 3 eggs
- ¾ cup sugar
- 1 tablespoon molasses
- 1 teaspoon honey

- 2 cups mayonnaise
- 1 tablespoon mustard seed, optional

- In a small bowl, combine mustard and vinegar. Cover and let stand at room temperature for 8 hours or overnight.

- In a large saucepan, whisk the eggs, sugar, molasses, honey and mustard mixture. Cook and stir over low heat until mixture is thickened and a thermometer reads 160°, about 20 minutes. Cool. Stir in mayonnaise and mustard seed if desired. Cover and refrigerate for up to 3 weeks.

Yield: 4 cups.

WILD PLUM JELLY

I've had this recipe in my collection for ages. Each year when the wild plums are ripe, I'll fill my pail and make this jelly. It's so good served with toast, pancakes or waffles.
—**Ludell Heuser** *Mt. Horeb, Wisconsin*

PREP: 55 MIN. **PROCESS:** 5 MIN.

- 5 pounds wild plums, halved and pitted
- 4 cups water
- 1 package (1¾ ounces) powdered fruit pectin
- 7½ cups sugar

- In a stockpot, simmer plums and water until tender, about 30 minutes. Line a strainer with four layers of cheesecloth and place over a bowl. Place plum mixture in strainer; cover with edges of cheesecloth. Let stand for 30 minutes or until liquid measures 5½ cups.

- Return liquid to the pan. Add pectin; stir and bring to a boil. Add sugar; bring to a full rolling boil. Boil for 1 minute, stirring constantly. Remove from the heat; skim off any foam. Carefully ladle hot mixture into hot sterilized half-pint jars, leaving ¼-in. headspace. Remove air bubbles; wipe rims and adjust lids. Process for 5 minutes in a boiling-water canner.

EDITOR'S NOTE: The processing time listed is for altitudes of 1,000 feet or less. Add 1 minute to the processing time for each 1,000 feet of additional altitude.

Yield: about 8 half-pints.

ITALIAN BASIL PASTA SALAD

Ready for a big bite of summertime? Pass around this garden-fresh pasta salad. I suggest serving it at your next dinner party, potluck or luncheon.

—**Charlotte Gehle** *Brownstown, Michigan*

PREP: 30 MIN. + CHILLING

1 package (16 ounces) bow tie pasta	½ cup fresh basil leaves, thinly sliced
2 cups grape tomatoes	DRESSING:
7 ounces fresh mozzarella cheese, cubed	¾ cup olive oil
1 medium sweet yellow pepper, chopped	¾ cup red wine vinegar
1 small red onion, chopped	1 garlic clove, minced
½ cup pickled banana pepper rings	1 teaspoon salt
1 can (2¼ ounces) sliced ripe olives, drained	½ teaspoon pepper
4 thin slices hard salami, diced	¼ teaspoon dried basil

◦ Cook pasta according to package directions; drain and rinse in cold water. In a large bowl, combine the pasta, tomatoes, cheese, yellow pepper, onion, pepper rings, olives, salami and basil.

◦ In a small bowl, whisk the dressing ingredients. Pour over salad and toss to coat. Cover and refrigerate for at least 1 hour before serving.

Yield: 18 servings.

OVERNIGHT ASPARAGUS STRATA

I've made this tasty egg dish for breakfast, brunch and even as a Christmas dinner side dish. With its English-muffin crust, this is not your run-of-the-mill strata. Friends *always* ask for the recipe!
—Lynn Licata *Sylvania, Ohio*

PREP: 15 MIN. + CHILLING **BAKE:** 40 MIN. + STANDING

1 pound fresh asparagus, trimmed and cut into 1-inch pieces

4 English muffins, split and toasted

2 cups (8 ounces) shredded Colby-Monterey Jack cheese, *divided*

1 cup cubed fully cooked ham

½ cup chopped sweet red pepper

8 eggs, lightly beaten

2 cups 2% milk

1 teaspoon salt

1 teaspoon ground mustard

¼ teaspoon pepper

○ In a large saucepan, bring 8 cups water to a boil. Add asparagus; cover and cook for 3 minutes. Drain and immediately place asparagus in ice water. Drain and pat dry.

○ Arrange six English muffin halves, cut side up, in a greased 13-in. x 9-in. baking dish. Fill in spaces with remaining muffin halves. Layer with 1 cup cheese, asparagus, ham and red pepper.

○ In a small bowl, whisk the eggs, milk, salt, mustard and pepper; pour over English muffins. Cover and refrigerate overnight.

○ Remove from the refrigerator 30 minutes before baking. Sprinkle with remaining cheese.

○ Bake, uncovered, at 375° for 40-45 minutes or until a knife inserted near the middle comes out clean. Let stand for 5 minutes before cutting.

Yield: 6-8 servings.

SUNDAY DINNER MASHED POTATOES

Sour cream and cream cheese add a silky richness to these spuds. They're special enough to serve guests, and busy hostesses can prepare them in advance.
—**Melody Mellinger** *Myerstown, Pennsylvania*

PREP: 35 MIN. **BAKE:** 20 MIN.

- 5 pounds potatoes, peeled and cubed
- 1 cup (8 ounces) sour cream
- 2 packages (3 ounces *each*) cream cheese, softened
- 3 tablespoons butter, *divided*
- 1 teaspoon salt
- 1 teaspoon onion salt
- ¼ teaspoon pepper

- Place potatoes in a Dutch oven; cover with water. Cover and bring to a boil. Cook for 20-25 minutes or until very tender; drain well.

- In a large bowl, mash potatoes. Add the sour cream, cream cheese, 2 tablespoons butter, salt, onion salt and pepper; beat until fluffy.

- Transfer to a greased 2-qt. baking dish. Dot with the remaining butter. Bake, uncovered, at 350° for 20-25 minutes or until heated through.

Yield: 8 servings.

> ❝Wow, these are delicious! If you go to the trouble of making real mashed potatoes, use this recipe!❞

—KDHCOOKS FROM TASTEOFHOME.COM

SCALLOPED CORN

Sunny corn kernels are tucked into a creamy custard for this super-yummy side. My mom got this recipe, and many other excellent ones, from her mother. By the time this scrumptious corn dish made it around the table, my father, sister, brothers and I would have almost scraped it clean!
—**Sandy Jenkins** *Elkhorn, Wisconsin*

PREP: 10 MIN. **BAKE:** 1 HOUR

- 4 cups fresh *or* frozen corn
- 3 eggs, lightly beaten
- 1 cup 2% milk
- 1 cup crushed saltines (about 30 crackers), *divided*
- 3 tablespoons butter, melted
- 1 tablespoon sugar
- 1 tablespoon finely chopped onion

Salt and pepper to taste

- In a large bowl, combine the corn, eggs, milk, ¾ cup cracker crumbs, butter, sugar, onion, salt and pepper. Transfer to a greased 1½-qt. baking dish. Sprinkle with remaining cracker crumbs.

- Bake, uncovered, at 325° for 1 hour or until a thermometer reads 160°.

Yield: 6 servings.

PEPPERONI PASTA SALAD

Bottled Italian dressing and pepperoni add zip to this colorful combination. Serve it right away or assemble it ahead of time. The longer this salad chills, the yummier it tastes!
—**Shannon Lommen** *Kaysville, Utah*

PREP/TOTAL TIME: 30 MIN.

QUICK & EASY

- 2 cups uncooked tricolor spiral pasta
- 1 cup cubed cheddar cheese
- 1 cup coarsely chopped cucumber
- 1 small tomato, chopped
- 2 green onions, chopped
- 28 pepperoni slices
- ½ cup zesty Italian salad dressing

● Cook pasta according to package directions; drain and rinse in cold water. In a large bowl, combine the pasta, cheese, cucumber, tomato, onions and pepperoni. Add salad dressing and toss to coat. Cover and refrigerate until serving.

Yield: 4-6 servings.

KITCHEN TIP

To easily remove seeds from a cucumber, cut it in half lengthwise, then run a melon baller down the length of both halves to scoop out the seeds. This is much faster than using a knife and wastes little of the cucumber.
—**Sally M.,** *Neligh, Nebraska*

GREEN BEAN CASSEROLE

I love this traditional no-fuss favorite because it can be prepared in advance and refrigerated until ready to bake. It's creamy and the french-fried onions add a delicious crunch.
—**Anna Baker** *Blaine, Washington*

PREP: 15 MIN. **BAKE:** 35 MIN.

- 2 cans (10¾ ounces *each*) condensed cream of mushroom soup, undiluted
- 1 cup milk
- 2 teaspoons soy sauce
- ⅛ teaspoon pepper
- 2 packages (16 ounces *each*) frozen whole *or* cut green beans, cooked and drained
- 1 can (6 ounces) french-fried onions, *divided*

● In a bowl, combine soup, milk, soy sauce and pepper. Gently stir in beans. Spoon half of the mixture into a 13-in. x 9-in. baking dish. Sprinkle with half of the onions. Spoon remaining bean mixture over the top.

● Bake at 350° for 30 minutes or until heated through. Sprinkle with remaining onions. Bake 5 minutes longer or until the onions are brown and crispy.

Yield: 10 servings.

CRAN-ORANGE RELISH

With its festive ruby-red color and refreshing citrus-cranberry flavor, this lovely relish works well at large holiday gatherings. It's so simple and so delicious served with ham or poultry.
—**Clara Honeyager** *North Prairie, Wisconsin*

PREP/TOTAL TIME: 25 MIN.

QUICK & EASY

- 8 packages (12 ounces *each*) fresh cranberries
- 6 large unpeeled navel oranges, cut into wedges
- 4 cups sugar

● In a food processor, process the cranberries and oranges in batches until finely chopped. Place in a large container; stir in sugar. Cover and refrigerate until serving.

Yield: 4½ quarts.

CUCUMBER: STOCKBYTE/PUNCHSTOCK

SALADS, SIDES & MORE

PEPPERED SQUASH RELISH

Here's an eye-catching medley that's an instant flavor booster. It always goes fast whenever I take it to a dinner or picnic, and I get multiple requests for the recipe. You can dress up everything from hot dogs and brats to grilled chicken breasts or pork chops with this fantastic relish.
—Rose Cole *Salem, West Virginia*

PREP: 15 MIN. + CHILLING **COOK:** 20 MIN. + COOLING

3 pounds yellow summer squash, finely chopped

3 pounds zucchini, finely chopped

6 large onions, finely chopped

3 medium green peppers, finely chopped

3 medium sweet red peppers, finely chopped

¼ cup salt

2 cups sugar

2 cups packed brown sugar

2 cups white vinegar

4 teaspoons celery seed

1 teaspoon ground turmeric

1 teaspoon ground mustard

○ In a large bowl, combine the first six ingredients. Cover and refrigerate overnight.

○ Drain vegetable mixture. Rinse in cold water and drain again. Place vegetables in a Dutch oven. Add the sugars, vinegar, celery seed, turmeric and mustard. Bring to a boil. Reduce the heat; simmer, uncovered, for 15-20 minutes or until liquid is clear.

○ Remove from the heat; cool. Spoon into containers. Cover and refrigerate for up to 3 weeks.

Yield: 4 quarts.

ROASTED CHICKEN WITH ROSEMARY, PAGE 98

96

90

101

MAIN DISHES

The centerpiece for any home-cooked meal is always the main course. But sometimes the greatest challenge is just deciding what to make. The mouthwatering beef, poultry, pork and seafood creations on the pages that follow are guaranteed to take the guesswork out of supper time for any busy family cook. So whether you're scrambling to whip up a no-fuss entree on a hectic weeknight or planning an elegant menu for the holidays, turn to these tried-and-true mainstays. Shared by family cooks just like you, these dishes make digging into the goodness of a piping hot dinner as easy as can be!

SAUCY PORK CHOPS

I'm always short on time and don't have a lot to spend on meal prep, so I take full advantage of the convenience of my slow cooker. I fix these tangy chops at least once a week. The meat is so tender, you can cut it with a fork!
—**Jennifer Ruberg** *Two Harbors, Minnesota*

PREP: 15 MIN. **COOK:** 4¼ HOURS

- 4   bone-in pork loin chops (8 ounces *each*)
- 1   teaspoon garlic powder
- ½   teaspoon salt
- ¼   teaspoon pepper
- 2   tablespoons canola oil
- 2   cups ketchup
- ½   cup packed brown sugar
- 1   teaspoon liquid smoke, optional

● Sprinkle pork chops with garlic powder, salt and pepper. In a large skillet, brown chops in oil on both sides; drain.

● In a small bowl, combine the ketchup, brown sugar and liquid smoke if desired. Pour half of the sauce into a 3-qt. slow cooker. Top with pork chops and remaining sauce. Cover and cook on low for 4-5 hours or until meat is tender.

Yield: 4 servings.

"This was very good and easy. I should have doubled the recipe. Everyone wanted to have seconds!"
—JENNIFERGARNETT FROM TASTEOFHOME.COM

PEACH-GLAZED SALMON

A local restaurant used fresh peaches to garnish a salmon dish, which gave me an idea for grilling the fish we catch. It makes a beautiful presentation and is so quick to prepare.
—**Valerie Dawley Horner** *Juneau, Alaska*

PREP: 10 MIN. + MARINATING **GRILL:** 15 MIN.

- 1   cup butter, cubed
- 1   cup peach preserves
- 1   tablespoon lime juice
- 1   garlic clove, minced
- ½   teaspoon prepared mustard
- 2   salmon fillets (1 pound *each*)
- ½   cup chopped peeled fresh peaches *or* frozen unsweetened sliced peaches, thawed

● In a microwave-safe bowl, combine butter and preserves. Cover and microwave on high for 45-60 seconds. Stir in the lime juice, garlic and mustard until blended. Cool. Set aside 1 cup for basting and serving.

● Place salmon in a resealable plastic bag; add remaining peach mixture. Seal bag and turn to coat. Marinate for 20 minutes.

● Drain and discard marinade. Using long-handled tongs, moisten a paper towel with cooking oil and lightly coat the grill rack. Place salmon skin side down on grill rack.

● Grill, covered, over medium heat for 5 minutes. Spoon half of reserved peach mixture over salmon. Grill 10-15 minutes longer or until fish flakes easily with a fork, basting frequently. Serve with sliced peaches and remaining peach mixture.

EDITOR'S NOTE: This recipe was tested in a 1,100-watt microwave.

Yield: 8 servings.

FRIED CHICKEN WITH PAN GRAVY

Mom's traditional fried chicken always cooked up golden brown and crispy. Drizzled with the pan gravy, the classic entree is finger-licking good!
—**Ginny Werkmeister** *Tilden, Nebraska*

PREP: 15 MIN. **COOK:** 45 MIN.

1 cup all-purpose flour	Oil for frying
¾ teaspoon salt	GRAVY:
¼ teaspoon dried thyme	2 tablespoons all-purpose flour
¼ teaspoon rubbed sage	⅛ teaspoon salt
¼ teaspoon pepper	1⅓ cups 2% milk
1 broiler/fryer chicken (3½ to 4 pounds), cut up	

◉ In a large resealable plastic bag, combine the first five ingredients. Add chicken, a few pieces at a time, and shake to coat.

◉ In a large skillet over medium-high heat, heat ¼ in. of oil; fry chicken until browned on all sides. Reduce heat; cover and cook for 30-35 minutes or until juices run clear, turning occasionally. Uncover and cook 5 minutes longer. Remove chicken to paper towels and keep warm.

◉ Pour off excess fat from the skillet, reserving the browned bits and 2 tablespoons of drippings. Stir in flour and salt until blended; gradually add the milk. Bring to a boil; cook and stir for 1-2 minutes or until thickened. Serve with chicken.

HERBED FRIED CHICKEN WITH GRAVY: Omit sage. Add 1 teaspoon each dried tarragon, oregano, paprika and ground mustard, and ½ teaspoon each onion powder and garlic powder to the flour mixture. Proceed as directed.

Yield: 6 servings (1½ cups gravy).

ROASTED TURKEY A L'ORANGE

My turkey recipe accomplishes every cook's Thanksgiving wish—a bird that brings the flavors of citrus and seasonings in every bite. It's the perfect, mouthwatering centerpiece for your celebration, and it's very easy.
—**Robin Haas** *Cranston, Rhode Island*

PREP: 40 MIN. **BAKE:** 3½ HOURS + STANDING

- 1 whole garlic bulb, cloves separated and peeled
- 1 large navel orange
- ¼ cup orange marmalade
- 2 tablespoons lemon juice
- 1 tablespoon honey
- 2 teaspoons dried parsley flakes
- 1 teaspoon paprika
- 1 teaspoon dried oregano
- ½ teaspoon salt
- ½ teaspoon dried thyme
- ½ teaspoon pepper
- 1 turkey (14 pounds)
- 4 celery ribs, quartered
- 4 large carrots, quartered
- 1 large onion, quartered
- 1 large potato, peeled and cut into 2-inch cubes
- 1 large sweet potato, peeled and cut into 2-inch cubes

○ Mince four garlic cloves; transfer to a small bowl. Juice half of the orange; add to bowl. Stir in the marmalade, lemon juice, honey, parsley, paprika, oregano, salt, thyme and pepper. With fingers, carefully loosen skin from the turkey; rub ½ cup marmalade mixture under the skin.

○ Thinly slice remaining orange half; place under the skin. Brush turkey with remaining marmalade mixture. Place remaining garlic cloves inside the cavity. Tuck wings under turkey; tie drumsticks together.

○ Combine celery, carrots, onion and potatoes in roasting pan. Set turkey, breast side up, over vegetables.

○ Bake at 325° for 3½ to 4 hours or until a thermometer reads 180°, basting with pan drippings. Cover loosely with foil if turkey browns too quickly. Cover and let stand for 20 minutes before carving.

Yield: 28 servings.

GLAZED PORK CHOPS

I serve these tasty chops for birthdays, Easter dinner and everyday meals. The recipe is easy to double or even triple to feed a crowd.
—*Sondra Warson* Madrid, Iowa

PREP: 10 MIN. + MARINATING **GRILL:** 10 MIN.

- ⅔ cup apricot preserves
- ½ cup Italian salad dressing
- 2 tablespoons Dijon mustard
- 4 boneless pork loin chops (1 inch thick and 6 ounces *each*)

In a small bowl, combine the preserves, dressing and mustard to create marinade. Pour ¾ cup of this marinade into a large resealable bag; add the pork. Seal bag and turn to coat; refrigerate for 8 hours or overnight. Cover and refrigerate the remaining unused marinade for basting.

Drain and discard the marinade used to coat pork. Using long-handled tongs, moisten a paper towel with cooking oil and lightly coat the grill rack.

Grill, covered, over medium heat or broil 4-5 in. from the heat for 4-5 minutes on each side or until a thermometer reads 145°, basting frequently with the reserved marinade. Let meat stand for 5 minutes before serving.

Yield: 4 servings.

> **"**These were so good. I used peach preserves as I didn't have any apricot. Turned out great!**"**
>
> —RACHELLESTRATTON FROM TASTEOFHOME.COM

EASY CRAB CAKES

Canned crabmeat makes these delicate patties simple enough for busy weeknight dinners. For a change of pace, try forming the crab mixture into four thick patties instead of eight cakes.
—*Charlene Spelock* Apollo, Pennsylvania

QUICK & EASY

PREP/TOTAL TIME: 25 MIN.

- 2 cans (6 ounces *each*) crabmeat, drained, flaked and cartilage removed
- 1 cup seasoned bread crumbs, *divided*
- 1 egg, lightly beaten
- ¼ cup finely chopped green onions
- ¼ cup finely chopped sweet red pepper
- ¼ cup reduced-fat mayonnaise
- 1 tablespoon lemon juice
- ½ teaspoon garlic powder
- ⅛ teaspoon cayenne pepper
- 1 tablespoon butter

In a large bowl, combine the crab, ⅓ cup bread crumbs, egg, onions, red pepper, mayonnaise, lemon juice, garlic powder and cayenne.

Divide mixture into eight portions; shape into 2-in. balls. Roll in remaining bread crumbs. Flatten to ½-in. thickness.

In a large nonstick skillet, cook crab cakes in butter for 3-4 minutes on each side or until golden brown.

Yield: 4 servings.

SLOW-COOKED PEPPER STEAK

After a long, grueling day, I appreciate coming home to this juicy, peppery steak simmering in the slow cooker. It has a down-home taste that can't be beat.
—**Sue Gronholz** *Beaver Dam, Wisconsin*

PREP: 10 MIN. **COOK:** 6½ HOURS

1½ pounds beef top round steak
  2 tablespoons canola oil
  1 cup chopped onion
  ¼ cup reduced-sodium soy sauce
  1 garlic clove, minced
  1 teaspoon sugar
  ½ teaspoon salt
  ¼ teaspoon ground ginger
  ¼ teaspoon pepper
  4 medium tomatoes, cut into wedges *or* 1 can
     (14½ ounces) diced tomatoes, undrained
  1 large green pepper, cut into strips
  1 tablespoon cornstarch
  ½ cup cold water
Hot cooked noodles *or* rice

● Cut beef into 3-in. x 1-in. strips. In a large skillet, brown beef in oil. Transfer to a 3-qt. slow cooker. Combine the onion, soy sauce, garlic, sugar, salt, ginger and pepper; pour over beef. Cover and cook on low for 5-6 hours or until meat is tender. Add tomatoes and green pepper; cook on low 1 hour longer or until vegetables are tender.

● Combine cornstarch and cold water until smooth; gradually stir into slow cooker. Cover and cook on high for 20-30 minutes until thickened. Serve with noodles or rice.

Yield: 6 servings.

LIME CHICKEN TACOS

You won't be able to get enough of my fun, zesty tacos! They're great for a casual fiesta with friends or family. For variety, use any leftover filling as a topping for a tasty taco salad.
—**Tracy Gunter** *Boise, Idaho*

PREP: 10 MIN. **COOK:** 5½ HOURS

1½ pounds boneless skinless chicken breasts
  3 tablespoons lime juice
  1 tablespoon chili powder
  1 cup frozen corn
  1 cup chunky salsa
 12 flour tortillas (6 inches), warmed
Sour cream, shredded cheddar cheese and shredded lettuce,
  optional

● Place the chicken in a 3-qt. slow cooker. Combine lime juice and chili powder; pour over chicken. Cover and cook on low for 5-6 hours or until chicken is tender.

● Remove chicken; cool slightly. Shred meat with two forks and return to the slow cooker; heat through. Stir in corn and salsa.

● Cover and cook on low for 30 minutes or until heated through. Serve in tortillas with sour cream, cheese and lettuce if desired.

Yield: 12 tacos.

> ❝Yum! Simple and delicious. I added some fresh cilantro when I added the salsa and corn.❞
>
> —**JESSICA DIDION** FROM TASTEOFHOME.COM

JALAPENO RIBS

These ribs are unique because of the zesty rub and the combination of sweet brown sugar and spicy jalapeno peppers in the sauce. I always make them for my husband's birthday.
—Shirley Manthey *Omaha, Nebraska*

PREP: 1 HOUR 35 MIN. **GRILL:** 10 MIN.

4 teaspoons brown sugar	
2 teaspoons chili powder	
1 teaspoon salt	
1 teaspoon paprika	
1 teaspoon pepper	
⅛ teaspoon garlic powder	
3½ to 4 pounds pork spareribs	

JALAPENO BARBECUE SAUCE:

2 cans (8 ounces *each*) tomato sauce
⅔ cup packed brown sugar
⅓ cup lemon juice
¼ cup Worcestershire sauce
1 small onion, finely chopped
2 jalapeno peppers, seeded and finely chopped
2 teaspoons beef bouillon granules

● In a small bowl, combine the first six ingredients; rub onto both sides of ribs. Place ribs, meat side up, on a rack in a foil-lined roasting pan. Bake at 325° for 1½ to 1¾ hours or until tender.

● Meanwhile, in a large saucepan, combine sauce ingredients; simmer, uncovered, for 30-40 minutes or until thickened.

● Grill ribs, uncovered, over medium heat for 10-15 minutes or until browned, basting with sauce and turning several times. Reheat remaining sauce and serve with ribs.

EDITOR'S NOTE: Ribs may be baked and sauce may be prepared a day ahead and refrigerated. Then grill and baste for 15 minutes or until heated through and nicely glazed.

Yield: 4 servings.

MEXICAN STUFFED PEPPERS

This nutritious yet economical summer meal makes the most of my homegrown peppers. I like to top it with sour cream and serve with tortilla chips and salsa, but it's wonderful on its own, too.
—**Kim Coleman** *Columbia, South Carolina*

PREP: 25 MIN. **BAKE:** 30 MIN.

8 medium green peppers
1 pound lean ground beef (90% lean)
1 can (14½ ounces) diced tomatoes and green chilies, undrained

1½ cups water
1 envelope (5.4 ounces) Mexican-style rice and pasta mix
2 cups (8 ounces) shredded Mexican cheese blend

⊚ Cut tops off peppers and remove seeds. In a Dutch oven, cook peppers in boiling water for 3-5 minutes. Drain and rinse in cold water; set aside.

⊚ In a large skillet, cook beef over medium heat until no longer pink; drain. Add the diced tomatoes, water and pasta mix. Bring to a boil. Reduce heat; cover and simmer for 6-8 minutes or until liquid is absorbed.

⊚ Place ⅓ cup pasta mixture in each pepper; sprinkle each with 2 tablespoons cheese. Top with remaining pasta mixture. Place in a greased 13-in. x 9-in. baking dish. Cover and bake at 375° for 25 minutes. Sprinkle with remaining cheese; bake 5-10 minutes longer or until the cheese is melted and peppers are tender.

Yield: 8 servings.

CHICKEN QUESADILLAS

Bring some Southwestern flair to your dinner table tonight with these scrumptious chicken quesadillas.
—**Linda Wetzel** *Woodland Park, Colorado*

PREP/TOTAL TIME: 30 MIN.

QUICK & EASY

- 2½ cups shredded cooked chicken
- ⅔ cup salsa
- ⅓ cup sliced green onions
- ¾ to 1 teaspoon ground cumin
- ½ teaspoon salt
- ½ teaspoon dried oregano
- 6 flour tortillas (8 inches)
- ¼ cup butter, melted
- 2 cups (8 ounces) shredded Monterey Jack cheese

Sour cream and guacamole

- In a large skillet, combine the first six ingredients. Cook, uncovered, over medium heat for 10 minutes or until heated through, stirring occasionally.

- Brush one side of tortillas with butter; place buttered side down on a lightly greased baking sheet. Spoon ⅓ cup chicken mixture over half of each tortilla; sprinkle with ⅓ cup cheese.

- Fold plain side of tortilla over cheese. Bake at 375° for 9-11 minutes or until crisp and golden brown. Cut into wedges; serve with sour cream and guacamole.

Yield: 6 servings.

MOM'S OVEN-BARBECUED RIBS

My mom made these tender ribs for Sunday dinner when I was growing up. A few common ingredients are all it takes to make the zesty sauce. Now that I have a family of my own, I love watching their eyes light up when I bring this sensation to the table!
—**Yvonne White** *Williamson, New York*

PREP: 10 MIN. **BAKE:** 2¾ HOURS

- 3 to 4 pounds country-style pork ribs
- 1½ cups water
- 1 cup ketchup

- ⅓ cup Worcestershire sauce
- 1 teaspoon salt
- 1 teaspoon chili powder
- ½ teaspoon onion powder
- ⅛ teaspoon hot pepper sauce

- Place ribs in a greased roasting pan. Bake, uncovered, at 350° for 45 minutes. Meanwhile, in a saucepan, combine the remaining ingredients. Bring to a boil; cook for 1 minute. Drain ribs. Spoon sauce over ribs. Cover and bake for 1½ hours. Uncover; bake 30 minutes longer, basting once.

Yield: 4-6 servings.

BACON-WRAPPED CHICKEN

Tender chicken becomes extra-special when coated in a creamy filling and wrapped with bacon strips. It's an easy entree that tastes as good as it looks.
—**MarlaKaye Skinner** *Tucson, Arizona*

PREP: 25 MIN. **BAKE:** 35 MIN.

- 6 boneless skinless chicken breast halves (4 ounces each)
- 1 carton (8 ounces) spreadable chive and onion cream cheese
- 1 tablespoon butter

Salt to taste

- 6 bacon strips

- Flatten chicken to ½-in. thickness. Spread 3 tablespoons cream cheese over each. Dot with butter and sprinkle with salt; roll up. Wrap each with bacon strip.

- Place, seam side down, in a greased 13-in. x 9-in. baking pan. Bake, uncovered, at 400° for 35-40 minutes or until a thermometer reads 170°. Broil 6 in. from the heat for 5 minutes or until bacon is crisp.

Yield: 6 servings.

ROASTED CHICKEN WITH ROSEMARY

Herbs, garlic and butter give this hearty meal in one a classic just-like-mom-used-to-make appeal. It's one succulent entree you're sure to make time and again!
—**Isabel Zienkosky** *Salt Lake City, Utah*

PREP: 20 MIN. **BAKE:** 2 HOURS + STANDING

- ½ cup butter, cubed
- 4 tablespoons minced fresh rosemary *or* 2 tablespoons dried rosemary, crushed
- 2 tablespoons minced fresh parsley
- 3 garlic cloves, minced
- 1 teaspoon salt
- ½ teaspoon pepper
- 1 whole roasting chicken (5 to 6 pounds)
- 6 small red potatoes, halved
- 6 medium carrots, halved lengthwise and cut into 2-inch pieces
- 2 medium onions, quartered

● In a small saucepan, melt butter; stir in the seasonings. Place chicken, breast side up, on a rack in a shallow roasting pan; tie drumsticks together with kitchen string. Spoon half of the butter mixture over chicken. Place the potatoes, carrots and onions around chicken. Drizzle remaining butter mixture over the vegetables.

● Cover and bake at 350° for 1½ hours, basting every 30 minutes. Uncover; bake 30-60 minutes longer or until a thermometer reads 180°, basting occasionally.

● Cover with foil and let stand for 10-15 minutes before carving. Serve with vegetables.

Yield: 9 servings.

CRISPY COD WITH VEGGIES

Take the chill off brisk evenings and warm the body and soul with this light but nourishing entree. Round out your meal with a crisp green salad and a loaf of crusty French bread.
—**Taste of Home Test Kitchen**

PREP: 15 MIN. **BAKE:** 25 MIN.

- 2 cups broccoli coleslaw mix
- ½ cup chopped fresh tomato
- 4 teaspoons chopped green onion
- 2 garlic cloves, minced
- 2 cod fillets (6 ounces *each*)

Pepper to taste

- ¼ cup crushed potato sticks
- 3 tablespoons seasoned bread crumbs
- 2 tablespoons grated Parmesan cheese
- 4 teaspoons butter, melted

● In a large bowl, combine the coleslaw mix, tomato, onion and garlic; spread into an 11-in. x 7-in. baking pan coated with cooking spray. Top with cod fillets; sprinkle with pepper.

● Combine the potato sticks, bread crumbs, cheese and butter; sprinkle over fillets. Bake, uncovered, at 450° for 25-30 minutes or until fish flakes easily with a fork.

Yield: 2 servings.

KITCHEN TIP

It's a cinch to peel fresh garlic. Using the blade of a chef's knife, crush garlic clove. Peel away skin. Chop or mince as directed in the recipe.

GARLIC: STOCKBYTE/PUNCHSTOCK

COOL-KITCHEN MEAT LOAF

Looking for a no-fuss meal to serve on a hot summer's night? Try this juicy, grilled meat loaf that's smothered in a homemade sweet-and-sour sauce.
—Susan Taul *Birmingham, Alabama*

PREP: 10 MIN. **GRILL:** 30 MIN.

- 1 cup soft bread crumbs
- 1 medium onion, chopped
- ½ cup tomato sauce
- 1 egg
- 1½ teaspoons salt
- ¼ teaspoon pepper
- 1½ pounds lean ground beef (90% lean)

SAUCE:

- ½ cup ketchup
- 3 tablespoons brown sugar
- 3 tablespoons Worcestershire sauce
- 2 tablespoons white vinegar
- 2 tablespoons prepared mustard

In a large bowl, combine the first six ingredients. Crumble beef over mixture and mix well. Shape into two loaves; place each loaf in a disposable 8-in. x 4-in. loaf pan. Cover with foil.

Prepare grill for indirect heat. Grill, covered, over medium heat for 30 minutes or until the meat is no longer pink and a thermometer reads 160°.

Meanwhile, in a small saucepan, combine sauce ingredients. Cook and stir over low heat until sugar is dissolved. Spoon over meat loaves before serving.

Yield: 2 loaves (3 servings each).

CAJUN SHRIMP SKEWERS

Fresh herbs and Cajun seasoning enhance these delicious shrimp, accompanied by a spicy Cajun butter sauce. You can serve them as a main entree or as appetizers. You'll love them either way!
—Dwayne Veretto *Roswell, New Mexico*

PREP: 20 MIN. + MARINATING **GRILL:** 5 MIN.

- ¾ cup canola oil
- 1 medium onion, finely chopped
- 2 tablespoons Cajun seasoning
- 6 garlic cloves, minced
- 2 teaspoons ground cumin
- 1 teaspoon minced fresh rosemary
- 1 teaspoon minced fresh thyme
- 2 pounds uncooked large shrimp, peeled and deveined

CAJUN BUTTER:

- 1 cup butter, cubed
- 1 teaspoon minced fresh basil
- 1 teaspoon minced fresh tarragon
- 1 teaspoon Cajun seasoning
- ½ teaspoon garlic powder
- 3 drops hot pepper sauce

In a small bowl, combine the first seven ingredients. Place the shrimp in a large resealable plastic bag; add half of the marinade. Seal bag and turn to coat; refrigerate for 1-2 hours. Cover and refrigerate remaining marinade for basting.

In a small saucepan, combine the Cajun butter ingredients; heat until butter is melted. Keep warm.

Drain and discard marinade. Thread shrimp onto eight metal or soaked wooden skewers. Grill, uncovered, over medium heat for 2-4 minutes on each side or until shrimp turn pink, basting once with reserved marinade. Serve with Cajun butter.

Yield: 8 servings.

PRIME RIB WITH HORSERADISH SAUCE

When midnight bells ring in the New Year, you'll find us celebrating with friends at our annual dinner party. I create a menu featuring this tender prime rib as the main star. A pepper rub and mild horseradish sauce complement the beef's great flavor.
—**Paula Zsiray** *Logan, Utah*

PREP: 5 MIN. **BAKE:** 3 HOURS

1 bone-in beef rib roast (4 to 6 pounds)	**HORSERADISH SAUCE:**
1 tablespoon olive oil	1 cup (8 ounces) sour cream
1 to 2 teaspoons coarsely ground pepper	3 to 4 tablespoons prepared horseradish
	1 teaspoon coarsely ground pepper
	⅛ teaspoon Worcestershire sauce

● Brush roast with oil; rub with pepper. Place roast, fat side up, on a rack in a shallow roasting pan. Bake, uncovered, at 450° for 15 minutes.

● Reduce heat to 325°. Bake for 2¾ hours or until meat reaches desired doneness (for medium-rare, a thermometer should read 145°; medium, 160°; well-done, 170°), basting with pan drippings every 30 minutes.

● Let stand for 10-15 minutes before slicing. Meanwhile, in a small bowl, combine the sauce ingredients. Serve with beef.

Yield: 6-8 servings.

SLOW-COOKED SOUTHWEST CHICKEN

With just 15 minutes of prep, you'll be out of the kitchen in no time. This deliciously low-fat dish gets even better served with reduced-fat sour cream and chopped cilantro.
—**Brandi Castillo** *Santa Maria, California*

PREP: 15 MIN. **COOK:** 6 HOURS

- 2 cans (15 ounces *each*) black beans, rinsed and drained
- 1 can (14½ ounces) reduced-sodium chicken broth
- 1 can (14½ ounces) diced tomatoes with mild green chilies, undrained
- ½ pound boneless skinless chicken breast
- 1 jar (8 ounces) chunky salsa
- 1 cup frozen corn
- 1 tablespoon dried parsley flakes
- 1 teaspoon ground cumin
- ¼ teaspoon pepper
- 3 cups hot cooked rice

● In a 2- or 3-qt. slow cooker, combine the beans, broth, tomatoes, chicken, salsa, corn and seasonings. Cover and cook on low for 6-8 hours or until a thermometer reads 170°.

● Shred chicken with two forks and return to the slow cooker; heat through. Serve with rice.

Yield: 6 servings.

> ❝Delicious! I just followed the recipe, and it came out great. A definite keeper at our house!❞
> —SKYMOM747 FROM TASTEOFHOME.COM

BAKED LOBSTER TAILS

Lobster tails make a rich and filling entree, especially when paired with steak for a special-occasion surf 'n' turf meal. With this perfectly seasoned, tender, juicy creation, you'll have mouths watering with sweet anticipation!
—**Taste of Home Test Kitchen**

PREP: 15 MIN. **BAKE:** 20 MIN.

- 3 lobster tails (8 to 10 ounces *each*)
- 1 cup water
- 1 tablespoon minced fresh parsley
- ⅛ teaspoon salt
- Dash pepper
- 1 tablespoon butter, melted
- 2 tablespoons lemon juice
- Lemon wedges and additional melted butter, optional

● Split the lobster tails in half lengthwise. With cut side up and using scissors, cut along the edge of the shell to loosen the cartilage covering the tail meat from the shell; remove and discard cartilage.

● Pour water into a 13-in. x 9-in. baking dish; place lobster tails in dish. Combine the parsley, salt and pepper; sprinkle over lobster. Drizzle with butter and lemon juice.

● Bake, uncovered, at 375° for 20-25 minutes or until the meat is firm and opaque. Serve with lemon wedges and melted butter if desired.

Yield: 6 servings.

TURKEY ENCHILADAS

We hosted a Mexican-themed party, and these creamy enchiladas were the hands-down star of the show. I was thrilled when four of our friends asked for the recipe. The best part was that no one figured out my secret—it's actually a light recipe!
—**Kimberly Bish** *Vandalia, Ohio*

PREP: 30 MIN. **BAKE:** 25 MIN.

- 1 large onion, chopped
- 1 large green pepper, chopped
- 2 teaspoons canola oil
- 3 tablespoons all-purpose flour
- 1¼ teaspoons ground coriander
- ¼ teaspoon pepper
- 1 can (14½ ounces) reduced-sodium chicken broth
- 1 cup (8 ounces) fat-free sour cream
- 1 cup (4 ounces) shredded reduced-fat cheddar cheese, *divided*
- 3 cups cubed cooked turkey breast
- ¾ cup salsa
- 8 flour tortillas (6 inches), warmed

● In a large nonstick saucepan coated with cooking spray, cook and stir onion and green pepper in oil until tender. Sprinkle with flour, coriander and pepper; stir until blended. Gradually stir in broth. Bring to a boil; cook and stir for 2 minutes or until thickened. Remove from the heat. Stir in the sour cream and ¾ cup cheese.

● In a large bowl, combine the turkey, salsa, and 1 cup cheese mixture. Spoon ⅓ cup turkey mixture down the center of each tortilla. Roll up and place seam side down in a 13-in. x 9-in. baking dish coated with cooking spray. Pour remaining cheese mixture over the top.

● Cover and bake at 350° for 20 minutes. Sprinkle with remaining cheese. Bake, uncovered, 5-10 minutes longer or until heated through and cheese is melted.

Yield: 8 servings.

BAKED TILAPIA

My baked tilapia brings the health benefits of fish into my family's diet in a delicious way. Just add a side of vegetables for a nutritious, no-fuss meal everyone will love.
—**Hope Stewart** *Raleigh, North Carolina*

PREP/TOTAL TIME: 20 MIN.

QUICK & EASY

- 4 tilapia fillets (6 ounces *each*)
- 3 tablespoons butter, melted
- 3 tablespoons lemon juice
- 1½ teaspoons garlic powder
- ⅛ teaspoon salt
- 2 tablespoons capers, drained
- ½ teaspoon dried oregano
- ⅛ teaspoon paprika

● Place tilapia in an ungreased 13-in. x 9-in. baking dish. In a small bowl, combine the butter, lemon juice, garlic powder and salt; pour over the fillets. Sprinkle tilapia with capers, oregano and paprika.

● Bake, uncovered, at 425° for 10-15 minutes or until fish flakes easily with a fork.

Yield: 4 servings.

CLASSIC CABBAGE ROLLS

I've always enjoyed cabbage rolls but was reluctant to try my hand at making them because most recipes seemed too complicated. Then I found this simple version and now I make the tasty delights for my family all the time.
—**Beverly Zehner** *McMinnville, Oregon*

PREP: 30 MIN. **COOK:** 1½ HOURS

- 1 medium head cabbage
- 1½ cups chopped onion, *divided*
- 1 tablespoon butter
- 2 cans (14½ ounces each) Italian stewed tomatoes
- 4 garlic cloves, minced
- 2 tablespoons brown sugar
- 1½ teaspoons salt, *divided*
- 1 cup cooked rice
- ¼ cup ketchup
- 2 tablespoons Worcestershire sauce
- ¼ teaspoon pepper
- 1 pound lean ground beef (90% lean)
- ¼ pound bulk Italian sausage
- ½ cup V8 juice, optional

◦ In a Dutch oven, cook cabbage in boiling water for 10 minutes or until outer leaves are tender; drain. Rinse in cold water; drain. Remove eight large outer leaves (refrigerate remaining cabbage for another use); set aside.

◦ In a large saucepan, saute 1 cup onion in butter until tender. Add the tomatoes, garlic, brown sugar and ½ teaspoon salt. Simmer for 15 minutes, stirring occasionally.

◦ Meanwhile, in a large bowl, combine the rice, ketchup, Worcestershire sauce, pepper and remaining onion and salt. Crumble beef and sausage over mixture and mix well.

◦ Remove thick vein from cabbage leaves for easier rolling. Place about ½ cup meat mixture on each leaf; fold in sides. Starting at an unfolded edge, roll up leaf to completely enclose filling. Place seam side down in a skillet. Top with the sauce.

◦ Cover and cook over medium-low heat for 1 hour. Add V8 juice if desired. Reduce heat to low; cook 20 minutes longer or until rolls are heated through and a thermometer inserted in the filling reads 160°.

Yield: 4 servings.

BEEF TENDERLOIN IN MUSHROOM SAUCE

It doesn't take much fuss to fix a special meal for two. This home-style classic is the delicious proof.
—**Denise McNab** *Warminster, Pennsylvania*

PREP/TOTAL TIME: 30 MIN.

QUICK & EASY

- 1 teaspoon canola oil
- 4 tablespoons butter, *divided*
- 2 beef tenderloin steaks (8 ounces *each*)
- ½ cup chopped fresh mushrooms
- 1 tablespoon chopped green onion
- 1 tablespoon all-purpose flour
- ⅛ teaspoon salt

Dash pepper

- ⅔ cup chicken *or* beef broth
- ⅛ teaspoon browning sauce, optional

◦ In a large skillet, heat oil and 2 tablespoons of butter over medium-high heat. Cook steaks for 6-7 minutes on each side or until meat reaches desired doneness (for medium-rare, a thermometer should read 145°; medium, 160°; well-done, 170°). Remove to a serving platter; keep warm.

◦ To pan juices, add the mushrooms, onion and remaining butter; saute until vegetables are tender. Add the flour, salt and pepper; gradually stir in broth until smooth. Add browning sauce if desired. Bring to a boil; cook and stir for 2 minutes or until thickened. Serve with the steaks.

Yield: 2 servings.

BEEF SIRLOIN TIP ROAST

The robust flavor of this meaty main course, served with a mouthwatering mushroom gravy, makes this a recipe you're going to repeat. It's a snap to assemble and pop in the oven.
—Mrs. Burgess Marshbanks *Buies Creek, North Carolina*

PREP: 10 MIN. **BAKE:** 2½ HOURS

- 1 beef sirloin tip roast (3 pounds)
- 1¼ cups water, *divided*
- 1 can (8 ounces) mushroom stems and pieces, drained
- 1 envelope onion soup mix
- 2 tablespoons cornstarch

● Place a large piece of heavy-duty foil (21-in. x 17-in.) in a shallow roasting pan. Place roast on foil. Pour 1 cup water and mushrooms over roast. Sprinkle with soup mix. Wrap foil around roast; seal tightly.

● Bake at 350° for 2½ to 3 hours or until meat reaches desired doneness (for medium-rare, a thermometer should read 145°; medium, 160°; well-done, 170°).

● Remove roast to a serving platter and keep warm. Pour drippings and mushrooms into a saucepan. Combine cornstarch and remaining water until smooth; gradually stir into drippings. Bring to a boil; cook and stir for 2 minutes or until thickened. Serve with sliced beef.

Yield: 10-12 servings.

APPLESAUCE-GLAZED PORK CHOPS

These tasty, tender chops are glazed with a sweet, smoky, apple-flavored sauce. They're on the table in no time at all, so they're perfect for busy weeknights.
—Brenda Campbell *Olympia, Washington*

QUICK & EASY

PREP/TOTAL TIME: 30 MIN.

- 4 bone-in pork loin chops (7 ounces *each*)
- 1 cup unsweetened applesauce
- ¼ cup packed brown sugar
- 1 tablespoon barbecue sauce
- 1 tablespoon Worcestershire sauce
- 1 garlic clove, minced
- ½ teaspoon salt
- ½ teaspoon pepper

● Place pork chops in a 13-in. x 9-in. baking dish coated with cooking spray. In a small bowl, combine the remaining ingredients; spoon over chops.

● Bake, uncovered, at 350° for 20-25 minutes or until a thermometer reads 160°.

Yield: 4 servings.

MAIN DISHES

BEEF-STUFFED ZUCCHINI

Tender zucchini boats serve as nifty holders for the hearty beef filling in this recipe. For a change of pace, substitute your favorite barbecue sauce for the marinara sauce.
—*Taste of Home Test Kitchen*

PREP/TOTAL TIME: 25 MIN.

QUICK & EASY

4 medium zucchini	¼ teaspoon salt
1 pound lean ground beef (90% lean)	¼ teaspoon pepper
½ cup chopped onion	1 cup (4 ounces) shredded Monterey Jack cheese, *divided*
1 egg	
¾ cup marinara *or* spaghetti sauce	Additional marinara *or* spaghetti sauce
¼ cup seasoned bread crumbs	

● Cut zucchini in half lengthwise; cut a thin slice from the bottom of each with a sharp knife to allow zucchini to sit flat. Scoop out pulp, leaving ¼-in. shells.

● Place shells in an ungreased 3-qt. microwave-safe dish. Cover and microwave on high for 3 minutes or until crisp-tender; drain and set aside.

● Meanwhile, in a large skillet, cook beef and onion over medium heat until meat is no longer pink; drain. Remove from the heat; stir in the egg, marinara sauce, bread crumbs, salt, pepper and ½ cup cheese.

● Spoon about ¼ cup into each shell. Microwave, uncovered, on high for 4 minutes. Sprinkle with remaining cheese. Microwave 3-4 minutes longer or until a thermometer inserted into filling reads 160° and zucchini are tender. Serve with additional marinara sauce.

EDITOR'S NOTE: This recipe was tested in a 1,100-watt microwave.

Yield: 4 servings.

MAIN DISHES

SWEET-AND-SOUR MEATBALLS

A tangy sauce, green pepper and pineapple transform premade meatballs into something special. Serve them over rice for a satisfying main dish.
—**Ruth Andrewson** *Leavenworth, Washington*

PREP/TOTAL TIME: 30 MIN.

QUICK & EASY

- 1 can (20 ounces) pineapple chunks
- ⅓ cup water
- 3 tablespoons vinegar
- 1 tablespoon soy sauce
- ½ cup packed brown sugar
- 3 tablespoons cornstarch
- 1 batch of 30 meatballs (frozen *or* thawed)
- 1 large green pepper, cut into 1-inch pieces

Hot cooked rice

◉ Drain pineapple, reserving juice. Set pineapple aside. Add water to juice if needed to measure 1 cup; pour into a large skillet. Add ⅓ cup water, vinegar, soy sauce, brown sugar and cornstarch; stir until smooth. Cook over medium heat until thick, stirring constantly. Add the pineapple, meatballs and green pepper. Simmer, uncovered, for 20 minutes or until heated through. Serve with rice.

Yield: 6 servings.

HAM WITH CHERRY SAUCE

Easter dinner just wouldn't be the same without this juicy, mouthwatering ham on the table. My recipe features a flavorful rub and a sweet cherry sauce with a hint of almond.
—**Lavonn Bormuth** *Westerville, Ohio*

PREP: 10 MIN. **BAKE:** 1¾ HOURS

- 1 fully cooked bone-in ham (6 to 8 pounds)
- 1 cup packed brown sugar
- 3 tablespoons maple syrup
- 1 teaspoon ground mustard
- ½ cup sugar
- 3 tablespoons cornstarch
- 1 cup cold water
- 1 can (16 ounces) pitted dark sweet cherries, undrained

- 2 tablespoons lemon juice
- 1 teaspoon almond extract

◉ Place ham in a roasting pan. Score surface of ham with shallow diagonal cuts, making diamond shapes. Combine the brown sugar, syrup and mustard; rub over ham and press into cuts.

◉ Cover roasting pan and bake at 325° for 1¾ to 2 hours or until a thermometer reads 140° and ham is heated through.

◉ For cherry sauce, in a small saucepan, combine the sugar, cornstarch and water until smooth. Add cherries. Bring to a boil; cook and stir for 2 minutes or until thickened. Remove from the heat; stir in lemon juice and extract. Serve with ham.

Yield: 8-10 servings.

MELT-IN-YOUR-MOUTH POT ROAST

Slow-simmered and seasoned with rosemary, mustard and thyme, this tender and tasty pot roast is so easy to make and always a hit. You can also substitute burgundy or brandy plus a half cup of water for the broth.
—**Jeannie Klugh** *Lancaster, Pennsylvania*

PREP: 10 MIN. **COOK:** 6 HOURS

- 1 pound medium red potatoes, quartered
- 1 cup fresh baby carrots
- 1 boneless beef chuck roast (3 to 4 pounds)
- ¼ cup Dijon mustard
- 2 teaspoons dried rosemary, crushed
- 1 teaspoon garlic salt
- ½ teaspoon dried thyme
- ½ teaspoon pepper
- ⅓ cup chopped onion
- 1½ cups beef broth

◉ Place potatoes and carrots in a 5-qt. slow cooker. Cut roast in half. In a small bowl, combine the mustard, rosemary, garlic salt, thyme and pepper; rub over roast.

◉ Place in slow cooker; top with onion and broth. Cover and cook on low for 6-8 hours or until meat and vegetables are tender.

Yield: 6-8 servings.

CUBED STEAKS WITH GRAVY

Here's a hearty, home-style dinner your family will love after a busy day. The slow-cooked beef is wonderful served over mashed potatoes or noodles!
—*Judy Long* *Limestone, Tennessee*

PREP: 15 MIN. **COOK:** 8½ HOURS

⅓ cup all-purpose flour
6 beef cubed steaks (4 ounces *each*)
1 tablespoon canola oil
1 large onion, sliced and separated into rings
3 cups water, *divided*
1 envelope brown gravy mix
1 envelope mushroom gravy mix
1 envelope onion gravy mix
Hot mashed potatoes *or* cooked noodles

◉ Place flour in a large resealable plastic bag. Add steaks, a few at a time, and shake until completely coated.

◉ In a skillet, cook steaks in oil until lightly browned on each side. Transfer to a 3-qt. slow cooker. Add the onion and 2 cups water. Cover and cook on low for 8 hours or until meat is tender.

◉ In a bowl, whisk together gravy mixes with remaining water. Add to slow cooker; cook 30 minutes longer. Serve over mashed potatoes or noodles.

Yield: 6 servings.

KITCHEN TIP

Unless the recipe instructs you to stir in or add ingredients, refrain from lifting the lid while the slow cooker is cooking. Every time you lift the lid, steam is lost and you add 15 to 30 minutes of cooking time.

BRISKET IN A BAG

This tender brisket is served with a savory cranberry gravy that's made right in the bag. You'll want to serve the slices with mashed potatoes just so you can drizzle the gravy over them.
—*Peggy Stigers* *Fort Worth, Texas*

PREP: 15 MIN. **BAKE:** 2½ HOURS

3 tablespoons all-purpose flour, *divided*
1 large oven roasting bag
1 fresh beef brisket (5 pounds), trimmed
1 can (14 ounces) whole-berry cranberry sauce
1 can (10¾ ounces) condensed cream of mushroom soup, undiluted
1 can (8 ounces) tomato sauce
1 envelope onion soup mix

◉ Place 1 tablespoon flour in oven bag; shake to coat. Place bag in an ungreased 13-in. x 9-in. baking pan; place brisket in bag.

◉ Combine the cranberry sauce, soup, tomato sauce, soup mix and remaining flour; pour over beef. Seal bag. Cut slits in top of bag according to package directions.

◉ Bake at 325° for 2½ to 3 hours or until meat is tender. Carefully remove brisket from bag. Let stand 5 minutes before slicing. Thinly slice meat across the grain; serve with gravy.

EDITOR'S NOTE: This is a fresh beef brisket, not corned beef.

Yield: 12 servings.

CROCK POT: RDA-MKE

SAUSAGE PIE, PAGE 124

117
129
126

CASSEROLES &
ONE-POT WONDERS

It's no wonder casseroles are so popular! Not only are they comfort food at its very best, they're convenient, freezer-friendly, can easily be assembled in advance and many call for ingredients you already have stocked in the pantry. Plus, cleanup is snap because you don't use every pot and pan in the kitchen! From bubbly lasagnas to classic potpies to stuffed pasta shells, you won't be able to get enough of the warm oven-baked goodness inside these timeless meal-in-one favorites!

POTATO-CRUSTED CHICKEN CASSEROLE

An herb-enhanced filling is surrounded by a sliced potato "crust" in this unique casserole. It tastes rich and satisfying, even though it calls for several lighter ingredients.
—**Becky Matheny** *Strasburg, Virginia*

PREP: 30 MIN. **BAKE:** 40 MIN.

- 1 large potato, thinly sliced
- 1 tablespoon olive oil
- ½ teaspoon salt
- ¼ teaspoon pepper

FILLING:

- 1½ pounds chicken tenderloins, cut into ½-inch cubes
- 2 teaspoons olive oil
- 1 medium onion, chopped
- 1 tablespoon butter
- 2 tablespoons all-purpose flour
- 1½ cups fat-free milk
- ¼ cup shredded part-skim mozzarella cheese
- ¼ cup grated Parmesan cheese
- 2 tablespoons shredded reduced-fat cheddar cheese
- 2 cups frozen peas and carrots
- ½ teaspoon salt
- ½ teaspoon dried thyme
- ¼ teaspoon dried basil

Dash rubbed sage

CRUMB TOPPING:

- 1 cup soft bread crumbs
- 1 tablespoon butter, melted
- ½ teaspoon garlic powder

○ In a large bowl, toss potato slices with oil, salt and pepper. Arrange slices on the bottom and sides of an 11-in. x 7-in. baking dish coated with cooking spray. Bake at 400° for 20-25 minutes or until potato is tender. Reduce heat to 350°.

○ Meanwhile, for filling, in a large skillet over medium heat, cook chicken in oil until no longer pink. Remove from skillet. In the same skillet, saute onion in butter. Stir in flour until blended; gradually add milk. Bring to a boil; cook and stir for 2 minutes or until thickened. Reduce heat; stir in cheeses until melted. Stir in vegetables, seasonings and chicken. Spoon into potato crust.

○ Combine topping ingredients; sprinkle over chicken mixture. Bake, uncovered, for 40-45 minutes or until bubbly and topping is golden brown.

Yield: 6 servings.

HAMBURGER SHEPHERD'S PIE

Transform leftovers into a light but filling meal. This easy one-dish wonder makes the perfect amount to feed a twosome.
—**Elaine Williams** *Surrey, British Columbia*

PREP: 20 MIN. **BAKE:** 30 MIN.

- ½ pound lean ground beef (90% lean)
- 2 tablespoons chopped onion
- 1 cup frozen cut green beans, thawed
- ⅔ cup condensed tomato soup, undiluted
- ¼ teaspoon Italian seasoning
- ⅛ teaspoon pepper
- 1 cup mashed potatoes (prepared with milk)

Dash paprika

○ In a small skillet, cook beef and onion over medium heat until meat is no longer pink; drain. Add the beans, soup, Italian seasoning and pepper. Transfer to a 7-in. pie plate coated with cooking spray.

○ Spread the mashed potatoes over the top; sprinkle with paprika. Bake, uncovered, at 350° for 30-35 minutes or until heated through.

Yield: 2 servings.

CHICKEN ALFREDO

Broccoli, zucchini and sweet red pepper lend a fresh taste to this classic pasta entree. And cream cheese makes the smooth sauce a snap to stir up!
—*Jody Stewart* *Goldsboro, North Carolina*

QUICK & EASY

PREP/TOTAL TIME: 15 MIN.

- 1 package (8 ounces) cream cheese, cubed
- 6 tablespoons butter, cubed
- ½ cup milk
- ½ teaspoon garlic powder

Salt and pepper to taste

- 2 boneless skinless chicken breast halves, cooked and cubed (about 1½ cups)
- 2 cups frozen chopped broccoli, thawed
- 2 small zucchini, julienned
- ½ cup julienned sweet red pepper
- 6 ounces cooked fettuccine

• In a large skillet over low heat, melt cream cheese and butter; stir until smooth. Add the milk, garlic powder, salt and pepper. Cook and stir for 3 minutes or until mixture is thickened.

• Add the chicken, broccoli, zucchini and red pepper. Cook over medium heat for 3 minutes. Reduce heat; cover and cook 5 minutes longer or until vegetables are tender. Serve with fettuccine.

Yield: 4-6 servings.

QUICK CHICKEN AND DUMPLINGS

Using precooked chicken and ready-made biscuits, this hearty dish is comfort food made simple. It's the perfect way to warm up on chilly nights.
—*Lakeya Astwood* *Schenectady, New York*

QUICK & EASY

PREP/TOTAL TIME: 30 MIN.

- 6 individually frozen biscuits
- ¼ cup chopped onion
- ¼ cup chopped green pepper
- 1 tablespoon olive oil
- 4 cups shredded rotisserie chicken
- 2 cans (14½ ounces *each*) reduced-sodium chicken broth
- 1 can (4 ounces) mushroom stems and pieces, drained
- 1 teaspoon chicken bouillon granules
- 1 teaspoon minced fresh parsley
- ½ teaspoon dried sage leaves
- ¼ teaspoon dried rosemary, crushed
- ¼ teaspoon pepper

• Cut each biscuit into fourths; set aside. In a large saucepan, saute onion and green pepper in oil until tender. Stir in the chicken, broth, mushrooms, bouillon granules, parsley, sage, rosemary and pepper.

• Bring to a boil. Reduce heat; add biscuits for dumplings. Cover and simmer for 10 minutes or until a toothpick inserted near the center of a dumpling comes out clean (do not lift cover while simmering).

Yield: 6 servings.

ALFREDO CHICKEN TORTELLINI

I'm always trying to come up with new recipes. For this one, I just started combining ingredients I had handy. The result was so rich and creamy, I knew it was a keeper.
—*Tiffany Treanor* *Waukomis, Oklahoma*

PREP/TOTAL TIME: 30 MIN.

QUICK & EASY

- 1½ cups frozen cheese tortellini
- 1 boneless skinless chicken breast half (6 ounces), cut into 1-inch cubes
- 3 bacon strips, chopped
- ⅛ teaspoon adobo seasoning
- ⅓ cup chopped onion
- ⅓ cup chopped sweet red pepper
- 3 teaspoons minced garlic
- 1 can (10¾ ounces) condensed cream of chicken soup, undiluted
- ½ cup 2% milk
- ⅓ cup sour cream
- 2 tablespoons grated Parmesan cheese
- 1 cup frozen chopped broccoli, thawed and drained

- Cook tortellini according to package directions. Meanwhile, in a large saucepan, cook and stir the chicken, bacon and adobo seasoning over medium heat until chicken is no longer pink. Add onion and red pepper; cook and stir until tender. Add garlic; cook 1 minute longer.

- In a small bowl, combine the soup, milk, sour cream and cheese; stir into chicken mixture. Bring to a boil. Reduce heat; simmer, uncovered, for 5-7 minutes.

- Drain tortellini; add to chicken mixture. Stir in broccoli; heat through.

Yield: 3 servings.

GARDEN PIZZA SUPREME

This pizza is so delicious and colorful. Feel free to toss on any fresh vegetables from your garden.
—*Pamela Shank* *Parkersburg, West Virginia*

PREP: 20 MIN. **BAKE:** 20 MIN.

- 1 loaf (1 pound) frozen bread dough, thawed
- 6 slices part-skim mozzarella cheese
- 1 can (8 ounces) pizza sauce
- 2 cups (8 ounces) shredded part-skim mozzarella cheese, *divided*
- ½ cup *each* finely chopped fresh cauliflowerets, mushrooms and broccoli florets
- ¼ cup *each* finely chopped red onion, green pepper and sweet red pepper
- ½ cup pickled pepper rings

- Roll dough into a 15-in. circle. Transfer to a greased 14-in. pizza pan, building up edges slightly. Place cheese slices on dough. Spread sauce over cheese. Sprinkle with 1 cup shredded cheese, cauliflower, mushrooms, broccoli, onion, peppers and pepper rings.

- Bake at 425° for 15 minutes. Sprinkle with remaining cheese. Bake 5-10 minutes longer or until cheese is melted and crust is golden brown.

Yield: 8 slices.

BAKED MOSTACCIOLI

Here's a casserole that is a trusted standby for church suppers and other potluck functions. Add a tossed green salad and breadsticks to round out a memorable meal.
—**Darlene Carlson** *Jamestown, North Dakota*

PREP: 35 MIN. **BAKE:** 30 MIN.

8 ounces uncooked mostaccioli	1 to 1¼ teaspoons salt
1½ pounds lean ground beef (90% lean)	1 teaspoon sugar
½ cup chopped onion	1 teaspoon dried basil
1 garlic clove, minced	⅛ teaspoon pepper
1 can (28 ounces) diced tomatoes	1 bay leaf
1 can (8 ounces) tomato sauce	2 cups (8 ounces) shredded part-skim
1 can (6 ounces) tomato paste	mozzarella cheese
1 can (4 ounces) sliced mushrooms	½ cup grated Parmesan cheese
½ cup water	

○ Cook mostaccioli according to package directions; drain and set aside. In a large saucepan, cook beef and onion over medium heat until no longer pink. Add garlic; cook 1 minute longer. Drain.

○ Stir in the tomatoes, tomato sauce and paste, mushrooms, water, salt, sugar, basil, pepper and bay leaf. Bring to a boil. Reduce heat; simmer, uncovered, for 30 minutes, stirring occasionally.

○ Discard bay leaf. Stir in mostaccioli. Spoon half into a 13-in. x 9-in. baking dish. Sprinkle with mozzarella cheese; layer with remaining meat mixture. Sprinkle with Parmesan cheese.

○ Cover and bake at 350 ° for 30-35 minutes or until heated casserole is through. Let stand for 5 minutes before serving.

Yield: 10-12 servings.

PESTO SHRIMP PASTA TOSS

You can whip up this elegant entree in just 30 minutes. Coated in pesto and topped with walnuts and Parmesan, the blend of pasta, shrimp and vegetables adds a dressy touch to any weeknight meal.
—**Fran Scott** Birmingham, Michigan

PREP/TOTAL TIME: 30 MIN.

QUICK & EASY

- 9   ounces uncooked linguine
- 1   pound cooked medium shrimp, peeled and deveined
- 1   pound fresh asparagus, trimmed and cut into 2-inch pieces
- 1   medium yellow summer squash, sliced
- 1   cup fresh baby carrots, halved lengthwise
- 1   tablespoon butter, melted
- ½   teaspoon lemon pepper seasoning
- ¼   teaspoon salt
- ½   cup prepared pesto
- ½   cup shredded Parmesan cheese
- ½   cup chopped walnuts, toasted, optional

◉ Cook linguine according to package directions, adding shrimp during the last minute. Meanwhile, in a greased 15-in. x 10-in. x 1-in. baking pan, combine the asparagus, squash and carrots. Drizzle with butter; sprinkle with lemon-pepper and salt.

◉ Bake, uncovered, at 450° for 15-20 minutes or until vegetables are tender, stirring once.

◉ Drain linguine and shrimp; transfer to a serving bowl. Add the vegetable mixture and pesto; toss gently. Sprinkle with cheese and walnuts if desired.

Yield: 6 servings.

KITCHEN TIP

To cook pasta more evenly, prevent it from sticking together and avoid boil-overs, always cook it in a large kettle or Dutch oven. Unless you have a very large kettle, don't cook more than two pounds of pasta at a time.

CHEESY SHELL LASAGNA

This zesty layered casserole is a real crowd-pleaser. It was one of our children's favorites when they were young...now our grandchildren love it! As an added bonus, it's easier to prepare than traditional lasagna.
—**Mrs. Leo Merchant** Jackson, Mississippi

PREP: 25 MIN. **BAKE:** 45 MIN. + STANDING

- 1½   pounds lean ground beef (90% lean)
- 2   medium onions, chopped
- 1   garlic clove, minced
- 1   can (14½ ounces) diced tomatoes, undrained
- 1   jar (14 ounces) meatless spaghetti sauce
- 1   can (4 ounces) mushroom stems and pieces, undrained
- 8   ounces uncooked small shell pasta
- 2   cups (16 ounces) reduced-fat sour cream
- 11   slices (8 ounces) reduced-fat provolone cheese
- 1   cup (4 ounces) shredded part-skim mozzarella cheese

◉ In a nonstick skillet, cook beef and onions over medium heat until meat is no longer pink. Add garlic; cook 1 minute longer. Drain. Stir in the tomatoes, spaghetti sauce and mushrooms. Bring to a boil. Reduce heat; simmer, uncovered, for 20 minutes.

◉ Meanwhile, cook the pasta according to the package directions; drain.

◉ Place half of the pasta in an ungreased 13-in. x 9-in. baking dish. Top with half of the meat sauce, sour cream and provolone cheese. Repeat layers. Sprinkle with mozzarella cheese.

◉ Cover and bake at 350° for 35-40 minutes. Uncover; bake 10 minutes longer or until the cheese begins to brown. Let stand for 10 minutes before cutting.

Yield: 12 servings.

MEATY RIGATONI BAKE

Here's a super-easy Italian entree perfect for two or three. I created this dish one night just using ingredients I had on hand.
—**Mary Grossman** *Cloquet, Minnesota*

PREP: 20 MIN. **BAKE:** 25 MIN.

- 1 cup uncooked rigatoni *or* large tube pasta
- ½ pound bulk Italian sausage
- 1½ cups spaghetti sauce
- 1 can (4 ounces) mushroom stems and pieces, drained
- ½ cup shredded Italian cheese blend
- 8 slices pepperoni

● Cook pasta according to package directions. Meanwhile, crumble sausage into a large skillet. Cook over medium heat until no longer pink; drain. Stir in the spaghetti sauce and mushrooms. Drain pasta; add to sausage mixture.

● Transfer to a 1-qt. baking dish coated with cooking spray. Top with cheese and pepperoni. Cover and bake at 350° for 25-30 minutes or until heated through.

Yield: 3 servings.

SPICY BEAN AND BEEF PIE

My daughter helped me create this recipe one day when we wanted a one-dish meal that offered a change of pace from typical casseroles. It slices nicely and is fun and filling!
—**Debra Dohy** *Newcomerstown, Ohio*

PREP: 20 MIN. **BAKE:** 30 MIN.

- 1 pound lean ground beef (90% lean)
- 2 to 3 garlic cloves, minced
- 1 can (11½ ounces) condensed bean with bacon soup, undiluted
- 1 jar (16 ounces) thick and chunky picante sauce, *divided*
- ¼ cup cornstarch
- 1 tablespoon chopped fresh parsley
- 1 teaspoon paprika
- 1 teaspoon salt
- ¼ teaspoon pepper
- 1 can (16 ounces) kidney beans, rinsed and drained
- 1 can (15 ounces) black beans, rinsed and drained
- 2 cups (8 ounces) shredded cheddar cheese, *divided*
- ¾ cup sliced green onions, *divided*
- Pastry for double-crust pie (10 inches)
- 1 cup (8 ounces) sour cream
- 1 can (2¼ ounces) sliced ripe olives, drained

● In a large skillet, cook beef over medium heat until beef is no longer pink. Add garlic; cook 1 minute longer. Drain.

● In a large bowl, combine the soup, 1 cup of picante sauce, cornstarch, parsley, paprika, salt and pepper. Fold in the beans, 1½ cups of cheese, ½ cup onions and the beef mixture.

● Line pie plate with bottom pastry; fill with bean mixture. Top with remaining pastry; seal and flute edges. Cut slits in top crust.

● Bake at 425° for 30-35 minutes or until lightly browned. Let stand for 5 minutes before cutting. Garnish with the sour cream, olives and remaining picante sauce, cheese and onions.

TO FREEZE: Before baking, cover and freeze the pie for up to 3 months.

TO USE FROZEN PIE: Remove from the freezer 30 minutes before baking. Cover edges of crust loosely with foil; place on a baking sheet. Bake at 425° for 30 minutes. Reduce heat to 350°; remove foil. Bake 55-60 minutes longer or until golden brown. Garnish with sour cream, olives, picante sauce, cheese and onions.

Yield: 8 servings.

BROCCOLI MAC AND CHEESE BAKE

My husband made a version of this casserole for me on our first date. Over the years we've been married, we've made several changes to the ingredients, and now it's even better than his original!
—**Lisa DeMarsh** Mt. Solon, Virginia

PREP: 25 MIN. **BAKE:** 20 MIN.

3 cups uncooked elbow macaroni	¼ teaspoon pepper
4 cups fresh broccoli florets	⅛ teaspoon salt
½ cup butter, cubed	2 cans (12 ounces *each*) evaporated milk
3 tablespoons all-purpose flour	2½ cups (10 ounces) shredded cheddar cheese, *divided*
½ teaspoon garlic powder	
½ teaspoon onion powder	½ cup crushed cornbread-flavored crackers (about 6 crackers)

- Cook macaroni according to package directions, adding broccoli during the last 3-4 minutes; drain.

- In a large saucepan, melt butter. Stir in the flour, garlic powder, onion powder, pepper and salt until smooth; gradually stir in evaporated milk. Bring to a boil; cook and stir for 2 minutes or until thickened. Remove from the heat; stir in 2 cups cheese.

- Place half of the macaroni and broccoli in a greased 13-in. x 9-in. baking dish. Top with half of the cheese sauce. Repeat layers. Sprinkle with cracker crumbs and remaining cheese.

- Bake, uncovered, at 375° for 20-25 minutes or until bubbly.

Yield: 12 servings.

ITALIAN SPAGHETTI AND MEATBALLS

My cousin's wife, who is from Italy, shared this authentic gem of a recipe with me. It's so hearty and satisfying, everyone's eyes light up when I tell them we're having this for supper!
—**Etta Winter** *Pavillion, New York*

PREP: 30 MIN. **COOK:** 1½ HOURS

- 2 cans (28 ounces *each*) diced tomatoes, undrained
- 1 can (12 ounces) tomato paste
- 1½ cups water, *divided*
- 3 tablespoons grated onion
- 1 tablespoon sugar
- 1½ teaspoons dried oregano
- 1 bay leaf
- 1¼ teaspoons salt, *divided*
- 1 teaspoon minced garlic, *divided*
- ¾ teaspoon pepper, *divided*
- 6 slices day-old bread, torn into pieces
- 2 eggs, lightly beaten
- ½ cup grated Parmesan cheese
- 2 tablespoons minced fresh parsley
- 1 pound lean ground beef (90% lean)

Hot cooked spaghetti

Additional Parmesan cheese, optional

- In a Dutch oven, combine the tomatoes, tomato paste, 1 cup water, onion, sugar, oregano, bay leaf and ½ teaspoon each of the salt, garlic and pepper. Bring to a boil. Reduce the heat and simmer, uncovered, for 1¼ hours.

- Meanwhile, soak bread in remaining water. Squeeze out excess moisture. In a large bowl, combine the bread, eggs, Parmesan cheese, parsley and remaining salt, garlic and pepper. Crumble beef over mixture and mix well. Shape into thirty-six 1½-in. meatballs.

- Place meatballs on a rack in a shallow baking pan. Bake,

uncovered, at 400° for 20 minutes or until no longer pink; drain. Transfer to spaghetti sauce. Simmer, uncovered, until heated through, stirring occasionally. Discard bay leaf. Serve with spaghetti with additional Parmesan if desired.

TO MAKE ITALIAN MEATBALL SANDWICHES: Serve meatballs on split submarine, hoagie or French bread rolls. Place on a baking sheet, leaving sandwich open. Sprinkle each with ¼ to ⅓ cup shredded mozzarella cheese. Bake, uncovered, at 350° for 10-15 minutes or until cheese is melted.

Yield: 6 servings.

ENCHILADA CASSEROLE

I get great reviews every time I serve this zesty Southwestern creation. The casserole calls for only six easy ingredients and smells so delicious while baking! If you like, add a few chili peppers on top for a festive garnish.
—**Nancy VanderVeer** *Knoxville, Iowa*

PREP: 20 MIN. **BAKE:** 30 MIN.

- 1 pound lean ground beef (90% lean)
- 1 can (10 ounces) enchilada sauce
- 1 cup salsa
- 6 flour tortillas (10 inch)
- 2 cups fresh *or* frozen corn
- 4 cups (16 ounces) shredded cheddar cheese

- In a large skillet, cook ground beef over medium heat until no longer pink; drain. Stir in enchilada sauce and salsa; set aside.

- Place two tortillas, overlapping as necessary, in the bottom of a greased 13-in. x 9-in. baking dish. Cover with one-third of the meat mixture; top with 1 cup corn; sprinkle with 1⅓ cups cheese. Repeat layers once, then top with remaining tortillas, meat and cheese.

- Bake, uncovered, at 350° for 30 minutes or until bubbly.

Yield: 6-8 servings.

CHILI MAC CASSEROLE

With wagon wheel pasta and popular Tex-Mex ingredients, this beefy main dish is sure to be a hit. It's never failed to please at potlucks and bring-a-dish gatherings.
—**Janet Kanzler** *Yakima, Washington*

PREP: 20 MIN. **BAKE:** 25 MIN.

- 1 cup uncooked wagon wheel pasta
- 1 pound lean ground beef (90% lean)
- ½ cup chopped onion
- ½ cup chopped green pepper
- 1 can (15 ounces) turkey chili with beans
- 1 can (14½ ounces) stewed tomatoes, undrained
- 1 cup crushed baked tortilla chip scoops
- 1 cup (4 ounces) shredded reduced-fat cheddar cheese, *divided*
- ¼ cup uncooked instant rice
- 1 teaspoon chili powder
- ¼ teaspoon salt
- ⅛ teaspoon pepper

● Cook pasta according to package directions. Meanwhile, in a large nonstick skillet, cook the beef, onion and green pepper over medium heat until meat is no longer pink; drain. Stir in the chili, tomatoes, chips, ½ cup cheese, rice, chili powder, salt and pepper. Drain pasta; add to beef mixture.

● Transfer to a 2-qt. baking dish coated with cooking spray. Sprinkle with remaining cheese. Bake, uncovered, at 350° for 25-30 minutes or until cheese is melted.

Yield: 6 servings.

PEPPERONI LASAGNA ROLL-UPS

My husband is in the military, and when he is away from home, it's hard to come up with meals just for myself. After finding I had some leftover items from making lasagna, I came up with this recipe.
—**Jennifer Juday** *Copperas Cove, Texas*

PREP: 25 MIN. **BAKE:** 25 MIN.

- 3 lasagna noodles
- ¾ cup ricotta cheese
- ½ teaspoon minced chives
- ½ teaspoon dried oregano
- ½ teaspoon dried basil
- 24 slices pepperoni
- 3 slices Swiss cheese, cut into thirds
- 1 cup meatless spaghetti sauce
- ¼ cup shredded Parmesan cheese

● Cook noodles according to package directions; drain. Combine the ricotta cheese, chives, oregano and basil; spread ¼ cup over each noodle to within ½ in. of edges. Top with pepperoni and Swiss cheese; carefully roll up.

● Place seam side down in a greased shallow 1-qt. baking dish; top with spaghetti sauce. Cover and bake at 350° for 20-25 minutes or until bubbly.

● Sprinkle with Parmesan cheese. Let stand for 5 minutes before serving.

Yield: 3 servings.

CHICKEN POTPIES

Pie for supper? If it's this cook-once-eat-twice classic, then yes, please! I received this cherished recipe from my aunt and tweaked it to fit my family's tastes. They love the addition of sage, which adds a unique flavor.
—Lysa Davis *Pine Bluff, Arkansas*

PREP: 20 MIN. **BAKE:** 35 MIN. + STANDING

2 cans (9¾ ounces each) chunk white chicken, drained

1 can (15¼ ounces) lima beans, drained

1 can (15 ounces) sliced carrots, drained

1 jar (4½ ounces) sliced mushrooms, drained

1 can (14½ ounces) sliced potatoes, drained

1 can (10¾ ounces) condensed cream of chicken soup, undiluted

1 can (10¾ ounces) condensed cream of mushroom soup, undiluted

1½ teaspoons rubbed sage

¼ teaspoon salt

¼ teaspoon pepper

2 packages (15 ounces each) refrigerated pie pastry

1 tablespoon butter, melted

○ In a large bowl, combine the first 10 ingredients. Line two 9-in. pie plates with bottom crusts. Add filling. Roll out remaining pastry to fit tops of pies; place over filling. Trim, seal and flute edges. Cut slits in pastry; brush with butter.

○ Cover and freeze one potpie for up to 3 months. Bake the remaining potpie at 375° for 35-40 minutes or until golden brown. Let stand for 10 minutes before cutting.

TO USE FROZEN POTPIE: Remove from freezer 30 minutes before baking. Cover edges of crust loosely with foil; place on baking sheet. Bake at 425° for 30 minutes. Reduce heat to 375°; remove foil. Bake 55-60 minutes longer or until golden brown. Let stand for 10 minutes before cutting.

Yield: 2 pies (6 servings each).

PASTA CARBONARA

My hungry clan can't get enough of this creamy, cheesy recipe. Serve it alongside a fresh green salad and your favorite rolls to round out the meal.

—*Cindi Bauer* *Marshfield, Wisconsin*

PREP/TOTAL TIME: 30 MIN.

- 2½   cups uncooked mostaccioli
- 8   bacon strips, diced
- 1   jar (4½ ounces) whole mushrooms, drained
- ¾   cup half-and-half cream
- ⅓   cup butter, cubed
- 1   teaspoon dried parsley flakes
- 1   teaspoon minced garlic
- 6   to 8 drops hot pepper sauce
- ½   teaspoon salt, optional
- ⅓   cup grated Parmesan cheese
- ¼   cup sliced green onions

● Cook mostaccioli according to package directions.

● Meanwhile, in a large skillet, cook bacon over medium heat until crisp. Using a slotted spoon, remove to paper towels to drain. Brown mushrooms in drippings; remove to paper towels. Drain drippings from pan.

● Add the cream, butter, parsley, garlic, pepper sauce and salt if desired to the skillet; cook and stir over medium heat until butter is melted. Drain mostaccioli; add to cream mixture. Stir in the bacon, mushrooms and cheese; heat through. Remove from the heat. Sprinkle with green onions.

Yield: 4 servings.

LASAGNA DELIZIOSA

Everyone loves this lasagna. It's often requested as a birthday treat or served to guests. I've lightened it up a lot from the original, but no one can tell the difference!

—*Heather O'Neill* *Troy, Ohio*

PREP: 45 MIN. **BAKE:** 50 MIN. + STANDING

- 9   uncooked lasagna noodles
- 1   package (19½ ounces) Italian turkey sausage links, casings removed
- ½   pound lean ground beef (90% lean)
- 1   large onion, chopped
- 2   garlic cloves, minced
- 1   can (28 ounces) diced tomatoes, undrained
- 1   can (12 ounces) tomato paste
- ¼   cup water
- 2   teaspoons sugar
- 1   teaspoon dried basil
- ½   teaspoon fennel seed
- ¼   teaspoon pepper
- 1   egg, lightly beaten
- 1   carton (15 ounces) reduced-fat ricotta cheese
- 1   tablespoon minced fresh parsley
- ½   teaspoon salt
- 2   cups (8 ounces) shredded part-skim mozzarella cheese
- ¾   cup grated Parmesan cheese

● Cook noodles according to package directions. Meanwhile, in a Dutch oven, cook the sausage, beef and onion over medium heat until meat is no longer pink; add garlic and cook 1 minute longer. Drain.

● Stir in the tomatoes, tomato paste, water, sugar, basil, fennel and pepper. Bring to a boil. Reduce heat; cover and simmer for 15-20 minutes, stirring occasionally.

● In a small bowl, combine the egg, ricotta cheese, parsley and salt. Drain noodles and rinse in cold water. Spread 1 cup of meat sauce into a 13-in. x 9-in. baking dish coated with cooking spray. Top with three noodles, 2 cups meat sauce, ⅔ cup ricotta cheese mixture, ⅔ cup mozzarella and ¼ cup Parmesan. Repeat layers twice.

● Cover and bake at 375° for 40 minutes. Uncover; bake 10-15 minutes longer or until bubbly. Let lasagna stand for 10 minutes before cutting.

Yield: 12 servings.

HEARTY PENNE BEEF

Here's comfort food at its finest! Packed with ground beef, pasta and cheese, this casserole is a great way to sneak some spinach into dinner for extra nutrition.
—Taste of Home Test Kitchen

QUICK & EASY

PREP/TOTAL TIME: 30 MIN.

> 1¾ cups uncooked penne pasta
> 1 pound lean ground beef (90% lean)
> 1 teaspoon minced garlic
> 1 can (15 ounces) tomato puree
> 1 can (14½ ounces) beef broth
> 1½ teaspoons Italian seasoning
> 1 teaspoon Worcestershire sauce
> ¼ teaspoon salt
> ¼ teaspoon pepper
> 2 cups chopped fresh spinach
> 2 cups (8 ounces) shredded part-skim mozzarella cheese

● Cook pasta according to the package directions. Meanwhile, in a Dutch oven, cook beef over medium heat until meat is no longer pink. Add garlic; cook 1 minute longer. Drain. Stir in the tomato puree, broth, Italian seasoning, Worcestershire sauce, salt and pepper.

● Bring to a boil. Reduce heat; simmer, uncovered, for 10-15 minutes or until slightly thickened. Add spinach; cook for 1-2 minutes or until spinach is wilted.

● Drain pasta; stir into beef mixture. Sprinkle with cheese; cover and cook for 3-4 minutes or until cheese is melted.

● Serve immediately, or cool before placing in a freezer container. Cover and freeze for up to 3 months.

TO USE FROZEN CASSEROLE: Thaw in the refrigerator overnight. Place in a Dutch oven; heat through. Sprinkle with additional cheese.

Yield: 4 servings.

SCALLOPED POTATOES 'N' HAM CASSEROLE

I'm a home health nurse and got this recipe from one of my elderly clients, who had used it for years. Now, it's one of my family's favorites. It will never curdle, thanks to the secret ingredient of powdered nondairy creamer.
—Kathy Johnson *Lake City, South Dakota*

PREP: 25 MIN. **BAKE:** 1 HOUR

> ¾ cup powdered nondairy creamer
> 1¾ cups water
> 3 tablespoons butter
> 3 tablespoons all-purpose flour
> 2 tablespoons dried minced onion
> 1 teaspoon salt
> ¾ teaspoon paprika
> 6 large potatoes, peeled and thinly sliced
> 2 cups diced fully cooked ham
> 1 cup (4 ounces) shredded cheddar cheese

● In a small bowl, combine creamer and water until smooth. In a small saucepan, melt butter. Stir in the flour, onion, salt and paprika until smooth; gradually add creamer mixture. Bring to a boil; cook and stir for 1-2 minutes or until thickened.

● In a greased shallow 2½-qt. baking dish, combine potatoes and ham. Pour sauce over the top.

● Cover and bake at 350° for 15 minutes. Uncover; bake 40-50 minutes longer or until potatoes are tender. Sprinkle with cheese; bake for 5-10 minutes or until edges are bubbly and cheese is melted.

Yield: 6 servings.

KITCHEN TIP

To add a little more zip to scalloped potatoes, sprinkle canned chopped green chilies between the potatoes, cheese and sauce.
—Kathleen M., Lemoore, California

POTATOES: BRAND X PICTURES

BAKED SPAGHETTI

You'll get requests for this yummy spaghetti casserole again and again. It's especially popular with my grandchildren, who just love all the cheese!
—**Louise Miller** *Westminster, Maryland*

PREP: 25 MIN. **BAKE:** 1 HOUR

1 package (16 ounces) spaghetti	⅓ cup grated Parmesan cheese
1 pound lean ground beef (90% lean)	5 tablespoons butter, melted
1 medium onion, chopped	2 cups (16 ounces) 4% cottage cheese
1 jar (24 ounces) meatless spaghetti sauce	4 cups (16 ounces) part-skim shredded
½ teaspoon seasoned salt	mozzarella cheese
2 eggs	

○ Cook spaghetti according to package directions. Meanwhile, in a large skillet, cook beef and onion over medium heat until meat is no longer pink; drain. Stir in spaghetti sauce and seasoned salt; set aside.

○ In a large bowl, whisk the eggs, Parmesan cheese and butter. Drain spaghetti; add to egg mixture and toss to coat.

○ Place half of the spaghetti mixture in a greased 13-in. x 9-in. baking dish. Top with half of the cottage cheese, meat sauce and mozzarella cheese. Repeat layers.

○ Cover and bake at 350° for 40 minutes. Uncover; bake 20-25 minutes longer or until cheese is melted.

Yield: 10 servings.

TACO PASTA SHELLS

Here's a kid-friendly dish so flavorful and fun, nobody is likely to guess that it's also lower in fat. It's an ideal family supper for busy weeknights.
—**Anne Thomsen** *Westchester, Ohio*

PREP: 25 MIN. **BAKE:** 25 MIN.

- 18 uncooked jumbo pasta shells
- 1½ pounds lean ground beef (90% lean)
- 1 bottle (16 ounces) taco sauce, *divided*
- 3 ounces fat-free cream cheese, cubed
- 2 teaspoons chili powder
- ¾ cup shredded reduced-fat Mexican cheese blend, *divided*
- 20 baked tortilla chip scoops, coarsely crushed

◎ Cook pasta according to package directions. Meanwhile, in a large nonstick skillet over medium heat, cook beef until no longer pink; drain. Add ½ cup taco sauce, cream cheese and chili powder; cook and stir until blended. Stir in ¼ cup of the cheese blend.

◎ Drain pasta and rinse in cold water; stuff each shell with about 2 tablespoons beef mixture. Arrange in an 11-in. x 7-in. baking dish coated with cooking spray. Spoon remaining taco sauce over the top.

◎ Cover and bake at 350° for 20 minutes. Uncover; sprinkle with remaining cheese blend. Bake 5-10 minutes longer or until heated through and cheese is melted. Sprinkle with chips.

Yield: 6 servings.

MEXICAN CASSEROLE

I created this recipe one day while attempting to clear my fridge of leftovers. Choose your favorite taco seasoning and salsa to make the casserole as spicy or as mild as you like.
—**David Mills** *Indianapolis, Indiana*

PREP: 20 MIN. **BAKE:** 40 MIN.

- 1½ pounds lean ground beef (90% lean)
- 1 envelope taco seasoning

- ¾ cup water
- 1 can (16 ounces) refried beans
- ½ cup salsa
- 6 flour tortillas (6 inches)
- 2 cups frozen corn, thawed
- 2 cups (8 ounces) shredded cheddar cheese

Shredded lettuce, chopped tomatoes, sliced ripe olives and sour cream, optional

◎ In a large skillet, cook beef over medium heat until no longer pink; drain. Stir in taco seasoning and water. Bring to a boil. Reduce heat; simmer, uncovered, for 5 minutes.

◎ Meanwhile, in a microwave-safe bowl, combine beans and salsa. Cover and microwave for 1-2 minutes or until spreadable.

◎ Place three tortillas in a greased round 2½-qt. baking dish. Layer with half of the beef, bean mixture, corn and cheese; repeat layers.

◎ Bake, uncovered, at 350° for 40-45 minutes or until cheese is melted. Let stand for 5 minutes. Serve with lettuce, tomatoes, olives and sour cream if desired.

EDITOR'S NOTE: This recipe was tested in a 1,100-watt microwave.

Yield: 6 servings.

> ❝I really liked the flavors and simplicity of this recipe. My guests loved it, too, and took some of the leftovers home with them.❞
>
> —**UMYAZNEMO** FROM TASTEOFHOME.COM

SAUSAGE PIE

When I was growing up, Mom made this tasty casserole often in summer for our family and guests. It's a perfect way to use up those garden vegetables, and the sausage adds comforting flavor. I'm sure you'll enjoy it as much as we do.
—**Sally Holbrook** *Pasadena, California*

PREP: 20 MIN. **BAKE:** 30 MIN.

        16 fresh pork sausage links (about 1 pound)
        ½ medium green pepper, chopped
        ½ medium sweet red pepper, chopped
        1 tablespoon canola oil
        3 cups cooked long grain rice
        4 to 5 medium tomatoes, peeled and chopped
        1 package (10 ounces) frozen corn, thawed
        1 cup (4 ounces) shredded cheddar cheese
        2 tablespoons minced fresh parsley
        1 tablespoon Worcestershire sauce
        1 teaspoon salt
        1 teaspoon dried basil
        1 cup soft bread crumbs
        2 tablespoons butter, melted

● Place sausages on a rack in a baking pan. Bake at 350° for 15 minutes or until lightly browned and no longer pink. Cut into 1-in. pieces; set aside.

● In a large skillet, saute peppers in oil for 3 minutes or until crisp-tender. Transfer to a 3-qt. baking dish. Add the sausages and the next eight ingredients.

● Combine bread crumbs and butter; sprinkle over top. Bake, uncovered, at 350° for 30-40 minutes or until heated through.

Yield: 6-8 servings.

BROCCOLI SHRIMP ALFREDO

After tasting fettuccine Alfredo at a restaurant, I tried to duplicate the recipe at home. You can't imagine how pleased I was when I came up with this delicious version. Not only does my family love the creamy dish, but my husband prefers it to the one at the restaurant. That makes me one happy cook!
—**Rae Natoli** *Kingston, New York*

PREP/TOTAL TIME: 30 MIN.

        1 package (16 ounces) fettuccine
        1 pound uncooked medium shrimp, peeled and deveined
        3 garlic cloves, minced
        ½ cup butter, cubed
        1 package (8 ounces) cream cheese, cubed
        1 cup milk
        ½ cup shredded Parmesan cheese
        6 cups frozen broccoli florets
        ½ teaspoon salt
Dash pepper

● Cook fettuccine according to package directions. Meanwhile, in a large skillet, saute shrimp and garlic in butter until shrimp turn pink. Remove and keep warm. In the same skillet, combine the cream cheese, milk and Parmesan cheese; cook and stir until cheeses are melted and mixture is smooth.

● Place 1 in. of water in a saucepan; add broccoli. Bring to a boil. Reduce heat; cover and simmer for 6-8 minutes or until tender. Drain. Stir the broccoli, shrimp, salt and pepper into the cheese sauce; cook until heated through. Drain fettuccine; top with shrimp mixture.

Yield: 4 servings.

CHICAGO-STYLE PAN PIZZA

I developed a love for Chicago's deep-dish pizzas while attending college in the Windy City. This simple recipe relies on frozen bread dough, so I can indulge in the mouthwatering sensation without leaving home.
—**Nikki MacDonald** *Sheboygan, Wisconsin*

PREP: 20 MIN. **BAKE:** 30 MIN.

- 1 loaf (1 pound) frozen bread dough, thawed
- 1 pound bulk Italian sausage
- 2 cups (8 ounces) shredded part-skim mozzarella cheese
- ½ pound sliced fresh mushrooms
- 1 small onion, chopped
- 2 teaspoons olive oil
- 1 can (28 ounces) diced tomatoes, drained
- ¾ teaspoon dried oregano
- ½ teaspoon salt
- ½ teaspoon fennel seed, crushed
- ¼ teaspoon garlic powder
- ½ cup grated Parmesan cheese

◉ Press dough onto the bottom and up the sides of a greased 13-in. x 9-in. baking dish. In a large skillet, cook sausage over medium heat until no longer pink; drain. Sprinkle over dough. Top with mozzarella cheese.

◉ In a large skillet, saute mushrooms and onion in oil until onion is tender. Stir in the tomatoes, oregano, salt, fennel seed and garlic powder.

◉ Spoon over mozzarella cheese. Sprinkle with Parmesan cheese. Bake at 350° for 25-35 minutes or until crust is golden brown.

Yield: 6 slices.

SLOW COOKER BEEF STEW

I get giddy with excitement to make my slow-cooked stew as soon as I feel that first crisp chill in the air. Perfect for fall, it's chock-full of tender chunks of beef, potatoes and carrots.
—**Earnestine Wilson** *Waco, Texas*

PREP: 25 MIN. **COOK:** 7 HOURS

- 1½ pounds potatoes, peeled and cubed
- 6 medium carrots, cut into 1-inch slices
- 1 medium onion, coarsely chopped
- 3 celery ribs, coarsely chopped
- 3 tablespoons all-purpose flour
- 1½ pounds beef stew meat, cut into 1-inch cubes
- 3 tablespoons canola oil
- 1 can (14½ ounces) diced tomatoes, undrained
- 1 cup beef broth
- 1 teaspoon ground mustard
- ½ teaspoon salt
- ½ teaspoon pepper
- ½ teaspoon dried thyme
- ½ teaspoon browning sauce

◉ Layer the potatoes, carrots, onion and celery in a 5-qt. slow cooker. Place flour in a large resealable plastic bag. Add stew meat; seal and toss to coat evenly. In a large skillet, brown meat in oil in batches. Place over vegetables.

◉ In a large bowl, combine the tomatoes, broth, mustard, salt, pepper, thyme and browning sauce. Pour over beef. Cover and cook on high for 1½ hours. Reduce heat to low; cook 7-8 hours longer or until the meat and vegetables are tender.

Yield: 8 servings.

PIZZA CASSEROLE

Friends and family love my new spin on pizza. I load this hearty pasta casserole with ground beef, pepperoni, mozzarella cheese, mushrooms and a host of classic seasonings.
—**Nancy Foust** *Stoneboro, Pennsylvania*

PREP: 20 MIN. **BAKE:** 30 MIN.

- 3 cups uncooked spiral pasta
- 2 pounds lean ground beef (90% lean)
- 1 medium onion, chopped
- 2 cans (8 ounces *each*) mushroom stems and pieces, drained
- 1 can (15 ounces) tomato sauce
- 1 jar (14 ounces) pizza sauce
- 1 can (6 ounces) tomato paste
- ½ teaspoon sugar
- ½ teaspoon garlic powder
- ½ teaspoon onion powder
- ½ teaspoon dried oregano
- 4 cups (16 ounces) shredded part-skim mozzarella cheese, *divided*
- 1 package (3½ ounces) sliced pepperoni
- ½ cup grated Parmesan cheese

◉ Cook pasta according to package directions. Meanwhile, in a Dutch oven, cook beef and onion over medium heat until meat is no longer pink; drain. Stir in the mushrooms, tomato sauce, pizza sauce, tomato paste, sugar and seasonings. Drain pasta; stir into meat sauce.

◉ Divide half of the mixture between two greased 11-in. x 7-in. baking dishes; sprinkle each with 1 cup mozzarella cheese. Repeat layers. Top each with pepperoni and Parmesan cheese.

◉ Cover and bake at 350° for 20 minutes. Uncover; bake 10-15 minutes longer or until heated through.

Yield: 2 casseroles (8 servings each).

ZUCCHINI PIZZA CASSEROLE

My husband has a hearty appetite, our two kids never tire of pizza, and I grow lots of zucchini. So trying this casserole was a no-brainer! Everyone loves it.
—**Lynn Bernstetter** *White Bear Lake, Minnesota*

PREP: 20 MIN. **BAKE:** 40 MIN.

    4   cups shredded unpeeled zucchini
    ½   teaspoon salt
    2   eggs
    ½   cup grated Parmesan cheese
    2   cups (8 ounces) shredded part-skim mozzarella
        cheese, *divided*
    1   cup (4 ounces) shredded cheddar cheese, *divided*
    1   pound lean ground beef (90% lean)
    ½   cup chopped onion
    1   can (15 ounces) Italian tomato sauce
    1   medium green pepper, chopped

● Place zucchini in strainer; sprinkle with salt. Let stand for 10 minutes. Squeeze out moisture.

● Combine zucchini with the eggs, Parmesan and half of the mozzarella and cheddar cheeses. Press into a greased 13-in. x 9-in. baking dish.

● Bake, uncovered, at 400° for 20 minutes. Meanwhile, cook beef and onion over medium heat until meat is no longer pink; drain. Add tomato sauce; spoon over zucchini mixture.

● Sprinkle with remaining cheeses; add green pepper. Bake 20 minutes longer or until heated through.

Yield: 6-8 servings.

FAVORITE MEXICAN LASAGNA

Tortillas replace lasagna noodles in this beefy casserole featuring a south-of-the-border twist. With salsa, enchilada sauce, chilies, cheese and refried beans, it's a fiesta of flavors!
—**Tina Newhauser** *Peterborough, New Hampshire*

PREP: 25 MIN. **BAKE:** 40 MIN. + STANDING

    1¼ pounds lean ground beef (90% lean)
    1   medium onion, chopped
    4   garlic cloves, minced
    2   cups salsa
    1   can (16 ounces) refried beans
    1   can (15 ounces) black beans, rinsed and drained
    1   can (10 ounces) enchilada sauce
    1   can (4 ounces) chopped green chilies
    1   envelope taco seasoning
    ¼   teaspoon pepper
    6   flour tortillas (10 inches)
    3   cups (12 ounces) shredded Mexican cheese blend,
        divided
    2   cups crushed tortilla chips
Sliced ripe olives, guacamole, chopped tomatoes and sour
    cream, optional

● In a large skillet, cook beef and onion over medium heat until meat is no longer pink. Add garlic; cook 1 minute longer. Drain. Stir in the salsa, beans, enchilada sauce, chilies, taco seasoning and pepper; heat through.

● Spread 1 cup meat mixture in a greased 13-in. x 9-in. baking dish. Layer with two tortillas, a third of the remaining meat mixture and 1 cup cheese. Repeat layers. Top with remaining tortillas and meat mixture.

● Cover and bake at 375° for 30 minutes. Uncover; sprinkle with remaining cheese and top with tortilla chips.

● Bake 10-15 minutes longer or until cheese is melted. Let stand for 10 minutes before serving. Garnish with olives, guacamole, tomatoes and sour cream if desired.

Yield: 12 servings.

SUPREME PIZZA CASSEROLE

You can guarantee the pan will come home empty when you bring this ooey-gooey, pepperoni-topped casserole to a family gathering or potluck. It tastes just like pizza in a dish—and who wouldn't love that?
—Nancy Foust Stoneboro, Pennsylvania

PREP: 20 MIN. **BAKE:** 30 MIN.

8 ounces uncooked fettuccine	½ teaspoon sugar
2 pounds lean ground beef (90% lean)	½ teaspoon garlic powder
1 medium onion, chopped	½ teaspoon onion powder
2 cans (8 ounces each) mushroom stems and pieces, drained	½ teaspoon dried oregano
1 can (15 ounces) tomato sauce	4 cups (16 ounces) shredded part-skim mozzarella cheese, divided
1 jar (14 ounces) pizza sauce	1 package (3½ ounces) sliced pepperoni
1 can (6 ounces) tomato paste	½ cup grated Parmesan cheese

◉ Cook fettuccine according to package directions. Meanwhile, in a Dutch oven, cook beef and onion over medium heat until meat is no longer pink; drain. Stir in the mushrooms, tomato sauce, pizza sauce, tomato paste, sugar and seasonings. Drain pasta; stir into meat sauce.

◉ Divide half of the mixture between two greased 2-qt. baking dishes; sprinkle each with 1 cup mozzarella cheese. Repeat layers. Top each with pepperoni and Parmesan cheese.

◉ Cover and bake at 350° for 20 minutes. Uncover; bake 10-15 minutes longer or until heated through.

Yield: 2 casseroles (8 servings each).

DOUBLE-CHEESE MACARONI

A friend passed this recipe on to me, and I experimented with the ingredients to make it the grand-daddy of all mac and cheeses. I bring it to every family gathering, and I haven't found anyone, child or adult, who doesn't love its melty, cheesy appeal.
—**Sabrina DeWitt** *Cumberland, Maryland*

PREP: 25 MIN. **BAKE:** 20 MIN.

1 package (16 ounces) elbow macaroni	3 cups half-and-half cream
3 cups (24 ounces) 4% cottage cheese	1 cup 2% milk
½ cup butter, cubed	4 cups (16 ounces) shredded cheddar cheese
½ cup all-purpose flour	TOPPING:
1 teaspoon salt	1 cup dry bread crumbs
½ teaspoon white pepper	¼ cup butter, melted
¼ teaspoon garlic salt	

● Cook macaroni according to package directions. Meanwhile, place cottage cheese in a food processor; cover and process until smooth. Set aside.

● In a large saucepan, melt butter. Stir in the flour, salt, pepper and garlic salt until smooth. Gradually add cream and milk. Bring to a boil; cook and stir for 2 minutes or until thickened.

● Drain macaroni; transfer to a large bowl. Add the cheddar cheese, cottage cheese and white sauce; toss to coat. Transfer to a greased 13-in. x 9-in. baking dish. (Dish will be full.) Combine bread crumbs and butter; sprinkle over the top.

● Bake, uncovered, at 400° for 20-25 minutes or until bubbly.

Yield: 12 servings (1 cup each).

GREEK CHICKEN PASTA

This hearty main dish has great Mediterranean flavor. I left out the olives, and my family still loved it.
—**Susan Stetzel** *Gainesville, New York*

PREP/TOTAL TIME: 25 MIN.

QUICK & EASY

2	cups uncooked penne pasta
¼	cup butter, cubed
1	large onion, chopped
¼	cup all-purpose flour
1	can (14½ ounces) reduced-sodium chicken broth
3	cups cubed rotisserie chicken
1	jar (7½ ounces) marinated quartered artichoke hearts, drained
1	cup (4 ounces) crumbled feta cheese
½	cup chopped oil-packed sun-dried tomatoes
⅓	cup sliced pitted Greek olives
2	tablespoons minced fresh parsley

• Cook pasta according to package directions.

• Meanwhile, in a large ovenproof skillet, melt butter over medium-high heat. Add onion; cook and stir until tender. Stir in flour until blended; gradually add broth. Bring to a boil; cook and stir for 2 minutes or until thickened. Stir in the chicken, artichoke hearts, cheese, tomatoes and olives.

• Drain pasta; stir into the pan. Broil 3-4 in. from the heat for 5-7 minutes or until bubbly and golden brown. Sprinkle with parsley.

Yield: 5 servings.

ASPARAGUS BEEF STIR-FRY

I love filet mignon, but not its price. This stir-fry is a budget-friendly alternative. My husband loves it so much, I pack up any leftovers for his lunch the next day.
—**Linda Flynn** *Ellicott City, Maryland*

PREP/TOTAL TIME: 30 MIN.

QUICK & EASY

1	pound beef tenderloin roast, cubed
1	green onion, sliced
½	teaspoon salt
¼	teaspoon pepper
1	tablespoon canola oil
2	garlic cloves, minced
1	pound fresh asparagus, trimmed and cut into 2-inch pieces
½	pound sliced fresh mushrooms
¼	cup butter, cubed
1	tablespoon reduced-sodium soy sauce
1½	teaspoons lemon juice

Hot cooked rice

• In a wok or large skillet, stir-fry the beef, onion, salt and pepper in oil for 3-5 minutes. Add garlic; cook 1 minute longer. Remove and keep warm.

• In the same pan, stir-fry asparagus and mushrooms in butter until asparagus is tender. Return beef mixture to the pan. Stir in soy sauce and lemon juice; heat through. Serve with rice.

Yield: 4 servings.

EL SOMBERO CORN BREAD, PAGE 135

141

135

140

BREADS, ROLLS & MUFFINS

Mmm! Breathe in the aroma of freshly baked breads, muffins, coffee cakes, scones, dinner rolls and other from-scratch favorites, and you'll find yourself in the promised land of all things divine. Tender and delicate, drizzled with icing or dusted with sugar, there's simply nothing like the blissful, old-fashioned comfort of warm-from-the-oven specialties. The to-die-for goodness of these traditional delights is guaranteed to draw a crowd and will leave hungry tummies more than satisfied.

GARLIC POPPY SEED SPIRALS

This is a fast, easy way to dress up plain crescent rolls. Adjust the seasoning to your family's taste...or use a little powdered ranch dressing mix as an alternative.
—**Stacey Scherer** *Macomb, Michigan*

QUICK & EASY

PREP/TOTAL TIME: 25 MIN.

- 3 tablespoons butter, melted
- 1 teaspoon garlic powder
- 1 teaspoon dried minced onion
- ½ teaspoon poppy seeds
- 1 tube (8 ounces) refrigerated crescent rolls

● In a small bowl, combine the butter, garlic powder, onion and poppy seeds; set aside. Remove crescent dough from tube; do not unroll. Cut the dough into 10 slices; dip one side in the butter mixture.

● Place buttered side up in an ungreased 9-in. round baking pan. Brush with remaining butter mixture. Bake at 350° for 14-16 minutes or until golden brown. Serve warm.

Yield: 10 servings.

CHERRY CREAM CHEESE COFFEE CAKE

The texture of this tender coffee cake makes it hard to stop at one slice. The sour cream pairs well with the cherries, and the crunchy almonds make a nice accent.
—**Linda Guiles** *Belvidere, New Jersey*

PREP: 25 MIN. **BAKE:** 50 MIN. + COOLING

- 2¼ cups all-purpose flour
- ¾ cup sugar
- ¾ cup cold butter, cubed
- ½ teaspoon baking powder
- ½ teaspoon baking soda
- ½ teaspoon salt
- 1 egg, lightly beaten
- ¾ cup sour cream
- 1 teaspoon almond extract

FILLING:
- 1 package (8 ounces) cream cheese, softened
- ¼ cup sugar
- 1 egg, lightly beaten
- 1 can (21 ounces) cherry pie filling
- ½ cup slivered almonds

● In a large bowl, combine flour and sugar. Cut in butter until crumbly. Reserve ¾ cup crumb mixture. Add the baking powder, baking soda and salt to remaining crumb mixture. Stir in the egg, sour cream and almond extract until blended. Press onto the bottom and 1 in. up the sides of an ungreased 9-in. springform pan with removable bottom.

● For filling, in a large bowl, beat cream cheese and sugar for 1 minute. Add egg; beat just until combined. Spread over crust. Carefully top with pie filling. Sprinkle with almonds and reserved crumb mixture.

● Bake at 350° for 50-60 minutes or until center is set. Cool on a wire rack. Carefully run a knife around edge of pan to loosen; remove sides of pan. Store in the refrigerator.

APPLE CREAM CHEESE COFFEE CAKE: Substitute apple pie filling for the cherry filling and ½ cup chopped pecans or walnuts for the almonds.

BLUEBERRY CREAM CHEESE COFFEE CAKE: Substitute blueberry pie filling for the cherry filling.

Yield: 8-10 servings.

> ❝This cake is excellent. I served it with some whipped cream on the side and our dinner guests absolutely loved it!❞
>
> —**PARKSVILLE** FROM TASTEOFHOME.COM

PEACH COBBLER COFFEE CAKE

"Absolutely delicious" describes my coffee cake that boasts a peachy flavor and a delectable drizzle of frosting. Serve this warm from the oven for an extra-special Sunday treat.
—**Virginia Krites** *Cridersville, Ohio*

PREP: 25 MIN. **BAKE:** 70 MIN. + COOLING

1	cup butter, softened	1	can (15¼ ounces) sliced peaches, drained
1	cup sugar		**TOPPING:**
2	eggs	1	cup packed brown sugar
3	teaspoons vanilla extract	1	cup all-purpose flour
3	cups all-purpose flour	½	cup quick-cooking oats
1	teaspoon baking powder	¼	teaspoon ground cinnamon
1	teaspoon baking soda	½	cup cold butter, cubed
½	teaspoon salt		**GLAZE:**
1¼	cups sour cream	1	cup confectioners' sugar
1	can (21 ounces) peach pie filling	1	to 2 tablespoons 2% milk

⊚ In a large bowl, cream butter and sugar until light and fluffy. Add eggs, one at a time, beating well after each addition. Beat in vanilla. Combine flour, baking powder, baking soda and salt; add to creamed mixture alternately with sour cream. Beat just until combined.

⊚ Pour half of the batter into a greased 13-in. x 9-in. baking dish. Combine pie filling and peaches; spread over batter. Drop remaining batter by tablespoonfuls over filling.

⊚ For topping, combine the brown sugar, flour, oats and cinnamon in a bowl. Cut in butter until mixture is crumbly. Sprinkle over batter.

⊚ Bake at 350° for 70-75 minutes or until a toothpick inserted near the center comes out clean. Cool on a wire rack. In a small bowl, combine confectioner's sugar and enough milk to achieve desired consistency; drizzle over warm coffee cake.

Yield: 12 servings.

CHERRY CHOCOLATE CHIP MUFFINS

I made these yummy muffins for my husband, who considers himself a muffin expert, and he polished off four of them in one sitting. It's a good thing the recipe only makes six!
—**Joanne Minke** *St. Petersburg, Florida*

PREP: 15 MIN. **BAKE:** 20 MIN.

    1 cup all-purpose flour
    ⅓ cup sugar
    1 teaspoon baking powder
    ¼ teaspoon salt
    1 egg
    ⅓ cup 2% milk
    ¼ cup canola oil
    1 teaspoon almond extract
    ½ cup halved maraschino cherries
    ½ cup semisweet chocolate chips

● In a small bowl, combine the flour, sugar, baking powder and salt. In another bowl, whisk the egg, milk, oil and extract. Stir into dry ingredients just until moistened. Fold in cherries and chocolate chips.

● Fill paper-lined muffin cups three-fourths full. Bake at 350° for 20-25 minutes or until a toothpick inserted near the center comes out clean. Cool for 5 minutes before removing from pan to a wire rack. Serve warm.

Yield: 6 muffins.

KITCHEN TIP

When baking muffins or cupcakes in paper liners, I spray them with nonstick cooking spray. The liner peels off very nicely, leaving no crumbs behind!
—**Pamela K.**, *Martinsburg, West Virginia*

I WANT S'MORE MUFFINS

My fun muffins feature a fluffy marshmallow creme in the center. The s'more flavors are sure to bring back fond childhood memories of summertime campfires.
—**Sally Sibthorpe** *Shelby Township, Michigan*

PREP: 20 MIN. **BAKE:** 15 MIN.

    3 tablespoons butter, softened
    ¼ cup packed brown sugar
    4 teaspoons sugar
    1 egg
    ⅓ cup sour cream
    ⅔ cup all-purpose flour
    ½ cup graham cracker crumbs
    ¼ teaspoon salt
    ¼ teaspoon baking powder
    ¼ teaspoon ground cinnamon
    ⅛ teaspoon baking soda
    3 tablespoons 2% milk
    ⅓ cup milk chocolate chips
    6 tablespoons marshmallow creme

● In a small bowl, cream butter and sugars until light and fluffy. Beat in egg. Stir in sour cream. Combine the flour, graham cracker crumbs, salt, baking powder, cinnamon and baking soda; add to creamed mixture alternately with milk just until moistened. Fold in chocolate chips.

● Coat six muffin cups with cooking spray; fill one-fourth full with batter. Spoon 1 tablespoon marshmallow creme into each muffin cup. Top with remaining batter.

● Bake at 400° for 14-16 minutes or until a toothpick inserted neat the center comes out clean. Cool for 5 minutes before removing from pan to a wire rack. Serve warm.

Yield: 6 muffins.

CUPCAKE LINERS: RDA-GID

BAKER'S DOZEN YEAST ROLLS

Melted butter infused with a tantalizing blend of honey and garlic turns basic dinner rolls into something extraordinary. They're wonderful paired with your favorite homemade soup or chili.
—*Taste of Home Test Kitchen*

PREP: 25 MIN. + RISING **BAKE:** 15 MIN.

- 2 to 2½ cups all-purpose flour
- 2 tablespoons sugar
- 1 package (¼ ounce) quick-rise yeast
- ½ teaspoon salt
- ¾ cup warm water (120° to 130°)
- 2 tablespoons plus 4 teaspoons butter, melted, *divided*
- ¾ cup shredded sharp cheddar cheese
- 2 teaspoons honey
- ⅛ teaspoon garlic salt

● In a large bowl, combine 1½ cups flour, sugar, yeast and salt. Add water and 2 tablespoons butter; beat on medium speed for 3 minutes or until smooth. Stir in cheese and enough remaining flour to form a soft dough.

● Turn onto a lightly floured surface; knead until smooth and elastic, about 4-6 minutes. Cover and let rest for 10 minutes. Divide into 13 pieces. Shape each into a ball. Place in a greased 9-in. round baking pan. Cover and let rise in a warm place until doubled, about 30 minutes.

● Bake at 375° for 11-14 minutes or until lightly browned. Combine the honey, garlic salt and remaining butter; brush over rolls. Remove to a wire rack to cool.

Yield: 13 rolls.

EL SOMBRERO CORN BREAD

This moist, cheesy corn bread is easy to stir together and pop in the oven just before dinner. You can vary the number of peppers to suit your taste.
—*Joan Hallford* North Richland Hills, Texas

PREP: 10 MIN. **BAKE:** 35 MIN.

- 1½ cups cornmeal
- 3 teaspoons baking powder
- ½ teaspoon salt
- 2 eggs
- 1 can (14¾ ounces) cream-style corn
- 1 cup (8 ounces) sour cream
- ½ cup canola oil
- 1½ cups shredded cheddar cheese, *divided*
- 3 jalapeno peppers, seeded and finely chopped

● In a large bowl, combine the cornmeal, baking powder and salt. In another bowl, whisk the eggs, corn, sour cream and oil. Stir into dry ingredients just until moistened. Fold in 1 cup of cheese and jalapenos.

● Transfer to a greased 9-in. square baking pan. Sprinkle with remaining cheese. Bake at 350° for 35-40 minutes or until a toothpick inserted near the center comes out clean. Serve warm.

EDITOR'S NOTE: Wear disposable gloves when cutting hot peppers; the oils can burn skin. Avoid touching your face.

Yield: 9 servings.

HUNGARIAN NUT ROLLS

It isn't officially Christmas until I've made this treasured recipe from my husband's grandmother. The apple-walnut filling is so moist and flavorful.
—**Donna Bardocz** Howell, Michigan

PREP: 40 MIN. + RISING **BAKE:** 30 MIN. + COOLING

- 2 packages (¼ ounce *each*) active dry yeast
- ½ cup warm 2% milk (110° to 115°)
- ¼ cup plus 2 tablespoons sugar
- ¾ teaspoon salt
- 1 cup butter, softened
- 1 cup (8 ounces) sour cream
- 3 eggs, lightly beaten
- 6 to 6½ cups all-purpose flour

FILLING:

- 1¼ cups sugar
- ½ cup butter, cubed
- 1 egg
- ½ teaspoon ground cinnamon
- 4½ cups ground walnuts
- 1 large apple, peeled and grated

ICING:

- 2 cups confectioners' sugar
- 2 to 3 tablespoons 2% milk

● In a large bowl, dissolve yeast in warm milk. Add the sugar, salt, butter, sour cream, eggs and 3 cups flour. Beat on medium speed for 3 minutes. Beat until smooth. Stir in enough remaining flour to form a soft dough (dough will be sticky).

● Turn onto a floured surface; knead until smooth and elastic, about 6-8 minutes. Place in a greased bowl, turning once to grease top. Cover and let rise in a warm place until doubled, about 1 hour.

● Meanwhile, in a large saucepan, combine the sugar, butter, egg and cinnamon. Cook and stir over medium heat until mixture reaches 160° or is thick enough to coat the back of a

metal spoon. Remove from the heat; gently stir in walnuts and apple. Cool completely.

● Punch dough down. Turn onto a lightly floured surface; divide into four portions. Roll each into a 12-in. x 10-in. rectangle. Spread filling to within ½ in. of edges. Roll up jelly-roll style, starting with a long side; pinch seams to seal. Place seam side down on greased baking sheets. Cover and let rise until doubled, about 30 minutes.

● Bake at 350° for 30-40 minutes or until lightly browned. Remove from pans to wire racks to cool. Meanwhile, in a small bowl, combine confectioner's sugar and enough milk to achieve desired consistency; drizzle over warm loaves.

Yield: 4 loaves (12 slices each).

ALMOND BERRY MUFFINS

I made these tender muffins for a fun treat at work, and they were a hit. Sugared almonds give them a crunchy topping. If it's not strawberry season, simply use individual frozen strawberries (no thawing required).
—**Deborah Feinberg** Gulf Breeze, Florida

PREP: 20 MIN. **BAKE:** 20 MIN.

- 1¼ cups sliced almonds, *divided*
- 1 egg white, lightly beaten
- 1½ cups sugar, *divided*
- ¼ cup shortening
- ¼ cup butter, softened
- 2 eggs
- 1 teaspoon vanilla extract
- ½ teaspoon almond extract
- 2 cups all-purpose flour
- 1 teaspoon baking powder
- ½ teaspoon salt
- ¼ teaspoon baking soda
- ¾ cup buttermilk
- 1¼ cups fresh strawberries, chopped

- In a large bowl, combine 1 cup almonds and egg white. Add ½ cup sugar; toss to coat. Spoon into a greased 15-in. x 10-in. x 1-in. baking pan. Bake at 350° for 9-11 minutes or until golden brown, stirring occasionally.

- In a large bowl, cream the shortening, butter and remaining sugar until light and fluffy. Add eggs, one at a time, beating well after each addition. Beat in extracts. Combine the flour, baking powder, salt and baking soda; add to the creamed mixture alternately with buttermilk just until moistened. Fold in strawberries and remaining almonds.

- Fill greased or paper-lined muffin cups two-thirds full. Sprinkle with sugared almonds. Bake at 350° for 20-25 minutes or until a toothpick inserted near the center comes out clean. Cool for 5 minutes before removing from pans to wire racks. Serve warm.

Yield: 1½ dozen.

BASIC BISCUITS

You likely already have the ingredients for these biscuits stocked in your pantry. They're easy to make, and their from-scratch flavor is wonderful!
—**Jennifer Trenhaile** *Emerson, Nebraska*

QUICK & EASY

PREP/TOTAL TIME: 30 MIN.

2	cups all-purpose flour
4	teaspoons baking powder
3	teaspoons sugar
½	teaspoon salt
½	cup shortening
1	egg
⅔	cup milk
1	tablespoon honey

- In a bowl, combine the flour, baking powder, sugar and salt. Cut in shortening until the mixture resembles coarse crumbs. Combine the egg, milk and honey; stir into flour mixture just until combined. Turn onto a floured surface; knead 8-10 times. Roll out to ½-in. thickness. Cut with a floured 2½-in. biscuit cutter. Place 1 in. apart on an ungreased baking sheet. Bake at 425° for 10-12 minutes or until golden brown. Serve warm.

Yield: 10 biscuits.

BUTTERY CROISSANTS

A flaky croissant is always a welcome accompaniment to dinner. This recipe yields a big batch, so it's great for those times when you have to feed a crowd.
—**Loraine Meyer** *Bend, Oregon*

PREP: 1 HOUR + CHILLING **BAKE:** 15 MIN./BATCH

1½	cups butter, softened
⅓	cup all-purpose flour

DOUGH:

1	package (¼ ounce) active dry yeast
¼	cup warm water (110° to 115°)
1	cup warm 2% milk (110° to 115°)
¼	cup sugar

1	egg
1	teaspoon salt
3½	to 3¾ cups all-purpose flour

- In a bowl, beat butter and flour until combined; spread into a 12-in. x 6-in. rectangle on a piece of waxed paper. Cover with another piece of waxed paper; refrigerate for at least 1 hour.

- In a bowl, dissolve yeast in warm water. Add the milk, sugar, egg, salt and 2 cups flour; beat until smooth. Stir in enough remaining flour to form a soft dough. Turn onto a floured surface; knead until smooth and elastic, about 6-8 minutes.

- Roll dough into a 14-in. square. Remove top sheet of waxed paper from butter; invert onto half of dough. Remove waxed paper. Fold dough over butter; seal edges.

- Roll into a 20-in. x 12-in. rectangle. Fold into thirds. Repeat rolling and folding twice. (If butter softens, chill after folding.) Wrap in plastic wrap; refrigerate overnight.

- Unwrap dough. On a lightly floured surface, roll into a 25-in. x 20-in. rectangle. Cut into 5-in. squares. Cut each square diagonally in half, forming two triangles.

- Roll up triangles from the wide end; place 2 in. apart with point down on ungreased baking sheets. Curve ends down to form crescent shape. Cover dough and let rise until doubled, about 45 minutes.

- Bake at 375° for 12-14 minutes or until golden brown. Remove to wire racks. Serve warm.

Yield: about 3 dozen.

KITCHEN TIP

Envelopes of yeast generally weigh 1/4 ounce each and measure approximately 2-1/4 teaspoons. If your recipe calls for less yeast, just measure the amount called for in your recipe from an individual packet, then fold the packet closed and store remaining yeast in the fridge for next time.

Active Dry Yeast: RDA-MKE

CRANBERRY SCONES

You can use any dried fruit for these scones, but my favorite is a mix of dried cranberries and golden raisins. Be sure to not overmix the batter or your finished scone will be hard and dense.
—**Della Dunsieth** *New Castle, Pennsylvania*

QUICK & EASY

PREP/TOTAL TIME: 25 MIN.

  1 cup all-purpose flour
  ¼ cup sugar
 1½ teaspoons baking powder
  ⅛ teaspoon salt
  ¼ cup cold butter
  3 tablespoons 2% milk
  1 egg, beaten
  ¼ cup dried cranberries
  ¼ teaspoon coarse sugar

- In a small bowl, combine the flour, sugar, baking powder and salt. Cut in the butter until mixture resembles coarse crumbs. In a small bowl, combine milk and 2 tablespoons beaten egg; add to crumb mixture just until moistened. Stir in the dried cranberries.

- Turn onto a floured surface; knead gently 6-8 times. Pat into a 6-in. circle. Cut into four wedges. Separate wedges and place on a baking sheet coated with cooking spray. Brush with remaining egg; sprinkle with coarse sugar.

- Bake at 425° for 12-15 minutes or until golden brown. Serve warm.

Yield: 4 scones.

BEST CHEESE BREAD

My husband and I often make a meal of bread and salad. We enjoy the garlic, dill and cheddar flavors in this savory loaf. It's best served fresh from the oven.
—**Joanie Elbourn** *Gardner, Massachusetts*

PREP: 10 MIN. **BAKE:** 55 MIN. + COOLING

 3¾ cups all-purpose flour
 2½ cups (10 ounces) shredded cheddar cheese
  5 teaspoons baking powder
  ½ teaspoon garlic powder
  ½ teaspoon dill weed
  2 eggs
 1½ cups milk
  ⅓ cup canola oil
  3 tablespoons honey

- In a large bowl, combine the flour, cheese, baking powder, garlic powder and dill. In another bowl, whisk the eggs, milk, oil and honey. Stir into dry ingredients just until moistened.

- Pour into a greased 9-in. x 5-in. loaf pan. Bake at 350° for 55-65 minutes or until a toothpick inserted near the center comes out clean (top will have an uneven appearance). Cool for 10 minutes before removing from pan to a wire rack. Serve warm. Refrigerate leftovers.

Yield: 1 loaf (16 slices each).

ALMOND APRICOT BREAD

My mom, who is a big apricot and almond fan, was the inspiration behind this delectable creation. I often make multiple loaves to give away around the holidays. Everyone loves the sweet, home-baked flavor!
—**Kathy Cary** *Wildwood, Missouri*

PREP: 15 MIN. **BAKE:** 55 MIN. + COOLING

2½ cups all-purpose flour
½ cup sugar
½ cup packed brown sugar
3 teaspoons baking powder
1 teaspoon salt
1 package (7 ounces) apricots with mixed fruit baby food, *divided*

1 egg
¾ cup plus 1 teaspoon milk, *divided*
3 tablespoons canola oil
1⅛ teaspoons almond extract, *divided*
⅔ cup sliced almonds, coarsely chopped
½ cup diced dried apricots
½ cup confectioners' sugar

⊙ In a large bowl, combine the flour, sugars, baking powder and salt. Set aside 1 tablespoon baby food for glaze. In another bowl, beat the egg, ¾ cup milk, oil, 1 teaspoon almond extract and remaining baby food. Stir into dry ingredients just until moistened. Fold in almonds and apricots.

⊙ Pour batter into a greased 9-in. x 5-in. loaf pan. Bake at 350° for 55-65 minutes or until a toothpick inserted near the center comes out clean. Cool for 10 minutes before removing from the pan to a wire rack to cool completely.

⊙ For glaze, combine the confectioners' sugar, reserved baby food, and remaining milk and extract until smooth. Drizzle over bread.

Yield: 1 loaf (16 slices).

RICH COFFEE CAKE

Indulgent cinnamon-pecan swirls and a rich chocolate drizzle take this tender cake over the top on taste. Take one bite and you'll see why it's almost impossible to resist a second slice of this old-fashioned delight.
—**Gaytha Holloway** *Marion, Indiana*

PREP: 30 MIN. **BAKE:** 1 HOUR + COOLING

1 cup butter, softened	**TOPPING:**
2 cups sugar	1 cup chopped pecans
2 eggs	2 tablespoons sugar
2 cups all-purpose flour	1 teaspoon ground cinnamon
1½ teaspoons baking powder	**CHOCOLATE GLAZE:**
½ teaspoon salt	½ cup semisweet chocolate chips
1 cup (8 ounces) sour cream	¼ cup butter, cubed
½ teaspoon vanilla extract	

◦ In a large bowl, cream butter and sugar until light and fluffy. Add eggs, one at a time, beating well after each addition. Combine the flour, baking powder and salt. Combine sour cream and vanilla; add to creamed mixture alternately with dry ingredients just until combined.

◦ Combine topping ingredients; sprinkle 2 tablespoons into a greased and floured 10-in. tube pan. For glaze, in a microwave-safe bowl, melt chocolate chips and butter; stir until smooth. Spoon half of the batter over topping; sprinkle with half of the remaining topping. Drizzle with half of the glaze. Top with remaining batter; sprinkle with remaining topping.

◦ Bake at 350° for 60-70 minutes or until toothpick inserted near the center comes out clean. Cool for 10 minutes before removing from pan to a wire rack. Warm remaining glaze; drizzle over warm coffee cake. Serve warm if desired.

Yield: 12 servings.

PILLOW-SOFT DINNER ROLLS

These tender rolls will melt in your mouth! I was giddy with excitement when I came across this recipe in an old church cookbook—I love timeless gems like these that have graced the table of many a family cook before me.
—**Norma Harder** *Saskatoon, Saskatchewan*

PREP: 30 MIN. + RISING **BAKE:** 20 MIN.

- 4½ teaspoons active dry yeast
- ½ cup warm water (110° to 115°)
- 2 cups warm milk (110° to 115°)
- 6 tablespoons shortening
- 2 eggs
- ¼ cup sugar
- 1½ teaspoons salt
- 7 to 7½ cups all-purpose flour

- In a large bowl, dissolve yeast in warm water. Add the milk, shortening, eggs, sugar, salt and 3 cups flour. Beat until smooth. Stir in enough remaining flour to form a soft dough.

- Turn onto a floured surface; knead until smooth and elastic, about 6-8 minutes (dough will be sticky). Place in a greased bowl, turning once to grease top. Cover and let rise in a warm place until doubled, about 1 hour.

- Punch dough down. Turn onto a lightly floured surface; divide into 24 pieces. Shape each into a roll. Place 2 in. apart on greased baking sheets. Cover and let rise until doubled, about 30 minutes.

- Bake at 350° for 20-25 minutes or until golden brown. Remove to wire racks.

Yield: 2 dozen.

BROWN SUGAR OAT MUFFINS

With Kansas being one of the top wheat-producing states, it seems only fitting to share a recipe containing whole wheat flour. These are great muffins to have for breakfast or as a late night snack with a cup of hot cocoa.
—**Regina Stock** *Topeka, Kansas*

QUICK & EASY

PREP/TOTAL TIME: 30 MIN.

- 1 cup old-fashioned oats
- 1 cup whole wheat flour
- ¾ cup packed brown sugar
- ½ cup all-purpose flour
- 2 teaspoons baking powder
- ½ teaspoon salt
- 2 eggs
- ¾ cup 2% milk
- ¼ cup canola oil
- 1 teaspoon vanilla extract

- In a small bowl, combine the first six ingredients. In another small bowl, beat the eggs, milk, oil and vanilla. Stir into the dry ingredients just until moistened.

- Fill greased or paper-lined muffin cups two-thirds full. Bake at 400° for 15-17 minutes or until a toothpick inserted near the center comes out clean. Cool for 5 minutes before removing from pan to a wire rack. Serve warm.

Yield: 1 dozen.

SWEET POTATO CRESCENTS

These light-as-air crescents make a delightful accompaniment to any menu. They're always on my table at Thanksgiving, but I also like serving them with weeknight meals of pork or chicken.
—Rebecca Bailey *Fairbury, Nebraska*

PREP: 30 MIN. + RISING **BAKE:** 15 MIN.

2	packages (¼ ounce *each*) active dry yeast
1	cup warm water (110° to 115°)
1	can (15¾ ounces) cut sweet potatoes, drained and mashed
½	cup sugar
½	cup shortening
1	egg
1½	teaspoons salt
5	to 5½ cups all-purpose flour
¼	cup butter, melted

● In a large bowl, dissolve the yeast in water; let stand for 5 minutes. Beat in the sweet potatoes, sugar, shortening, egg, salt and 3 cups of the flour. Add enough remaining flour to form a stiff dough.

● Turn onto a floured surface; knead until smooth and elastic, about 6-8 minutes. Place in a greased bowl, turning once to grease top. Cover and let rise in a warm place until doubled, about 1 hour.

● Punch dough down; divide into thirds. Roll each portion into a 12-in. circle; cut each into 12 wedges. Brush with butter. Roll up from the wide end and place, pointed end down, 2 in. apart on greased baking sheets. Cover and let rise until doubled, about 40 minutes.

● Bake at 375° for 13-15 minutes or until golden brown. Remove from pans to wire racks.

Yield: 3 dozen.

ZUCCHINI BANANA BREAD

I got this recipe from a friend at work, and now it's one of my favorites. Share a mini loaf with a friend or store in the freezer.
—Donna Hall *Wolfforth, Texas*

PREP: 15 MIN. **BAKE:** 40 MIN. + COOLING

1½	cups all-purpose flour
1	cup sugar
1	teaspoon ground cinnamon
½	teaspoon baking powder
½	teaspoon baking soda
½	teaspoon salt
1	egg
1	cup mashed ripe bananas
½	cup canola oil
½	teaspoon banana extract
½	teaspoon vanilla extract
1	cup shredded zucchini
½	cup chopped walnuts

● In a large bowl, combine the first six ingredients. In a small bowl, beat the egg, bananas, oil and extracts. Stir into dry ingredients just until moistened. Fold in zucchini and walnuts.

● Transfer to three 5¾-in. x 3-in. x 2-in. loaf pans coated with cooking spray. Bake at 325° for 40-45 minutes or until a toothpick inserted near the center comes out clean. Cool for 10 minutes before removing from pans to wire racks.

Yield: 3 mini loaves (6 slices each).

KITCHEN TIP

Be sure to measure ingredients accurately when making banana bread or other quick breads. If there is not enough flour added compared to liquids, the bread could be underdone in the center.

LOAF PAN: RDA-GID

RHUBARB COFFEE CAKE WITH CARAMEL SAUCE

When I was growing up, I couldn't wait for the rhubarb to ripen so Mom could bake this luscious cake. Now I'm all grown up, and the recipe is part of my own collection—and I *still* wait in sweet anticipation!
—**Angie Fehr** Ottosen, Iowa

PREP: 20 MIN. **BAKE:** 35 MIN. + COOLING

½ cup shortening	TOPPING:
1½ cups sugar	½ cup packed brown sugar
1 egg	¼ cup all-purpose flour
2 cups all-purpose flour	1 teaspoon ground cinnamon
1 teaspoon baking soda	3 tablespoons cold butter
1 cup buttermilk	SAUCE:
1½ cups finely chopped fresh *or* frozen rhubarb	½ cup butter, cubed
	1 cup packed brown sugar
	½ cup heavy whipping cream

○ In a large bowl, cream shortening and sugar until light and fluffy. Add egg; beat well. Combine flour and baking soda; add to creamed mixture alternately with buttermilk. Fold in the rhubarb. Transfer to a greased 13-in. x 9-in. baking pan.

○ For topping, in a small bowl, combine the brown sugar, flour and cinnamon; cut in butter until crumbly. Sprinkle over batter.

○ Bake at 350° for 35-40 minutes or until a toothpick inserted near the center comes out clean. Cool for 10 minutes before serving.

○ For sauce, in a small saucepan, melt butter. Stir in brown sugar and cream; bring to a boil. Reduce heat; simmer for 3 to 4 minutes or until slightly thickened. Serve with warm coffee cake.

Yield: 18 servings (1⅔ cups sauce).

BANANA NUT MUFFINS

A scattering of chopped walnuts adds a pleasant crunch to these moist, taste-tempting muffins. They're great for breakfast or anytime you want a sweet treat.
—**Neva Starnes** *Summerville, Georgia*

PREP: 15 MIN. **BAKE:** 25 MIN.

¼ cup butter, softened	¾ teaspoon baking powder
½ cup sugar	¼ teaspoon salt
1 egg	⅛ teaspoon baking soda
¾ cup mashed ripe banana	⅛ teaspoon ground cinnamon
½ teaspoon vanilla extract	¼ cup chopped walnuts
1 cup all-purpose flour	

● In a small bowl, cream butter and sugar. Beat in the egg, banana and vanilla. Combine the flour, baking powder, salt, baking soda and cinnamon; add to creamed mixture just until moistened. Fold in walnuts.

● Coat muffin cups with cooking spray or use paper liners; fill two-thirds full with batter. Bake at 350° for 23-25 minutes or until a toothpick comes out clean. Cool for 5 minutes before removing from pan to a wire rack. Serve warm.

Yield: 6 muffins.

CARAMEL-PECAN MONKEY BREAD

No one can resist this tender, caramel-coated bread sprinkled with pecans. You can either cut it into generous slices, or let everyone pick off the ooey, gooey pieces themselves.
—Taste of Home Test Kitchen

PREP: 20 MIN. + CHILLING **BAKE:** 30 MIN. + COOLING

- 1 package (¼ ounce) active dry yeast
- ¼ cup water (110° to 115°)
- 1¼ cups warm 2% milk (110° to 115°)
- ⅓ cup butter, melted
- ¼ cup sugar
- 2 eggs
- 1 teaspoon salt
- 5 cups all-purpose flour

CARAMEL:
- ⅔ cup packed brown sugar
- ¼ cup butter, cubed
- ¼ cup heavy whipping cream

ASSEMBLY:
- ¾ cup chopped pecans
- 1 cup sugar
- 1 teaspoon ground cinnamon
- ½ cup butter, melted

- In a large bowl, dissolve the yeast in warm water. Add the milk, butter, sugar, eggs, salt and 3 cups flour. Beat on medium speed for 3 minutes. Stir in enough remaining flour to form a firm dough.

- Turn onto a floured surface; knead until smooth and elastic, about 6-8 minutes. Place in a greased bowl, turning once to grease the top. Cover and refrigerate overnight.

- For caramel, in a small saucepan, bring the brown sugar, butter and cream to a boil. Cook and stir for 3 minutes. Pour half into a greased 10-in. fluted tube pan; sprinkle with half of the pecans.

- Punch dough down; shape into 40 balls (about 1¼-in. diameter). In a shallow bowl, combine sugar and cinnamon. Place melted butter in another bowl. Dip balls in butter, then roll in sugar mixture.

- Place 20 balls in the tube pan; top with remaining caramel and pecans. Top with remaining balls. Cover and let rise until doubled, about 45 minutes.

- Bake at 350° for 30-35 minutes or until golden brown. (Cover loosely with foil if top browns too quickly.) Cool for 10 minutes before inverting onto a serving plate. Serve warm.

Yield: 1 loaf (20 servings).

KEY LIME BREAD

I first tasted this deliciously different bread at a friend's house, and she graciously shared the recipe with me. It's so easy to make and absolutely yummy!
—Joan Hallford *North Richland Hills, Texas*

PREP: 15 MIN. **BAKE:** 50 MIN. + COOLING

- ⅔ cup butter, softened
- 2 cups sugar
- 4 eggs
- 2 tablespoons grated lime peel
- 2 tablespoons key lime juice
- 1 teaspoon vanilla extract
- 3 cups all-purpose flour
- 3 teaspoons baking powder
- 1 teaspoon salt
- 1 cup milk
- 1 cup chopped walnuts

GLAZE:
- ⅔ cup confectioners' sugar
- 1 to 2 tablespoons key lime juice

- In a large bowl, cream butter and sugar until light and fluffy. Beat in eggs. Beat in the lime peel, juice and vanilla. Combine the flour, baking powder and salt; gradually add to creamed mixture alternately with milk, beating well after each addition. Fold in walnuts.

- Transfer to two greased 9-in. x 5-in. loaf pans. Bake at 350° for 50-55 minutes or until a toothpick inserted near the center comes out clean. Cool for 10 minutes before removing from pans to wire racks.

- Combine the confectioners' sugar and enough lime juice to achieve desired consistency; drizzle over warm bread. Cool completely.

Yield: 2 loaves (16 slices each).

SOFT GARLIC BREADSTICKS

I rely on the convenience of my bread machine to mix the dough for these buttery breadsticks that are mildly seasoned with garlic and basil. This dough works great for pizza, too. It yields two 12-inch crusts.

—Charles Smith *Baltic, Connecticut*

PREP: 30 MIN. + RISING **BAKE:** 20 MIN.

- 1 cup plus 2 tablespoons water (70° to 80°)
- 2 tablespoons olive oil
- 3 tablespoons grated Parmesan cheese
- 2 tablespoons sugar
- 3 teaspoons garlic powder
- 1½ teaspoons salt
- ¾ teaspoon minced fresh basil *or* ¼ teaspoon dried basil
- 3 cups bread flour
- 2 teaspoons active dry yeast
- 1 tablespoon butter, melted

- In bread machine pan, place the first nine ingredients in order suggested by manufacturer. Select dough setting (check dough after 5 minutes of mixing; add 1 to 2 tablespoons of water or flour if needed).

- When cycle is completed, turn dough onto a lightly floured surface. Divide into 20 portions. Shape each into a ball; roll each into a 9-in. rope. Place on greased baking sheets. Cover and let rise in a warm place for 40 minutes or until doubled.

- Bake breadsticks at 350° for 18-22 minutes or until golden brown. Remove to wire racks to cool. Brush warm breadsticks with butter.

Yield: 20 breadsticks.

KITCHEN TIP

Feel free to change up the pace of these traditional breadsticks with different flavor variations. Before baking, add rosemary or another fragrant herb of your choice in place of the basil.

SUGAR-DUSTED BLUEBERRY MUFFINS

My fruity golden-brown muffins are topped with cinnamon and sugar for a tasty treat you can enjoy any time of day.
—Janis Plagerman *Ephrata, Washington*

PREP: 15 MIN. **BAKE:** 20 MIN.

- ¼ cup old-fashioned oats
- ¼ cup orange juice
- 1 egg
- ¼ cup canola oil
- ¾ cup all-purpose flour
- ¼ cup plus 1 tablespoon sugar, *divided*
- ½ teaspoon baking powder
- ¼ teaspoon salt
- ⅛ teaspoon baking soda
- ½ cup fresh *or* frozen unsweetened blueberries
- ⅛ teaspoon ground cinnamon

- In a small bowl, combine the oats and orange juice; let stand for 5 minutes. Stir in egg and oil until blended. Combine the flour, ¼ cup sugar, baking powder, salt and baking soda; stir into oat mixture just until moistened. Fold in blueberries.

- Coat muffin cups with cooking spray or use paper liners; fill two-thirds full with batter. Combine cinnamon and remaining sugar; sprinkle over batter. Bake at 400° for 18-22 minutes or until a toothpick comes out clean. Cool for 5 minutes before removing from pan to a wire rack.

EDITOR'S NOTE: If using frozen blueberries, use without thawing to avoid discoloring the batter.

Yield: 6 muffins.

HERBS: RDA-MKE

CINNAMON SWIRL
QUICK BREAD

While cinnamon bread is a natural for breakfast, we love it so much we enjoy it all day long. This is a nice twist on traditional cinnamon swirl yeast breads.

—Helen Richardson *Shelbyville, Michigan*

PREP: 15 MIN. **BAKE:** 45 MIN. + COOLING

　2　cups all-purpose flour
1½　cups sugar, *divided*
　1　teaspoon baking soda
　½　teaspoon salt
　1　cup buttermilk
　1　egg
　¼　cup canola oil
　3　teaspoons ground cinnamon

GLAZE:
　¼　cup confectioners' sugar
1½　to 2 teaspoons milk

● In a large bowl, combine the flour, 1 cup sugar, baking soda and salt. Combine buttermilk, egg and oil; stir into dry ingredients just until moistened. In a small bowl, combine cinnamon and remaining sugar.

● Grease the bottom only of a 9-in. x 5-in. loaf pan. Pour half of the batter into pan; sprinkle with half of the cinnamon-sugar. Carefully spread with the remaining batter and sprinkle with the remaining cinnamon-sugar; cut through the batter with a knife to swirl.

● Bake at 350° for 45-50 minutes or until a toothpick inserted near the center comes out clean. Cool for 10 minutes before removing from pan to a wire rack to cool completely. Combine confectioners' sugar and enough milk to reach desired consistency; drizzle over loaf.

Yield: 1 loaf.

GLUTEN-FREE
BANANA BREAD

Tired of gluten-free baked goods that are dry and crumbly? This banana bread tastes like the real thing and goes over well with everyone at your table.

—Gladys Arnold *Pittsburgh, Pennsylvania*

PREP: 20 MIN. **BAKE:** 45 MIN. + COOLING

　2　cups gluten-free all-purpose baking flour
　1　teaspoon baking soda
　¼　teaspoon salt
　4　eggs
　2　cups mashed ripe bananas (4-5 medium)
　1　cup sugar
　½　cup unsweetened applesauce
　⅓　cup canola oil
　1　teaspoon vanilla extract
　½　cup chopped walnuts

● In a large bowl, combine the flour, baking soda and salt. In a small bowl, whisk the eggs, bananas, sugar, applesauce, oil and vanilla. Stir into dry ingredients just until moistened.

● Transfer to two 8-in. x 4-in. loaf pans coated with cooking spray. Sprinkle with walnuts. Bake at 350° for 45-55 minutes or until a toothpick inserted near the center comes out clean. Cool for 10 minutes before removing from pans to wire racks.

EDITOR'S NOTE: Read all ingredient labels for possible gluten content prior to use. Ingredient formulas can change, and production facilities vary among brands. If you're concerned that your brand may contain gluten, contact the company.

Yield: 2 loaves (12 slices each).

“ **This gluten-free recipe really is good! It smells so delicious that you just want to dive in before it is finished baking. It has the perfect amount of moisture, and the flavor is great!** ”

—LENA B FROM TASTEOFHOME.COM

APPLE COFFEE CAKE

Tart apples and sour cream flavor this moist coffee cake covered with brown sugar and crunchy nuts. The recipe makes two pans, so you can serve one and freeze the other for a busy morning or unexpected company.
—**Dawn Fagerstrom** *Warren, Minnesota*

PREP: 20 MIN. **BAKE:** 30 MIN.

- ½ cup butter-flavored shortening
- 1 cup sugar
- 2 eggs
- 1 teaspoon vanilla extract
- 2 cups all-purpose flour
- 1 teaspoon baking powder
- 1 teaspoon baking soda
- ½ teaspoon salt
- 1 cup (8 ounces) sour cream
- 1¾ to 2 cups chopped peeled tart apples

TOPPING:

- ¾ cup packed brown sugar
- 1 teaspoon ground cinnamon
- 2 tablespoons cold butter
- ½ cup chopped walnuts

● In a large bowl, cream shortening and sugar until light and fluffy. Beat in eggs and vanilla. Combine the flour, baking powder, baking soda and salt; gradually add to the creamed mixture alternately with sour cream, mixing well after each addition. Stir in apples. Transfer to two greased 8-in. square baking dishes.

● For topping, combine brown sugar and cinnamon. Cut in butter until crumbly. Stir in nuts; sprinkle over batter. Bake at 350° for 30-35 minutes or until a toothpick inserted near the center comes out clean. Cool completely. Cover and freeze for up to 6 months.

TO USE FROZEN COFFEE CAKE: Thaw overnight in the refrigerator.

Yield: 2 coffee cakes (6-9 servings each).

BLUEBERRY STREUSEL COFFEE CAKE

Studded with juicy berries and pecans, this tender sensation is sure to become a family favorite. The sweet streusel sprinkled on top makes it absolutely irresistible!
—**Lori Snedden** *Sherman, Texas*

PREP: 20 MIN. **BAKE:** 35 MIN. + COOLING

- 2 cups all-purpose flour
- ¾ cup sugar
- 2 teaspoons baking powder
- ¼ teaspoon salt
- 1 egg
- ½ cup milk
- ½ cup butter, softened
- 1 cup fresh *or* frozen blueberries
- 1 cup chopped pecans

STREUSEL TOPPING:

- ½ cup sugar
- ⅓ cup all-purpose flour
- ¼ cup cold butter

● In a large bowl, combine the flour, sugar, baking powder and salt. Whisk the egg, milk and butter; stir into dry ingredients. Fold in blueberries and pecans. Spread into a greased 9-in. square baking pan.

● For topping, combine sugar and flour in a bowl; cut in butter until crumbly. Sprinkle over batter. Bake at 375° for 35-40 minutes or until a toothpick inserted near the center comes out clean. Cool on a wire rack.

EDITOR'S NOTE: If using frozen blueberries, use without thawing to avoid discoloring the batter.

Yield: 9 servings.

PECAN LEMON LOAF

A pretty glaze gives this moist bread an extra boost of citrus flavor. For variety, substitute grated orange peel and orange juice for lemon.
—**Laura Comitz** *Enola, Pennsylvania*

PREP: 20 MIN. **BAKE:** 50 MIN. + COOLING

- ½ cup butter, softened
- 1½ cups sugar, *divided*
- 2 eggs
- 2 cups all-purpose flour
- 1 teaspoon baking powder
- ½ teaspoon salt
- ¾ cup sour cream
- 1 cup chopped pecans, toasted
- 1 tablespoon grated lemon peel
- ¼ cup lemon juice

• In a large bowl, cream butter and 1 cup sugar until light and fluffy. Beat in eggs. Combine the flour, baking powder and salt; add to creamed mixture alternately with sour cream, beating well after each addition. Fold in pecans and lemon peel.

• Transfer to a greased 9-in. x 5-in. loaf pan. Bake at 350° for 50-60 minutes or until a toothpick inserted near the center comes out clean.

• In a small saucepan, combine lemon juice and remaining sugar. Cook and stir over medium heat until sugar is dissolved. Pour over warm bread. Cool completely on a wire rack before removing from pan.

Yield: 1 loaf (16 slices).

BASIL GARLIC BREAD

My family members are big on garlic bread, and they request this simple loaf time and again. If there is any left over, I toast it for a quick snack.
—**Christine Burger** *Grafton, Wisconsin*

PREP: 15 MIN. **BAKE:** 3-4 HOURS

- ⅔ cup warm milk (70° to 80°)
- ¼ cup warm water (70° to 80°)
- ¼ cup warm sour cream (70° to 80°)
- 1½ teaspoons sugar
- 1 tablespoon butter, softened
- 1 tablespoon grated Parmesan cheese
- 1 teaspoon salt
- ½ teaspoon minced garlic
- ½ teaspoon dried basil
- ½ teaspoon garlic powder
- 3 cups bread flour
- 2¼ teaspoons active dry yeast

• In bread machine pan, place all ingredients in order suggested by manufacturer. Select basic bread setting. Choose crust color and loaf size if available. Bake according to bread machine directions (check dough after 5 minutes of mixing; add 1 to 2 tablespoons of water or flour if needed).

EDITOR'S NOTE: We recommend you do not use a bread machine's time-delay feature for this recipe.

Yield: 1 loaf (16 slices).

COOKIE DOUGH TRUFFLES, PAGE 157

160

161

154

COOKIES, CANDIES & MORE

Want a cookie? Yes, please! How about a fudgy brownie, creamy mousse parfait or a munchable bite-sized truffle? Then turn the page to find a host of cookie-jar favorites, scrumptious brownies and bars, chocolate treasures, petite confections and other luscious indulgences that serve up a big batch of finger-licking satisfaction! With all this variety, you'll turn to these yummy morsels for any occasion—whether you need a bake-sale hit, a fuss-free potluck contribution or simply an easy after-supper surprise. Just as the family bakers who shared the recipes, you'll quickly discover that these unforgettable treats are sure to warm hearts and bring big smiles!

FUDGY BROWNIES

I love to bake these brownies to share with co-workers. When I was growing up, I helped my mother make delicious, hearty meals and desserts like this for our farm family of eight.
—**Judy Cunningham** *Max, North Dakota*

PREP: 15 MIN. **BAKE:** 25 MIN. + COOLING

1⅓ cups butter, softened
2⅔ cups sugar
4 eggs
3 teaspoons vanilla extract
2 cups all-purpose flour
1 cup baking cocoa
½ teaspoon salt
Confectioners' sugar, optional

● In a large bowl, cream butter and sugar until light and fluffy. Beat in eggs and vanilla. Combine the flour, cocoa and salt; gradually add to the creamed mixture.

● Spread into a greased 13-in. x 9-in. baking pan. Bake at 350° for 25-30 minutes or until the top is dry and the center is set. Cool completely. Dust with confectioners' sugar if desired.

Yield: 2½ dozen.

WHITE CHOCOLATE CRANBERRY COOKIES

These sweet cookies feature white chocolate and cranberries for a delightful taste! And the red and white coloring adds a festive feel to any cookie tray.
—**Donna Beck** *Scottdale, Pennsylvania*

PREP: 20 MIN. **BAKE:** 10 MIN./BATCH

⅓ cup butter, softened
½ cup packed brown sugar
⅓ cup sugar
1 egg
1 teaspoon vanilla extract
1½ cups all-purpose flour
½ teaspoon salt
½ teaspoon baking soda
¾ cup dried cranberries
½ cup white baking chips

● In a large bowl, beat butter and sugars until crumbly, about 2 minutes. Beat in egg and vanilla. Combine the flour, salt and baking soda; gradually add to butter mixture and mix well. Stir in cranberries and chips.

● Drop by heaping tablespoonfuls 2 in. apart onto baking sheets coated with cooking spray. Bake at 375° for 8-10 minutes or until lightly browned. Cool for 1 minute before removing to wire racks.

Yield: 2 dozen.

CHOCOLATE TRIFLE

For a fabulous finale when entertaining, this lovely layered trifle is a winner! It's an easy do-ahead dessert that serves a group, and even tastes great the next day.
—**Pam Botine** *Goldsboro, North Carolina*

PREP: 30 MIN. + CHILLING

1 package (18¼ ounces) chocolate fudge cake mix

1 package (6 ounces) instant chocolate pudding mix

½ cup strong coffee

1 carton (12 ounces) frozen whipped topping, thawed

6 Heath candy bars (1.4 ounces *each*), crushed

● Bake cake according to package directions. Cool. Prepare pudding according to package directions; set aside.

● Crumble cake; reserve ½ cup. Place half of the remaining cake crumbs in the bottom of a 4½- or 5-qt. trifle dish or decorative glass bowl.

● Layer with half of the coffee, half of the pudding, half of the whipped topping and half of the crushed candy bars. Repeat the layers of cake, coffee, pudding and whipped topping.

● Combine remaining crushed candy bars with reserved cake crumbs; sprinkle over top. Refrigerate 4-5 hours before serving.

Yield: 8-10 servings.

COCONUT CITRUS BARS

Sweet oranges are the key to my amazing bars with loads of orange flavor in every bite. The unique crust and vibrant orange zing make them different from regular lemon bars.
—Heather Rotunda *Saint Cloud, Minnesota*

PREP: 30 MIN. **BAKE:** 20 MIN. + COOLING

¾ cup butter, softened	⅓ cup orange juice
⅓ cup confectioners' sugar	¼ cup lemon juice
1½ cups all-purpose flour	2 tablespoons lime juice
½ cup crisp rice cereal	2 tablespoons all-purpose flour
FILLING:	3 teaspoons grated orange peel
4 eggs	2 teaspoons grated lemon peel
1½ cups sugar	1½ teaspoons grated lime peel
1 cup flaked coconut	Confectioners' sugar

○ In a small bowl, cream butter and confectioners' sugar until light and fluffy; gradually beat in flour until crumbly. Stir in cereal. Press into a greased 13-in. x 9-in. baking pan. Bake at 350° for 18-22 minutes or until lightly browned.

○ Meanwhile, in a large bowl, beat the eggs, sugar, coconut, juices, flour and peels until frothy. Pour over the hot crust. Bake for 18-22 minutes or until lightly browned. Cool on a wire rack. Dust with confectioners' sugar; cut into bars. Store in the refrigerator.

Yield: 2 dozen.

BLOND BROWNIES
A LA MODE

We have a lot of church socials, so I'm always looking for something new and different to prepare. Drizzled with a sweet maple sauce, these chewy brownies are wonderful with or without the ice cream.
—**Pat Parker** *Chester, South Carolina*

PREP: 25 MIN. **BAKE:** 25 MIN. + COOLING

- ¾ cup butter, softened
- 2 cups packed brown sugar
- 4 eggs
- 2 teaspoons vanilla extract
- 2 cups all-purpose flour
- 2 teaspoons baking powder
- 1 teaspoon salt
- 1½ cups chopped pecans

MAPLE CREAM SAUCE:

- 1 cup maple syrup
- 2 tablespoons butter
- ¼ cup evaporated milk

Vanilla ice cream and chopped pecans

● In a large bowl, cream butter and brown sugar until light and fluffy. Beat in the eggs and vanilla. Combine the flour, baking powder and salt; gradually add to the creamed mixture. Stir in the pecans.

● Spread into a greased 13-in. x 9-in. baking pan. Bake at 350° for 25-30 minutes or until a toothpick inserted near the center comes out clean. Cool on a wire rack.

● For the sauce, combine syrup and butter in a saucepan. Bring to a boil; cook and stir for 3 minutes. Remove from the heat; stir in milk. Cut brownies into squares; cut in half if desired.

● Place on dessert plates with a scoop of ice cream. Top with sauce; sprinkle with pecans.

Yield: 20 servings.

CHOCOLATE
CRUNCH BROWNIES

The first time I took these brownies to work, I knew I'd better start making copies of the recipe.
—**Pat Mueller** *Mitchell, South Dakota*

PREP: 30 MIN. **BAKE:** 25 MIN. + CHILLING

- 1 cup butter, softened
- 2 cups sugar
- 4 eggs
- 2 teaspoons vanilla extract
- 1½ cups all-purpose flour
- ½ cup baking cocoa
- ½ teaspoon salt
- 1 jar (7 ounces) marshmallow creme
- 1 cup creamy peanut butter
- 2 cups (12 ounces) semisweet chocolate chips
- 3 cups crisp rice cereal

● In a large bowl, cream butter and sugar until light and fluffy. Beat in eggs and vanilla. Combine the flour, cocoa and salt; gradually add to creamed mixture until blended.

● Spread into a greased 13-in. x 9-in. baking pan. Bake at 350° for 24-28 minutes or until a toothpick inserted near the center comes out clean (do not overbake). Cool in pan on a wire rack. Spread marshmallow creme over cooled brownies.

● In a small saucepan, melt peanut butter and chocolate chips over low heat, stirring constantly until smooth. Remove from the heat; stir in cereal. Spread over top. Refrigerate until set. Cut into bars.

Yield: 3 dozen.

KITCHEN TIP

I use my pizza cutter to cut sheet cakes, brownies and bars. It rolls along smoothly and simply, cutting nice clean squares.
—**CAROLYN O.**, BLAIRSVILLE, GEORGIA

PIZZA CUTTER: RDA-MKE

BUTTERSCOTCH PEANUT BARS

With lots of peanuts and butterscotch flavor plus a rich, buttery crust, these easy-to-make bars are crazy good!
—**Margery Richmond** *Fort Collins, Colorado*

PREP: 15 MIN. **BAKE:** 20 MIN. + COOLING

- ½ cup butter, softened
- ¾ cup packed brown sugar
- 1½ cups all-purpose flour
- ½ teaspoon salt
- 3 cups salted peanuts

TOPPING:

- 1 package (10 to 11 ounces) butterscotch chips
- ½ cup light corn syrup
- 2 tablespoons butter
- 1 tablespoon water

○ Line a 15-in. x 10-in. x 1-in. baking pan with aluminum foil. Coat the foil with cooking spray; set aside.

○ In a small bowl, cream butter and brown sugar until light and fluffy. Combine flour and salt; gradually add to creamed mixture and mix well.

○ Press into prepared pan. Bake at 350° for 6 minutes. Sprinkle with peanuts.

○ In a large saucepan, combine topping ingredients. Cook and stir over medium heat until chips and butter are melted. Spread over hot crust. Bake for 12-15 minutes longer or until topping is bubbly. Cool on a wire rack. Cut into bars.

Yield: 4 dozen.

KITCHEN TIP

Out of corn syrup? For each cup of light corn syrup in a recipe, you can substitute 1 cup of sugar and ¼ cup water. For each cup of dark corn syrup, substitute 1 cup of packed brown sugar and ¼ cup water.

BILTMORE'S BREAD PUDDING

This is a comforting heirloom dessert from the historic Biltmore Estate. The caramel sauce is something special.
—**Biltmore Estate** *Asheville, North Carolina*

PREP: 15 MIN. **BAKE:** 40 MIN.

- 8 cups cubed day-old bread
- 9 eggs
- 2¼ cups whole milk
- 1¾ cups heavy whipping cream
- 1 cup sugar
- ¾ cup butter, melted
- 3 teaspoons vanilla extract
- 1½ teaspoons ground cinnamon

CARAMEL SAUCE:

- 1 cup sugar
- ¼ cup water
- 1 tablespoon lemon juice
- 2 tablespoons butter
- 1 cup heavy whipping cream

○ Place bread cubes in a greased 13-in. x 9-in. baking dish. In a large bowl, whisk the eggs, milk, cream, sugar, butter, vanilla and cinnamon. Pour evenly over bread.

○ Bake, uncovered, at 350° for 40-45 minutes or until a knife inserted near the center comes out clean. Let stand for 5 minutes before cutting.

○ Meanwhile, in a small saucepan, bring the sugar, water and lemon juice to a boil. Reduce heat to medium; cook until sugar is dissolved and mixture turns a golden amber color. Stir in butter until melted. Add cream. Remove from the heat. Serve with bread pudding.

Yield: 12 servings.

SYRUPS: RDA-MKE

CARAMEL MARSHMALLOW TREATS

I created this candy by combining my husband's favorite cookie recipe and my mom's caramel dip. These sweets really appeal to kids—and they're so easy to make that kids of all ages should enjoy helping you put them together. Why not prepare a big batch along with some fun family memories?
—*Tamara Holschen* Anchor Point, Alaska

PREP/TOTAL TIME: 30 MIN.

QUICK & EASY

    5 cups crisp rice cereal, coarsely crushed
    1 can (14 ounces) sweetened condensed milk
    1 package (14 ounces) caramels
    1 cup butter, cubed
    1 teaspoon ground cinnamon
    ½ teaspoon vanilla extract
    1 package (16 ounces) large marshmallows

● Line two baking sheets with waxed paper; set aside. Place the rice cereal in a shallow bowl.

● In a large saucepan, cook and stir the milk, caramels and butter over low heat until the caramels are melted and the mixture is smooth. Remove from the heat; stir in the cinnamon and vanilla.

● Using a toothpick, pierce each marshmallow and dip into the warm caramel mixture; turn to coat. Press the marshmallow bottoms in cereal; place on prepared pans. Let stand until set.

Yield: 5 dozen.

COOKIE DOUGH TRUFFLES

The flavorful filling at the center of these yummy candies tastes just like genuine chocolate chip cookie dough...without the worry of raw eggs. They make a delectable addition to cookie trays or lovely hostess gifts around the holidays.
—*Lanita Dedon* Slaughter, Louisiana

PREP: 1 HOUR + CHILLING

    ½ cup butter, softened
    ¾ cup packed brown sugar
    1 teaspoon vanilla extract
    2 cups all-purpose flour
    1 can (14 ounces) sweetened condensed milk
    ½ cup miniature semisweet chocolate chips
    ½ cup chopped walnuts
    1½ pounds dark chocolate candy coating, coarsely chopped

● In a large bowl, cream the butter and brown sugar until light and fluffy. Beat in vanilla. Gradually add flour, alternately with milk, beating well after each addition. Stir in chocolate chips and walnuts.

● Shape into 1-in. balls; place on waxed paper-lined baking sheets. Loosely cover and refrigerate for 1-2 hours or until firm.

● In a microwave, melt candy coating; stir until smooth. Dip balls in coating; allow excess to drip off. Place on waxed paper-lined baking sheets. Refrigerate until firm, about 15 minutes. If desired, remelt remaining candy coating and drizzle over candies. Store in the refrigerator.

Yield: 5½ dozen.

WONTON KISSES

These wrapped bundles are filled with a sweet chocolate candy kiss and sure to delight guests at your next party or get-together.
—**Darlene Brenden** *Salem, Oregon*

QUICK & EASY

PREP/TOTAL TIME: 25 MIN.

  24 milk chocolate kisses
  24 wonton wrappers
Oil for frying
Confectioners' sugar

● Place a chocolate kiss in the center of a wonton wrapper. (Keep remaining wrappers covered with a damp paper towel until ready to use.) Moisten edges with water; fold opposite corners together over candy kiss and press to seal. Repeat.

● In an electric skillet, heat 1 in. of oil to 375°. Fry wontons for 2½ minutes or until golden brown, turning once. Drain on paper towels. Dust with confectioners' sugar.

Yield: 2 dozen.

KITCHEN TIP

Wonton kisses can also be baked if you prefer not to deep fry. Spritz both sides of the wrappers with refrigerated butter-flavored spray. Press into mini-muffin cups and bake at 350° for 5 minutes or until lightly browned. Then add kisses and bake 5 minutes longer.

MINI RASPBERRY MOUSSE PARFAITS

These elegant parfaits make the perfect finish to a special meal. An added bonus? Busy hostesses can assemble them in advance.
—**Taste of Home Test Kitchen**

PREP: 30 MIN. + CHILLING

1¾ cups fresh *or* frozen unsweetened raspberries, thawed
  3 tablespoons sugar
  2 teaspoons cornstarch
  2 teaspoons orange juice
1⅓ cups whipped topping
 12 cubes angel food cake (½-inch cubes)

● Press raspberries through a strainer and discard seeds and pulp. In a small saucepan, combine sugar and cornstarch; stir in raspberry juice. Bring to a boil; cook and stir for 2 minutes or until thickened. Refrigerate until chilled.

● Divide raspberry mixture in half. Stir orange juice into one portion; set aside. Place remaining mixture in a small bowl; fold in whipped topping.

● Divide angel food cake among four small cocktail glasses or dessert dishes. Layer each with a scant tablespoon of reserved raspberry-orange mixture and ⅓ cup creamy mixture. Refrigerate until serving.

Yield: 4 servings.

COOKIES, CANDIES & MORE

WONTON WRAPPER: RDA-GID

PEANUT BUTTER CUP COOKIES

With the classic combination of chocolate and peanut butter, it's no surprise these are my family's favorite cookies. Because of their ease of preparation, I'm able to make them at a moment's notice.
—**Faith Jensen** *Meridian, Idaho*

PREP: 20 MIN. **BAKE:** 10 MIN./BATCH

1	cup butter, softened	2¼	cups all-purpose flour
⅔	cup peanut butter	1	teaspoon baking soda
1	cup sugar	½	teaspoon salt
1	cup packed brown sugar	2	cups (12 ounces) semisweet chocolate chips
2	eggs		
2	teaspoons vanilla extract	2	cups chopped peanut butter cups (about six 1.6-ounce packages)

● In a large bowl, cream the butter, peanut butter and sugars until light and fluffy. Beat in eggs and vanilla. Combine the flour, baking soda and salt; gradually add to creamed mixture and mix well. Stir in chocolate chips and peanut butter cups.

● Drop by rounded tablespoonfuls 2 in. apart onto ungreased baking sheets. Bake at 350° for 10-12 minutes or until edges are lightly browned. Cool for 2 minutes before removing to wire racks.

EDITOR'S NOTE: Reduced-fat peanut butter is not recommended for this recipe.

Yield: 7½ dozen.

SPICY OATMEAL COOKIE MIX

Layer this sweet blend of spices, oats, chips and coconut flakes in pretty jars. The mix creates yummy, ready-to-bake cookies and makes a quick and easy gift any time of year. Be sure to include extra ingredients and prep directions with your gift tag!
—Taste of Home Test Kitchen

PREP: 15 MIN. **BAKE:** 10 MIN./BATCH

- 1 cup all-purpose flour
- 1 teaspoon ground cinnamon
- ¾ teaspoon baking soda
- ¼ teaspoon salt
- ⅛ teaspoon ground nutmeg
- ½ cup packed brown sugar
- ½ cup sugar
- 1 cup old-fashioned oats
- 1 cup swirled milk chocolate and caramel chips
- ½ cup flaked coconut

ADDITIONAL INGREDIENTS:

- ½ cup butter, softened
- 1 egg
- ¾ teaspoon vanilla extract

● In a small bowl, combine the first five ingredients. In a 1-qt. glass jar, layer the flour mixture, brown sugar, sugar, oats, chips and coconut, packing well between each layer. Cover and store in a cool, dry place for up to 6 months.

Yield: 1 batch (4 cups).

TO PREPARE COOKIES: In a large bowl, beat the butter, egg and vanilla. Add cookie mix and mix well. Drop by rounded teaspoonfuls 2 in. apart onto ungreased baking sheets. Bake at 350° for 9-11 minutes or until golden brown. Cool for 2 minutes before removing to wire racks.

Yield: about 3½ dozen.

FROZEN HOT CHOCOLATE

Make it an occasion for chocolate lovers with this icy treat! For a stiffer consistency, freeze a full 8 hours. Serve in frosted goblets for a pretty touch.
—Lily Julow *Gainesville, Florida*

PREP: 15 MIN. + FREEZING

- ¾ cup sugar
- ½ cup baking cocoa
- 2¾ cups 2% milk, *divided*
- ¼ cup reduced-fat whipped topping
- 4 teaspoons chocolate syrup

● In a large saucepan, combine sugar and cocoa. Gradually add milk, reserving 2 tablespoons for blending; cook and stir until heated through and sugar is dissolved. Remove from the heat and let cool.

● Transfer to an 8-in. square dish. Freeze for 2 hours or until edges begin to firm. Stir and return to freezer. Freeze 4 hours longer or until firm.

● Just before serving, transfer to a food processor; cover and process with remaining milk until smooth. Garnish with whipped topping and chocolate syrup.

Yield: 4 servings.

KITCHEN TIP

I love to garnish coffee drinks, desserts and cakes with a few sprinkles of grated chocolate, baking cocoa or instant chocolate drink mix for a pretty look. I keep it in a small shaker—like the ones that hold powdered sugar—for speedy sifting over pastries and desserts.

—RENEE Z., TACOMA, WASHINGTON

CHOCOLATE POWDER: RDA-GID

JUMBO CHOCOLATE CHIP COOKIES

These oversized delights are a cookie-jar favorite. No one can resist their sweet chocolaty taste.
—*Lori Sporer* *Oakley, Kansas*

PREP: 15 MIN. + CHILLING **BAKE:** 15 MIN./BATCH

- ⅔ cup shortening
- ⅔ cup butter, softened
- 1 cup sugar
- 1 cup packed brown sugar
- 2 eggs
- 2 teaspoons vanilla extract
- 3½ cups all-purpose flour
- 1 teaspoon baking soda
- 1 teaspoon salt
- 2 cups (12 ounces) semisweet chocolate chips
- 1 cup chopped pecans

● In a large bowl, cream shortening, butter and sugars until light and fluffy. Beat in eggs and vanilla. Combine the flour, baking soda and salt; add to creamed mixture and mix well. Fold in the chocolate chips and pecans. Chill for at least 1 hour.

● Drop by ¼ cupfuls at least 1½ in. apart onto greased baking sheets. Bake at 375° for 13-15 minutes or until golden brown. Cool for 5 minutes before removing to a wire rack.

Yield: 2 dozen.

> **❝**The name of these cookies is true to form, for sure. Jumbo is definitely what you get and they are PERFECT. Chewy gooey on the inside with a nice crisp outer edge.**❞**
>
> —TRIXIEJO302 FROM TASTEOFHOME.COM

STRAWBERRY TRIFLE

I won first prize in a dairy recipe contest with this luscious berry trifle. It's easy to double the ingredients and make two for potlucks or church suppers.
—*Norma Steiner* *Monroe, Wisconsin*

PREP: 20 MIN. + CHILLING

- 1 cup cold milk
- 1 cup (8 ounces) sour cream
- 1 package (3.4 ounces) instant vanilla pudding mix
- 1 teaspoon grated orange peel
- 2 cups heavy whipping cream, whipped
- 8 cups cubed angel food cake
- 4 cups sliced fresh strawberries

● In a large bowl, beat the milk, sour cream, pudding mix and orange peel on low speed until mixture is thickened. Fold in the whipped cream.

● Place half of the cake cubes in a 3-qt. glass bowl. Arrange a third of the strawberries around sides of bowl and over cake; top with half of the pudding mixture. Repeat layers once. Top with remaining berries. Refrigerate for 2 hours before serving.

Yield: 8-10 servings.

CHOCOLATE STRAWBERRY SHORTCAKES

Shortcake is one of summer's finest desserts—especially when you have just-picked strawberries on hand. And this recipe makes a mouthwatering treat to serve guests.
—*Taste of Home Test Kitchen*

PREP: 20 MIN. + CHILLING **BAKE:** 10 MIN. + COOLING

- 1 quart fresh strawberries, sliced
- ⅔ cup sugar, *divided*
- 2 cups all-purpose flour
- ¼ cup baking cocoa
- ½ teaspoon baking soda
- 2 teaspoons baking powder
- ¼ teaspoon salt
- ½ cup cold unsalted butter
- ⅔ cup plus 1 tablespoon miniature semisweet chocolate chips, *divided*
- ¾ cup half-and-half cream
- 1 egg white, lightly beaten
- 1 tablespoon coarse sugar
- ½ pint heavy whipping cream
- 3 tablespoons confectioners' sugar
- ¾ cup hot fudge ice cream topping
- 10 fresh strawberries *or* grated chocolate, optional

Grated chocolate, optional

• Combine strawberries and ⅓ cup sugar; refrigerate if desired. In a large bowl, combine the flour, cocoa, baking soda, baking powder, salt and remaining sugar. Cut in butter and ⅔ cup chips until crumbly. Add half-and-half and stir until just moistened.

• Divide dough into 8 patties, about ¾-in. thick. Place on parchment paper-lined baking sheets. Brush with egg white; sprinkle with coarse sugar and remaining chips.

• Bake at 450° for 13 minutes or until toothpick inserted near the center comes out clean. Cool. Meanwhile, in a small bowl, beat whipping cream and confectioners' sugar until stiff peaks form. Refrigerate.

• To assemble, split shortcakes in half. Place cake bottoms on dessert plates. Divvy up about two-thirds of the strawberries, whipped cream and fudge topping among them. Replace shortcake tops; top with remaining berries, cream and topping. Garnish with grated chocolate if desired.

Yield: 8 servings.

APPLE PEANUT BUTTER COOKIES

Featuring the flavors of peanut butter, apple and cinnamon, these cookies are ideal for fall gatherings.
—*Marjorie Benson* New Castle, Pennsylvania

PREP: 20 MIN. **BAKE:** 10 MIN./BATCH

- ½ cup shortening
- ½ cup chunky peanut butter
- ½ cup sugar
- ½ cup packed brown sugar
- 1 egg
- ½ teaspoon vanilla extract
- 1½ cups all-purpose flour
- ½ teaspoon baking soda
- ½ teaspoon salt
- ½ teaspoon ground cinnamon
- ½ cup grated peeled apple

In a large bowl, cream the shortening, peanut butter and sugars until light and fluffy. Beat in egg and vanilla. Combine the dry ingredients; gradually add to creamed mixture and mix well. Stir in apple.

Drop by rounded tablespoonfuls 2 in. apart onto greased baking sheets. Bake at 375° for 10-12 minutes or until golden brown. Cool for 5 minutes before removing to wire racks.

EDITOR'S NOTE: Reduced-fat peanut butter is not recommended for this recipe.

Yield: about 2½ dozen.

HAMBURGER COOKIES

My husband loves peppermint patties, and our son is crazy for vanilla wafers. So I put the two together to make a cool cookie that looks just like a burger. Kids of all ages get such a kick out of these adorable treats!
—*Julie Wellington* Youngstown, Ohio

QUICK & EASY

PREP/TOTAL TIME: 30 MIN.

- ½ cup vanilla frosting
- Red and yellow paste *or* gel food coloring
- 40 vanilla wafers
- 20 peppermint patties
- 1 teaspoon corn syrup
- 1 teaspoon sesame seeds

Place ¼ cup frosting in each of two small bowls. Tint one red and the other yellow. Frost the bottoms of 20 vanilla wafers yellow; top with a peppermint patty. Spread with red frosting. Brush tops of the remaining vanilla wafers with corn syrup; sprinkle with sesame seeds. Place over red frosting.

Yield: 20 cookies.

ALMOND VENETIAN DESSERT

These beautiful bars feature three colorful cake-like layers, an apricot filling and a chocolate topping.
—*Reva Becker* Farmington Hills, Michigan

PREP: 35 MIN. **BAKE:** 15 MIN. + CHILLING

- ½ cup almond paste
- ¾ cup butter, softened
- ½ cup sugar
- 2 eggs, *separated*
- ¼ teaspoon almond extract
- 1 cup all-purpose flour
- ⅛ teaspoon salt
- 5 drops green food coloring
- 4 drops red food coloring
- ⅔ cup apricot preserves
- 3 ounces semisweet chocolate, chopped

Grease the bottoms of three 8-in. square baking dishes. Line with waxed paper and grease the paper; set aside.

Place almond paste in a large bowl; break up with a fork. Add the butter, sugar, egg yolks and extract; beat until smooth and

fluffy. Stir in flour and salt. In another bowl, beat egg whites until soft peaks form. Stir a fourth of the whites into the dough, then fold in the remaining whites (dough will be stiff).

Divide dough evenly into three portions, about ⅔ cup each. Tint one portion green and one portion red; leave the remaining portion white. Spread each portion into a prepared pan. Bake at 350° for 13-15 minutes or until edges are golden brown. Immediately invert onto wire racks; remove waxed paper. Place another wire rack on top and turn over. Cool completely.

Place green layer on a large piece of plastic wrap. Spread evenly with ⅓ cup apricot preserves. Top with white layer and spread with remaining preserves. Top with red layer. Bring plastic over layers. Slide onto a baking sheet and set a cutting board on top to compress layers. Refrigerate overnight.

In a microwave-safe bowl, melt chocolate. Remove cutting board and unwrap dessert. Spread melted chocolate over top; let stand until set. With a sharp knife, trim edges. Cut into 2-in. x ⅝-in. bars. Store in an airtight container.

Yield: about 2 dozen.

66 These are fabulous and almost everyone else said so, too. I thought they were too much work to make again, but after tasting them... OMG! 99

—**FRUITGAL** FROM TASTEOFHOME.COM

MAMIE EISENHOWER'S FUDGE

My mother came across this effortless recipe in a newspaper some 40 years ago. One taste and you'll see why it's now a favorite at our house and doesn't take long for a big batch to disappear.
—**Linda First** *Hinsdale, Illinois*

PREP: 20 MIN. + CHILLING

1 tablespoon plus ½ cup butter, *divided*
3 milk chocolate candy bars (two 7 ounces, one 1.55 ounces), broken into pieces
4 cups (24 ounces) semisweet chocolate chips

1 jar (7 ounces) marshmallow creme
1 can (12 ounces) evaporated milk
4½ cups sugar
2 cups chopped walnuts

● Line a 13-in. x 9-in. pan with foil and butter the foil with 1 tablespoon butter; set aside. In a large heat-proof bowl, combine the candy bars, chocolate chips and marshmallow creme; set aside.

● In a large heavy saucepan over medium-low heat, combine the milk, sugar and remaining butter. Bring to a boil, stirring constantly. Boil and stir for 4½ minutes. Pour over chocolate mixture; stir until chocolate is melted and mixture is smooth and creamy. Stir in walnuts. Pour into prepared pan. Cover and refrigerate until firm.

● Using foil, lift fudge out of pan; cut into 1-in. squares. Store in an airtight container in the refrigerator.

Yield: about 6 pounds.

FUDGE-FILLED BROWNIE BARS

I always have the ingredients on hand to put together these soft chewy bars. They have been a hit at many potlucks, and someone is always asking for the recipe.
—**Nola Burski** *Lakeville, Minnesota*

PREP: 10 MIN. **BAKE:** 30 MIN. + COOLING

1½ cups all-purpose flour
¾ cup packed brown sugar
¾ cup butter, softened
1 egg yolk
¾ teaspoon vanilla extract

FILLING:

1 package fudge brownie mix (13-inch x 9-inch pan size)
1 egg
⅓ cup water
⅓ cup canola oil

TOPPING:

1 package (11½ ounces) milk chocolate chips, melted
¾ cup chopped walnuts, toasted

● In a large bowl, combine the first five ingredients. Press onto the bottom of a greased 15-in. x 10-in. x 1-in. baking pan. Bake at 350° for 15-18 minutes or until golden brown.

● Meanwhile, in a large bowl, combine the filling ingredients. Spread over hot crust. Bake for 15 minutes or until set. Cool on a wire rack for 30 minutes.

● Spread melted chocolate over filling; sprinkle with walnuts. Cool completely. Cut into bars.

Yield: 4 dozen.

> ❝ These were fantastic! They're by far the best cookie bars I have ever had. ❞
> —**DDISHER** FROM TASTEOFHOME.COM

OATMEAL CHIP COOKIES

My mom liked to mix up different spices in traditional recipes to create unique and unexpected flavors. Molasses and cinnamon make these cookies stand out from ordinary oatmeal cookies.
—**Susan Henry** *Bullhead City, Arizona*

PREP: 20 MIN. **BAKE:** 10 MIN.

QUICK & EASY

½ cup shortening
1 cup sugar
1 tablespoon molasses
1 egg
1 teaspoon vanilla extract
1 cup all-purpose flour
1 cup quick-cooking oats
1 teaspoon baking soda
1 teaspoon ground cinnamon
½ teaspoon salt
1 cup (6 ounces) semisweet chocolate chips

● In a large bowl, cream shortening and sugar until light and fluffy. Beat in the molasses, egg and vanilla. Combine the flour, oats, baking soda, cinnamon and salt; gradually add to creamed mixture and mix well. Stir in chocolate chips.

● Roll into 1½-in. balls. Place 2 in. apart on greased baking sheets. Bake at 350° for 8-10 minutes or until golden brown. Cool for 5 minutes before removing from pans to wire racks.

Yield: about 1½ dozen.

KITCHEN TIP

When a bottle of molasses is almost empty, warm it in the microwave for a few seconds. This thins the remaining liquid so it runs out easier.

—**CHARLENE T.,** WAINWRIGHT, ALBERTA

MOLASSES: RDA-MKE

PEANUT BUTTER COCONUT BALLS

Here's a recipe that's been a family "secret" for generations. But it's just too good to keep to ourselves. A glossy chocolate coating hides a crunchy coconut filling.
—**Jennifer Dignin** *Westerville, Ohio*

PREP: 45 MIN. + CHILLING

1	cup butter, softened
1	cup crunchy peanut butter
2	tablespoons vanilla extract
3½	cups confectioners' sugar
2	cups graham cracker crumbs
2	cups chopped walnuts
1⅓	cups flaked coconut
2½	cups (15 ounces) semisweet chocolate chips
4	teaspoons shortening

Chopped nuts *or* sprinkles

● In a large bowl, cream the butter and peanut butter until light and fluffy. Beat in vanilla. Gradually add confectioners' sugar and mix well. Stir in the cracker crumbs, walnuts and coconut. Shape into 1-in. balls. Place on baking sheets; cover and refrigerate for at least 1 hour.

● In a microwave, melt chocolate chips and shortening; stir until smooth.

● Dip balls into melted chocolate; allow excess to drip off. Roll in nuts or sprinkles. Place on waxed paper until set. Store in an airtight container in the refrigerator.

Yield: about 7 dozen.

CHOCOLATE PEANUT SQUARES

If you're a fan of peanut butter cups, you'll enjoy these two-layer treats. A slightly crunchy graham cracker and peanut butter layer is topped with a smooth coating of melted chocolate chips and peanut butter. Yum!
—**Nicole Trudell** *Fort Lanley, British Columbia*

PREP: 20 MIN. + COOLING

2	cups confectioners' sugar
¾	cup creamy peanut butter
⅔	cup graham cracker crumbs
½	cup butter, melted

TOPPING:

⅔	cup semisweet chocolate chips
4½	teaspoons creamy peanut butter
½	teaspoon butter

● Line a 9-in. square pan with foil and butter the foil; set aside. In a large bowl, combine confectioners' sugar, peanut butter, graham cracker crumbs and butter. Spread into prepared pan.

● Combine topping ingredients in a microwave-safe bowl; heat until melted. Spread over peanut butter layer. Refrigerate until cool. Using foil, left out of pan. Cut into 1-in. squares. Store in an airtight container in the refrigerator.

Yield: 1½ pounds.

BIG SOFT GINGER COOKIES

Easy and delicious. These nicely spiced, soft cookies are perfect for folks who like the old-time flavor of ginger but don't care for the crispy texture of gingersnaps.

—Barbara Gray *Boise, Idaho*

QUICK & EASY

PREP/TOTAL TIME: 25 MIN.

¾ cup butter, softened
1 cup sugar
1 egg
¼ cup molasses
2¼ cups all-purpose flour
2 teaspoons ground ginger

1 teaspoon baking soda
¾ teaspoon ground cinnamon
½ teaspoon ground cloves
¼ teaspoon salt
Additional sugar

- In a large bowl, cream butter and sugar until light and fluffy. Beat in egg and molasses. Combine the flour, ginger, baking soda, cinnamon, cloves and salt; gradually add to the creamed mixture and mix well.

- Roll into 1½-in. balls, then roll in sugar. Place 2 in. apart on ungreased baking sheets. Bake at 350° for 10-12 minutes or until puffy and lightly browned. Remove to wire racks to cool.

Yield: 2½ dozen.

> ❝Just made these for the first time, and they are amazing! I will be making tons more for Christmas for sure!❞
>
> —HHUNTER012 FROM TASTEOFHOME.COM

COCONUT CREAM ANGEL PIE, PAGE 188

179   173   174

CAKES & PIES

Forget boxed cake mixes and day-old store-bought pies. When you want to whip up
an oven-fresh treat just like Mom's, turn to any of these old-fashioned wonders. We've
gathered a delicious assortment of tried-and-true favorites from family bakers that make
the perfect finale to any meal...big or small. From classic layered cakes and cute cupcakes
to luscious fruit pies and tangy tarts, each and every one of these divine pleasures tastes
as irresistible as it sounds. So get ready to dig in! After all, with the 30+ recipes found here,
you can finally have the cake (or pie) of your dreams—and eat it, too!

AMBROSIA CUPCAKES

These unbeatable cupcakes taste just like the classic Southern salad, only sweeter! Pineapple, apricot, coconut...your taste buds will be dancing. Butter, shortening and sour cream in the batter guarantee a moist, tender crumb. Yum!
—*Zan Brock* *Jasper, Alabama*

PREP: 25 MIN. **BAKE:** 20 MIN./BATCH + COOLING

- ½ cup butter, softened
- ½ cup butter-flavored shortening
- 2 cups sugar
- 5 eggs, *separated*
- 1 teaspoon rum extract
- ½ cup sour cream
- ½ cup apricot nectar
- ¼ cup pineapple preserves
- ¼ cup apricot preserves
- 2 cups cake flour
- 1 teaspoon baking powder
- ½ teaspoon salt
- ¼ teaspoon baking soda
- 1 cup chopped pecans

FROSTING:

- ½ cup butter, softened
- 1 package (3 ounces) cream cheese, softened
- ½ teaspoon coconut extract
- ½ teaspoon almond extract
- ¼ cup pineapple preserves
- ¼ cup apricot preserves
- 3¾ cups confectioners' sugar
- 1 cup flaked coconut
- 36 maraschino cherries with stems

- In a large bowl, cream the butter, shortening and sugar until light and fluffy. Add egg yolks, one at a time, beating well after each addition. Beat in extract.

- In another bowl, whisk the sour cream, apricot nectar and preserves. Combine the flour, baking powder, salt and baking soda; add to creamed mixture alternately with sour cream mixture. Beat just until blended. Stir in pecans. Beat egg whites until stiff peaks form; fold into batter.

- Fill paper-lined muffin cups three-fourths full. Bake at 350° for 18-22 minutes or until a toothpick inserted near the center comes out clean. Cool for 10 minutes before removing from pans to wire racks to cool completely.

- For frosting, in a large bowl, cream the butter, cream cheese and extracts until light and fluffy. Beat in preserves. Gradually beat in confectioners' sugar until blended.

- Frost cupcakes; sprinkle with coconut. Garnish with cherries.

Yield: 3 dozen.

POUND CAKE

This pound cake is hands down the best! With its rich texture, buttery flavor and lovely golden crust, you won't be able to stop at just one slice.
—*Margie Dalton* *Chicago, Illinois*

PREP: 20 MIN. **BAKE:** 1 HOUR + COOLING

- 2 cups butter, softened
- 4 cups confectioners' sugar
- 6 eggs
- 1 teaspoon almond extract
- 3 cups all-purpose flour
- ½ teaspoon salt

Fresh raspberries and whipped cream, optional

- In a large bowl, cream butter and confectioners' sugar until light and fluffy, about 5 minutes. Add eggs, one at a time, beating well after each addition. Stir in extract. Combine flour and salt; gradually add to creamed mixture. Beat just until combined.

- Transfer to two greased 8-in. x 4-in. loaf pans. Bake at 325° for 60-70 minutes or until a toothpick inserted near the center comes out clean. Cool for 10 minutes before removing from pans to wire racks. Serve with raspberries and whipped cream if desired.

Yield: 2 cakes (12 servings each).

APRICOT ALMOND TORTE

This pretty cake takes a bit of effort, so I make the layers ahead of time and assemble them on the day I'll be serving my guests. This makes it an easier option for entertaining, and it's well worth the extra work!
—**Trisha Kruse** *Eagle, Idaho*

PREP: 45 MIN. **BAKE:** 25 MIN. + COOLING

3 eggs	**FROSTING:**
1½ cups sugar	1 package (8 ounces) cream cheese, softened
1 teaspoon vanilla extract	
1¾ cups all-purpose flour	1 cup sugar
1 cup ground almonds, toasted	⅛ teaspoon salt
2 teaspoons baking powder	1 teaspoon almond extract
½ teaspoon salt	1½ cups heavy whipping cream, whipped
1½ cups heavy whipping cream, whipped	1 jar (10 to 12 ounces) apricot preserves
	½ cup slivered almonds, toasted

○ In a large bowl, beat the eggs, sugar and vanilla on high speed until thick and lemon-colored. Combine the flour, almonds, baking powder and salt; gradually fold into egg mixture alternately with the whipped cream.

○ Transfer to two greased and floured 9-in. round baking pans. Bake at 350° for 22-28 minutes or until a toothpick inserted near the center comes out clean. Cool for 10 minutes before removing from pans to wire racks to cool completely.

○ In a large bowl, beat cream cheese, sugar and salt until smooth. Beat in extract. Fold in whipped cream.

○ Cut each cake horizontally into two layers. Place bottom layer on a serving plate; spread with 1 cup frosting. Top with another cake layer; spread with half of the preserves. Repeat layers. Frost sides of cake; decorate the top edge with remaining frosting. Sprinkle with almonds.

Yield: 12 servings.

GERMAN CHOCOLATE CREAM PIE

I've won quite a few awards in recipe contests over the years and was over the moon with delight when this luscious pie sent me to the Great American Pie Show finals. It will always be a winner in my recipe box!
—**Marie Rizzio** *Interlochen, Michigan*

PREP: 20 MIN. **BAKE:** 45 MIN. + COOLING

Pastry for single-crust pie (9 inches)

4 ounces German sweet chocolate, chopped
1/4 cup butter, cubed
1 can (12 ounces) evaporated milk
1-1/2 cups sugar
3 tablespoons cornstarch
Dash salt
2 eggs
1 teaspoon vanilla extract
1-1/3 cups flaked coconut
1/2 cup chopped pecans

TOPPING:

2 cups heavy whipping cream
2 tablespoons confectioners' sugar
1 teaspoon vanilla extract
Additional flaked coconut and chopped pecans

- Line a 9-in. pie plate with pastry; trim and flute edges.

- Place the chocolate and butter in a small saucepan. Cook and stir over low heat until smooth. Remove from the heat; stir in milk. In a large bowl, combine the sugar, cornstarch and salt. Add the eggs, vanilla and chocolate mixture; mix well. Pour into crust. Sprinkle with coconut and pecans.

- Bake at 375° for 45-50 minutes or until a knife inserted near the center comes out clean. Cool completely on a wire rack.

- For topping, in a large bowl, beat cream until it begins to thicken. Add confectioners' sugar and vanilla; beat until stiff peaks form. Spread over pie; sprinkle with additional coconut and pecans. Refrigerate pie until serving.

Yield: 8 servings.

CHOCOLATE TRUFFLE CAKE

This tender, luxurious layer cake is perfect for chocolate lovers. With a ganache glaze and a fabulous bittersweet filling, the indulgence is so worth it!

—Jo Ann Koerkenmeier *Damiansville, Illinois*

PREP: 35 MIN. + CHILLING **BAKE:** 25 MIN. + COOLING

- 2½ cups 2% milk
- 1 cup butter, cubed
- 8 ounces semisweet chocolate, chopped
- 3 eggs
- 2 teaspoons vanilla extract
- 2⅔ cups all-purpose flour
- 2 cups sugar
- 1 teaspoon baking soda
- ½ teaspoon salt

FILLING:

- 6 tablespoons butter, cubed
- 4 ounces bittersweet chocolate, chopped
- 2½ cups confectioners' sugar
- ½ cup heavy whipping cream

GANACHE:

- 10 ounces semisweet chocolate, chopped
- ⅔ cup heavy whipping cream

● In a large saucepan, cook the milk, butter and chocolate over low heat until it is melted. Remove from the heat; let stand for 10 minutes.

● In a large bowl, beat the eggs and vanilla; stir in chocolate mixture until smooth. Combine the flour, sugar, baking soda and salt; gradually add to chocolate mixture and mix well (batter will be thin).

● Transfer to three greased and floured 9-in. round baking pans. Bake at 325° for 25-30 minutes or until a toothpick inserted near the center comes out clean. Cool for 10 minutes before removing from pans to wire racks to cool completely.

● For filling, in a small saucepan, melt butter and chocolate. Stir in confectioners' sugar and cream until smooth.

● For ganache, place chocolate in a small bowl. In a small saucepan, bring cream just to a boil. Pour over chocolate; whisk until smooth. Cool, stirring occasionally, until ganache reaches a spreading consistency.

● Set aside ½ cup filling for garnish. Place one cake layer on a serving plate; spread with half of the remaining filling. Repeat layers. Top with remaining cake layer. Spread the ganache over the top and sides of cake. Decorate with reserved filling. Store in the refrigerator.

Yield: 16 servings.

HOT MILK CAKE

When I think back on my mom's delicious meals, her milk cake always comes to mind as the perfect dessert. It's a simple, old-fashioned treat that tastes so good, it will surprise you!

—Rosemary Pryor *Pasadena, Maryland*

PREP: 20 MIN. **BAKE:** 30 MIN. + COOLING

- 4 eggs
- 2 cups sugar
- 1 teaspoon vanilla extract
- 2¼ cups all-purpose flour
- 2¼ teaspoons baking powder
- 1¼ cups 2% milk
- 10 tablespoons butter, cubed

● In a large bowl, beat the eggs on high speed for 5 minutes or until thick and lemon-colored. Gradually add the sugar, beating until mixture is light and fluffy. Beat in the vanilla. Combine the flour and baking powder; gradually add to batter; beat at low speed until smooth.

● In a small saucepan, heat milk and butter just until butter is melted. Gradually add to batter; beat just until combined.

● Pour into a greased 13-in. x 9-in. baking pan. Bake at 350° for 30-35 minutes or until a toothpick inserted near the center comes out clean. Cool on a wire rack.

Yield: 12-16 servings.

TOASTED BUTTER PECAN CAKE

If you're a fan of butter pecan ice cream, you'll love this cake. Loads of nuts are folded into the batter, and even more are sprinkled over the delectable frosting.
—**Phyllis Edwards** *Fort Valley, Georgia*

PREP: 25 MIN. **BAKE:** 25 MIN. + COOLING

1 cup plus 2 tablespoons butter, softened, *divided*
2⅔ cups chopped pecans
2 cups sugar
4 eggs
2 teaspoons vanilla extract
3 cups all-purpose flour
2 teaspoons baking powder
½ teaspoon salt
1 cup 2% milk

FROSTING:

2 packages (one 8 ounces, one 3 ounces) cream cheese, softened
⅔ cup butter, softened
6½ cups confectioners' sugar
1½ teaspoons vanilla extract
1 to 2 tablespoons 2% milk

● In a small heavy skillet, melt 2 tablespoons butter. Add pecans; cook over medium heat until toasted, about 4 minutes. Set aside to cool.

● In a large bowl, cream sugar and remaining butter until light and fluffy. Add eggs, one at a time, beating well after each addition. Beat in vanilla. Combine the flour, baking powder and salt; add to creamed mixture alternately with milk. Beat just until combined. Fold in 2 cups of the reserved pecans.

● Spread batter evenly into three greased and waxed paper-lined 9-in. round baking pans. Bake at 350° for 25-30 minutes or until a toothpick inserted near the center comes out clean. Cool cake for 10 minutes before removing from pans to wire racks to cool completely.

● For frosting, in a large bowl, beat the cream cheese, butter, confectioners' sugar and vanilla until smooth. Beat in enough milk to achieve spreading consistency. Spread frosting between layers and over top and sides of cake. Sprinkle with remaining pecans. Store in the refrigerator.

Yield: 12-16 servings.

APPLE HARVEST CAKE

Tender apple slices and the subtle flavors of orange, vanilla and cinnamon make an old-fashioned cake a big hit with my family. It's great for fall, but you'll find me making it all year long.
—**E. Bartuschat** *Abington, Massachusetts*

PREP: 20 MIN. **BAKE:** 40 MIN. + COOLING

2¼ cups sugar, *divided*
1 cup canola oil
4 eggs
¼ cup orange juice
2½ teaspoons vanilla extract
3 cups all-purpose flour
3 teaspoons baking powder
½ teaspoon salt
4 medium tart apples, peeled and cubed
2 teaspoons ground cinnamon
Whipped cream and additional cinnamon, optional

● In a large bowl, beat 2 cups sugar, oil, eggs, orange juice and vanilla until well blended. Combine the flour, baking powder and salt; gradually beat into the sugar mixture until blended. Stir in the apples.

● Spread half of the batter into a greased 13-in. x 9-in. baking dish. Combine cinnamon and remaining sugar; sprinkle over batter. Carefully spread remaining batter over the top.

● Bake at 350° for 40-50 minutes or until a toothpick inserted near the center comes out clean. Cool on a wire rack. Garnish with whipped cream and additional cinnamon if desired.

Yield: 12-15 servings.

SURPRISE-INSIDE CUPCAKES

These cupcakes are so easy to whip up, but everyone will think you've slaved for hours because of the "secret" creamy filling inside. They're great for picnics and lunch boxes.
—**Susan Muehmer** *Delaware, Ontario*

PREP: 25 MIN. **BAKE:** 20 MIN.

CAKE:
- 2 cups sugar
- 2 cups water
- ⅔ cup canola oil
- 2 tablespoons white vinegar
- 2 teaspoons vanilla extract
- 3 cups all-purpose flour
- ½ cup baking cocoa
- 2 teaspoons baking soda

FILLING:
- 1 package (8 ounces) cream cheese, softened
- 1/3 cup sugar
- 1 egg

Dash salt

Chocolate frosting, optional

○ In a large bowl, beat the sugar, water, oil, vinegar and vanilla until well blended. In another large bowl, combine the flour, cocoa and baking soda; gradually beat into sugar mixture until blended. Fill paper-lined muffin cups two-thirds full.

○ For filling, in a small bowl, beat the cream cheese, sugar, egg and salt until smooth. Drop a teaspoonful of filling into each cupcake.

○ Bake at 350° for 20-24 minutes or until a toothpick inserted near the center comes out clean. Cool for 10 minutes before removing from pans to wire racks to cool completely. Pipe frosting on cupcakes if desired.

Yield: 2 dozen.

CHERRY-BERRY STREUSEL PIE

I entered this delicious pie in the Oklahoma State Fair and won a ribbon. It's very pretty and tastes great, especially when topped with a scoop of vanilla ice cream.
—**Rosalie Seebeck** *Bethany, Oklahoma*

PREP: 1 HOUR + CHILLING **BAKE:** 55 MIN. + COOLING

- 2½ cups all-purpose flour
- 1 tablespoon sugar
- 1 teaspoon salt
- 1 cup cold butter
- 7 to 8 tablespoons cold water

FILLING:
- 2 cans (21 ounces *each*) cherry pie filling
- 1 cup fresh *or* frozen raspberries
- ¼ cup packed brown sugar
- ¼ teaspoon ground cinnamon

TOPPING:
- 1 cup yellow cake mix
- ½ cup chopped pecans, toasted
- ½ cup flaked coconut
- ¼ cup butter, melted
- 2 tablespoons 2% milk
- 2 tablespoons sugar

- Place the flour, sugar and salt in a food processor; cover and pulse until blended. Add butter; cover and pulse until mixture resembles coarse crumbs. While processing, gradually add water until dough forms a ball.

- Divide dough in half so that one portion is slightly larger than the other; wrap each in plastic wrap. Refrigerate for 30 minutes or until easy to handle.

- On a lightly floured surface, roll out larger portion of dough to fit a 9-in. deep-dish pie plate. Transfer pastry to pie plate; trim pastry to ½ in. beyond edge of plate. Combine the filling ingredients; spoon into crust. Sprinkle with dry cake mix, pecans and coconut. Drizzle with butter.

- Roll out remaining pastry to a 13-inch circle; cut into strips for a lattice top. While creating the lattice top, twist the pastry strips for a decorative effect. Seal and flute edges of pie.

- Brush lattice top with milk; sprinkle with sugar. Cover edges loosely with foil. Bake at 375° for 55-65 minutes or until crust is golden brown and filling is bubbly.

EDITOR'S NOTE: To make this pretty flower pie, use a paring knife to cut the top pie dough into strips of various size. Use a 2- or 3-inch round cookie cutter to make the center of the flower. Lay the strips on top of the pie, sporadically overlapping them. Top with round center in the middle. Adhere strips together by dabbing with water, or brush egg wash over the finished pie. Sprinkle with coarse sugar and bake.

Yield: 8 servings.

FRESH RASPBERRY PIE

Here's a pretty raspberry pie that was practically a staple at our house during the late summer. It was always filled with fresh-picked berries, since my family had our own raspberry bushes.
—**Emily Dennis** *Hancock, Michigan*

PREP: 35 MIN. + CHILLING **BAKE:** 50 MIN. + COOLING

- 2 cups all-purpose flour
- 1 tablespoon sugar
- ½ teaspoon salt
- ¾ cup shortening
- 1 egg, lightly beaten
- 3 tablespoons cold water
- 1 tablespoon white vinegar

FILLING:
- 1⅓ cups sugar
- 2 tablespoons quick-cooking tapioca
- 2 tablespoons cornstarch
- 5 cups fresh *or* frozen unsweetened raspberries, thawed
- 1 tablespoon butter

TOPPING:

1 tablespoon 2% milk

1 tablespoon sugar

○ In a large bowl, combine the flour, sugar and salt; cut in shortening until mixture resembles coarse crumbs. Combine the egg, water and vinegar; stir into flour mixture just until moistened. Divide dough in half so that one ball is slightly larger than the other; wrap each in plastic wrap. Refrigerate for 30 minutes or until easy to handle.

○ Meanwhile, in another large bowl, combine the sugar, tapioca, cornstarch and raspberries; let stand for 15 minutes.

○ On a lightly floured surface, roll out larger ball of dough to fit a 9-in. pie plate. Transfer dough to pie plate; trim even with edge. Add raspberry filling; dot with butter.

○ Roll out remaining dough to fit top of pie; place over filling. Trim, seal and flute edges. Cut slits in top. Brush with milk; sprinkle with sugar.

○ Bake at 350° for 50-55 minutes or until crust is golden brown and filling is bubbly. Cool on a wire rack.

Yield: 6-8 servings.

APPLE TURNOVERS

Tender and flaky, these traditional turnovers feature an apple pie-like filling and a sweet, simple glaze. I freeze any extras and warm them up in the microwave.

—Dorothy Bayes *Sardis, Ohio*

PREP: 50 MIN. + CHILLING **BAKE:** 20 MIN.

1 cup all-purpose flour

½ teaspoon salt

½ cup cold butter, *divided*

¼ cup ice water

FILLING:

⅓ cup sugar

2 teaspoons cornstarch

⅛ teaspoon ground cinnamon

2 medium tart apples, peeled and thinly sliced

1 teaspoon lemon juice

2 tablespoons beaten egg

1½ teaspoons water

GLAZE:

¼ cup confectioners' sugar

1 teaspoon water

○ In a small bowl, combine flour and salt; cut in ¼ cup butter until crumbly. Gradually add water, tossing with a fork until a ball forms. On a lightly floured surface, roll dough into a 12-in. x 6-in. rectangle.

○ Cut remaining butter into thin slices. Starting at a short side of dough, arrange half of the butter slices over two-thirds of the rectangle to within ½ in. of the edges. Fold unbuttered third of dough over middle third. Fold remaining third over the middle, forming a 6-in. x 4-in. rectangle. Roll the dough into a 12-in. x 6-in. rectangle.

○ Repeat steps of butter layering and dough folding, ending with a 6-in. x 4-in. rectangle. Wrap in plastic wrap; refrigerate for 15 minutes. Roll dough into a 12-in. x 6-in. rectangle. Fold in half lengthwise and then widthwise. Wrap in plastic wrap; refrigerate for 1 hour.

○ Meanwhile, in a small saucepan, combine the sugar, cornstarch and cinnamon. Add apples and lemon juice; toss to coat. Bring to a boil over medium heat, stirring constantly. Reduce heat; simmer, uncovered, for 5-10 minutes or until apples are tender, stirring often. Remove from the heat.

○ In a small bowl, combine egg and water. Roll dough into a 12-in. square; cut into four squares. Brush with half of the egg mixture. Spoon about ¼ cup filling on half of each square; fold dough over filling. Press edges with a fork to seal. Place on an ungreased baking sheet. Brush lightly with remaining egg mixture. With a sharp knife, cut three small slits in the top of each turnover.

○ Bake at 450° for 17-22 minutes or until golden brown. Remove to a wire rack. Combine glaze ingredients; drizzle over turnovers. Serve warm.

QUICK APPLE TURNOVERS: Substitute 1 sheet frozen puff pastry, thawed, for the dough. Skip steps 1-3. Proceed as directed in steps 4-6. Check doneness after 15 minutes.

BLUEBERRY TURNOVERS: Omit filling. In a saucepan, combine ¼ cup blueberries, 1 tablespoon sugar, 1½ teaspoons cornstarch and 1 teaspoon grated lemon peel. Mash well with a fork. Bring to a boil over low heat; cook and stir for 2 minutes or until thickened. Remove from the heat. Stir in 1 tablespoon butter and ¾ cup blueberries. Fill and bake as directed.

Yield: 4 servings.

KITCHEN TIP

For dry ingredients such as flour, sugar or cornmeal, spoon ingredients into a dry measuring cup over a canister or waxed paper. Fill the cup to overflowing, then level by sweeping a metal spatula or the flat side of a knife across the top.

SUGAR AND MEASURING CUP: RDA-MKE

CARAMEL NUT TORTE

The original version of this recipe caught my eye many years ago because it calls for apple cider. My father has a small orchard and we all help pick, wash and sort the apples before they're pressed into cider. This delicious cake just feels like home.
—*Karla Stichter* New Paris, Indiana

PREP: 30 MIN. **BAKE:** 20 MIN. + COOLING

    3 eggs, *separated*
    ¼ cup apple cider *or* juice
    1 teaspoon vanilla extract
    ½ teaspoon baking powder
    ¼ teaspoon ground cinnamon
    ⅔ cup sugar, *divided*
    1 cup graham cracker crumbs
    ½ cup ground almonds
CARAMEL SAUCE:
    ¼ cup packed brown sugar
    1½ teaspoons cornstarch
    3 tablespoons butter
    2 tablespoons plus 2 teaspoons apple cider *or* juice,
       divided
    4 ounces cream cheese, softened
FROSTING:
    ½ cup heavy whipping cream
    1 tablespoon sugar
    ¼ teaspoon vanilla extract

● Line two 6-in. round baking pans with parchment paper; coat with cooking spray. In a small bowl, lightly beat egg yolks. Set aside 1 tablespoon. Add cider, vanilla, baking powder, cinnamon and ½ cup sugar to remaining yolks.

● In another bowl, beat egg whites on medium until soft peaks form. Beat in remaining sugar, about 1 tablespoon at a time on high, until stiff peaks form and sugar is dissolved. Fold a fourth of the whites into batter; then fold in remaining whites. Fold in crumbs and almonds.

● Gently spoon into prepared pans. Bake at 325° for 20-25 minutes or until cake springs back when lightly touched. Cool for 10 minutes; remove from pans to wire racks. Cool completely.

● In a saucepan, combine the brown sugar, cornstarch, butter and 2 tablespoons cider. Bring to a boil over medium heat, stirring constantly. Cook and stir for 2 minutes or until thickened. Stir a small amount into reserved yolk; return all to pan. Bring to a gentle boil, stirring constantly. Cool.

● In a small bowl, beat cream cheese until fluffy. Beat in 2 tablespoons caramel sauce until smooth. Spread over one cake; top with remaining cake. Add remaining cider to remaining caramel sauce to achieve drizzling consistency.

● Beat cream until it begins to thicken. Add sugar and vanilla; beat until soft peaks form. Frost top and sides of cake. Drizzle with caramel sauce.

Yield: 6 servings.

ICE CREAM SANDWICH CAKE

Here's a gooey, chocolaty dessert that's truly irresistible. No one will ever guess that you simply dressed up store-bought ice cream sandwiches. How easy is that?
—*Taste of Home Cooking School*

PREP: 20 MIN. + FREEZING

    19 ice cream sandwiches
    1 jar (16 ounces) hot fudge ice cream topping
    1½ cups salted peanuts
    3 Heath candy bars (1.4 ounces *each*)
    1 carton (8 ounces) frozen whipped topping, thawed

● Cut one ice cream sandwich in half. Place one whole and one half sandwich along a short side of an ungreased 13-in. x 9-in. dish. Arrange eight sandwiches in opposite direction in the dish. Remove lid from fudge topping. Microwave 15-30 seconds to warm; stir. Spread one-half of the fudge topping over the ice cream sandwiches.

● In a food processor, combine peanuts and candy bars. Cover and pulse until chopped. Sprinkle one-half of mixture over fudge layer. Repeat layer of ice cream sandwiches and fudge topping. Spread whipped topping over top of cake. Sprinkle with remaining peanut mixture.

● Cover and freeze for up to 2 months. Remove from the freezer 20 minutes before serving. Cut into squares.

Yield: 15 servings.

FRESH CHERRY PIE

This ruby-red showstopper is just sweet enough, with a hint of almond flavor and a tasty level of cinnamon. The cherries peeking out of the lattice crust make it so pretty, too.
—**Josie Bochek** *Sturgeon Bay, Wisconsin*

PREP: 25 MIN. **BAKE:** 55 MIN. + COOLING

1¼ cups sugar	¼ teaspoon almond extract
⅓ cup cornstarch	PASTRY:
1 cup cherry juice blend	2 cups all-purpose flour
4 cups fresh tart cherries, pitted *or* frozen pitted tart cherries, thawed	½ teaspoon salt
	⅔ cup shortening
½ teaspoon ground cinnamon	5 to 7 tablespoons cold water
¼ teaspoon ground nutmeg	

○ In a large saucepan, combine sugar and cornstarch; gradually stir in cherry juice until smooth. Bring to a boil; cook and stir for 2 minutes or until thickened. Remove from the heat. Add the cherries, cinnamon, nutmeg and extract; set aside.

○ In a large bowl, combine flour and salt; cut in shortening until crumbly. Gradually add cold water, tossing with a fork until a ball forms. Divide pastry in half so that one ball is slightly larger than the other.

○ On a lightly floured surface, roll out larger ball to fit a 9-in. pie plate. Transfer pastry to pie plate; trim even with edge of plate. Add filling. Roll out remaining pastry; make a lattice crust. Trim, seal and flute the edges of the crust.

○ Bake at 425° for 10 minutes. Reduce heat to 375°; bake 45-50 minutes longer or until crust is golden brown. Cool on a wire rack.

Yield: 8 servings.

LEMON CRUMB CAKE

If you like the tangy flavor of lemon, you won't be able to get enough of this citrus delight. The light, crumb-topped cake is the perfect finale to a special springtime brunch or dinner.
—**Katie Wollgast** *Florissant, Missouri*

PREP: 20 MIN. **BAKE:** 30 MIN. + COOLING

2 cups buttermilk
1 cup sugar
2 eggs
2 tablespoons butter, melted
2 teaspoons vanilla extract
3 cups all-purpose flour
1¼ teaspoons baking powder
1 teaspoon salt
½ teaspoon baking soda
1 can (15¾ ounces) lemon pie filling

TOPPING:
1 cup all-purpose flour
⅔ cup sugar
⅓ cup cold butter, cubed
¼ cup sliced almonds, toasted
Reduced-fat vanilla ice cream, optional

- In a large bowl, beat the first five ingredients until well blended. In a small bowl, combine the flour, baking powder, salt and baking soda; gradually beat into buttermilk mixture until blended. Pour into a 13-in. x 9-in. baking pan coated with cooking spray. Drop pie filling by teaspoonfuls over batter.

- In a small bowl, combine flour and sugar. Cut in butter until crumbly. Stir in almonds; sprinkle over batter. Bake at 350° for 30-35 minutes or until a toothpick inserted near the center comes out clean.

- Cool for 10 minutes on a wire rack. Serve warm with ice cream if desired.

Yield: 20 servings.

VANILLA FROSTING

Why settle for canned store-bought frosting when this four-ingredient recipe is so easy to make? The homemade taste just can't be beat.

—Mary Faulk *Cambridge, Wisconsin*

PREP/TOTAL TIME: 5 MIN.

QUICK & EASY

- 2 cups confectioners' sugar
- 2 tablespoons butter, softened
- 2 tablespoons milk
- ½ teaspoon vanilla extract

○ In a bowl, combine the sugar, butter, milk and vanilla. Beat on medium speed until smooth and fluffy. Frost cake or cupcakes.

Yield: 1 cup.

PEANUT BUTTER PUDDING DESSERT

Here's a fun, layered dessert that will appeal to all ages. If you want it even nuttier, you can use chunky peanut butter, and if you're not a fan of cashews, substitute your favorite nut.

—Barbara Schindler *Napoleon, Ohio*

PREP: 25 MIN. **BAKE:** 25 MIN. + CHILLING

- 1 cup all-purpose flour
- ½ cup cold butter, cubed
- 1½ cups chopped cashews, *divided*
- 1 package (8 ounces) cream cheese, softened
- ⅓ cup creamy peanut butter
- 1 cup confectioners' sugar
- 1 carton (12 ounces) frozen whipped topping, thawed, *divided*
- 2⅔ cups cold milk

- 1 package (3.9 ounces) instant chocolate pudding mix
- 1 package (3.4 ounces) instant vanilla pudding mix
- 1 milk chocolate candy bar (1.55 ounces), coarsely chopped

○ Place flour and butter in a food processor; cover and process until mixture resembles coarse crumbs. Add 1 cup cashews; pulse a few times until combined.

○ Press into a greased 13-in. x 9-in. baking dish. Bake at 350° for 25-28 minutes or until golden brown. Cool completely on a wire rack.

○ In a small bowl, beat the cream cheese, peanut butter and confectioners' sugar until smooth. Fold in 1 cup whipped topping. Spoon over crust.

○ In another bowl, whisk milk and both pudding mixes for 2 minutes. Let stand for 2 minutes or until soft-set. Spread over cream cheese layer. Top with remaining whipped topping. Sprinkle with chopped candy bar and remaining cashews. Cover and refrigerate for at least 1 hour before serving.

Yield: 12-16 servings.

KITCHEN TIP

For an easy way to measure 1/3 cup peanut butter, fill a measuring cup with 2/3 cup cold water. Then add enough peanut butter to raise the water level to the 1-cup measure mark, making sure the shortening is completely immersed. Pour off all of the water.

PEANUT BUTTER: RDA-MKE

LUSCIOUS ALMOND CHEESECAKE

Almond lovers rejoice! Take one bite of my tasty creation, and I promise you'll never go back to plain cheesecake again.
—**Brenda Clifford** *Overland Park, Kansas*

PREP: 15 MIN. **BAKE:** 1 HOUR + CHILLING

- 1¼ cups crushed vanilla wafers (about 40 wafers)
- ¾ cup finely chopped almonds
- ¼ cup sugar
- ⅓ cup butter, melted

FILLING:
- 4 packages (8 ounces each) cream cheese, softened
- 1¼ cups sugar
- 4 eggs, lightly beaten
- 1½ teaspoons almond extract
- 1 teaspoon vanilla extract

TOPPING:
- 2 cups (16 ounces) sour cream
- ¼ cup sugar
- 1 teaspoon vanilla extract
- ⅛ cup toasted sliced almonds

○ In a bowl, combine the wafer crumbs, almonds and sugar; stir in the butter and mix well. Press into the bottom of an greased 10-in. springform pan; set aside.

○ In a large bowl, beat cream cheese and sugar until smooth. Add eggs; beat on low speed just until combined. Stir in extracts. Pour into crust. Place on a baking sheet.

○ Bake at 350° for 50-55 minutes or until center is almost set. Remove from the oven; let stand for 5 minutes (leave oven on). Combine the sour cream, sugar and vanilla. Spoon around edge of cheesecake; carefully spread over filling. Bake 5 minutes longer. Cool on a wire rack for 10 minutes. Carefully run a knife

around edge of pan to loosen; cool 1 hour longer. Refrigerate cheesecake overnight.

○ Just before serving, sprinkle with almonds and remove sides of pan. Refrigerate leftovers.

Yield: 14-16 servings.

RASPBERRY CHOCOLATE CAKE

The classic flavors of chocolate and raspberry combine in this scrumptious triple-decker cake. It's guaranteed to impress.
—**Marlene Sanders** *Paradise, Texas*

PREP: 45 MIN. + STANDING **BAKE:** 35 MIN. + COOLING

- 3 cups sugar
- 2¾ cups all-purpose flour
- 1 cup baking cocoa
- 2 teaspoons baking soda
- 1½ teaspoons salt
- ¾ teaspoon baking powder
- 1¼ cups buttermilk
- ¾ cup canola oil
- 3 teaspoons vanilla extract
- 3 eggs
- 1½ cups strong brewed coffee, room temperature

FILLING:
- 3 tablespoons all-purpose flour
- 6 tablespoons 2% milk
- 6 tablespoons shortening
- 3 tablespoons butter, softened
- 3 cups confectioners' sugar
- 2 tablespoons raspberry liqueur
- ¼ teaspoon salt

2 drops red food coloring, optional

4 tablespoons seedless raspberry jam, melted

FROSTING:

1 package (8 ounces) cold cream cheese

⅓ cup butter, softened

½ cup baking cocoa

1 tablespoon raspberry liqueur

4 cups confectioners' sugar

○ Line three greased 9-in. round baking pans with waxed paper and grease paper; set aside. In a large bowl, combine the first six ingredients. Combine buttermilk, oil and vanilla; add to the dry ingredients. Add the eggs, one at a time, beating well after each addition; beat for 2 minutes. Gradually add coffee (batter will be thin).

○ Pour batter into prepared pans. Bake at 350° for 35-40 minutes or until a toothpick inserted near the center comes out clean. Cool for 10 minutes before removing from pans to wire racks to cool completely.

○ For filling, in a small saucepan, whisk together flour and milk until smooth. Cook over medium heat for 1 minute or until thickened, stirring constantly. Remove from the heat and let stand until cool.

○ In a large bowl, cream shortening and butter until light and fluffy. Gradually add confectioners' sugar and mix well. Gradually add cooled milk mixture; beat for 4 minutes or until light and fluffy. Beat in liqueur, salt and food coloring if desired.

○ Level tops of cakes if necessary. Place one layer on a serving plate; spread with about 2 tablespoons jam. Place remaining layers on waxed paper; spread one of the remaining layers with remaining jam. Let stand for 30 minutes.

○ Spread ½ cup filling over cake on the plate to within ¼ in. of edges. Top with jam-covered cake, then spread with remaining filling. Top with remaining cake layer.

○ In a large bowl, beat cream cheese and butter until smooth. Beat in cocoa and liqueur. Gradually beat in confectioners' sugar until light and fluffy. Frost the top and sides of cake. Store cake in the refrigerator.

Yield: 16 servings.

STRAWBERRY-RHUBARB CREAM DESSERT

A neighbor shared this recipe with me, and I created my own variation using garden-fresh rhubarb and strawberries. The shortbread crust and creamy sweet-tart layers went over big at a family party...not a crumb was left!
—**Sara Zignego** *Hartford, Wisconsin*

PREP: 45 MIN. **BAKE:** 20 MIN. + CHILLING

2 cups all-purpose flour

1 cup chopped pecans

1 cup butter, melted

¼ cup sugar

TOPPING:

1 cup packed brown sugar

3 tablespoons cornstarch

5 cups chopped fresh *or* frozen rhubarb

1 cup sliced fresh strawberries

1 package (8 ounces) cream cheese, softened

1 cup confectioners' sugar

1¼ cups heavy whipping cream, whipped, *divided*

Additional brown sugar, optional

○ In a small bowl, combine the flour, pecans, butter and sugar. Press into a greased 13-in. x 9-in. baking dish. Bake at 350° for 18-20 minutes or until golden brown. Cool on a wire rack.

○ In a large saucepan, combine brown sugar and cornstarch. Stir in rhubarb until combined. Bring to a boil over medium heat, stirring often. Reduce heat; cook and stir for 4-5 minutes or until thickened. Remove from the heat; cool. Stir in strawberries.

○ In a large bowl, beat cream cheese and confectioners' sugar until smooth. Fold in 1 cup whipped cream. Spread over crust; top with rhubarb mixture. Spread with remaining whipped cream. Refrigerate for 3-4 hours before serving. Garnish with additional brown sugar if desired.

Yield: 12 servings.

❝I love trying new rhubarb recipes, and this was a super-easy and very delicious one. My whole family loved it and requested I make it again!❞

—**ELLIEK** FROM TASTEOFHOME.COM

WHITE CHOCOLATE RASPBERRY TORTE

We grow raspberries, and this scrumptious torte is my all-time favorite way to make use of them. I get oohs and aahs as soon as it hits the table.
—**Martha Schwartz** *Sarasota, Florida*

PREP: 1 HOUR **BAKE:** 30 MIN. + COOLING

- ¾ cup butter, softened
- 2 cups sugar
- 4 eggs
- 1 cup white baking chips, melted and cooled
- 1 teaspoon vanilla extract
- 3 cups cake flour
- 1 teaspoon baking powder
- ½ teaspoon baking soda
- 1 cup buttermilk

FILLING:

- 2 cups fresh *or* frozen raspberries
- ¾ cup water
- ½ cup sugar
- 3 tablespoons cornstarch

FROSTING:

- 1 package (8 ounces) cream cheese, softened
- 1 cup vanilla *or* white chips, melted and cooled
- 1 carton (12 ounces) frozen whipped topping, thawed

Fresh raspberries, optional

● In a large bowl, cream butter and sugar until light and fluffy. Add eggs, one at a time, beating well after each addition. Beat in melted chips and vanilla. Combine the flour, baking powder and soda; add to creamed mixture alternately with buttermilk, beating well after each addition.

● Transfer to two greased and floured 9-in. round baking pans. Bake at 350° for 28-32 minutes or until a toothpick inserted near the center comes out clean. Cool 10 minutes before removing from pans to wire racks to cool completely.

● In a small saucepan, bring raspberries and water to a boil. Reduce heat; simmer 5 minutes. Remove from the heat. Press raspberries through a sieve; discard seeds. Cool.

● In the same pan, combine sugar and cornstarch; stir in raspberry puree until smooth. Bring to a boil; cook and stir for 2 minutes or until thickened. Cool. Spread between cake layers.

● In a large bowl, beat cream cheese until fluffy. Beat in melted chips; fold in whipped topping. Spread over top and sides of cake. Pipe frosting over top edge of cake and garnish with berries if desired. Store in the refrigerator.

Yield: 12 servings.

GLOSSY CHOCOLATE FROSTING

The original recipe for this thick chocolate frosting came from my grandmother. I lightened it up, but it still has all the flavor and richness of Grandma's.
—**Melissa Wentz** *Harrisburg, Pennsylvania*

PREP/TOTAL TIME: 15 MIN.

QUICK & EASY

- ½ cup sugar
- Sugar substitute equivalent to ½ cup sugar
- ½ cup baking cocoa
- 3 tablespoons cornstarch
- 1 cup cold water
- 4½ teaspoons butter
- 1 teaspoon vanilla extract

● In a saucepan, combine the sugar, sugar substitute, cocoa and cornstarch. Add water and stir until smooth. Bring to a boil; cook and stir for 1 minute or until thickened. Remove from the heat; stir in butter and vanilla until smooth. Spread over cupcakes or cake while frosting is still warm.

EDITOR'S NOTE: Recipe makes enough to frost 12 cupcakes or the top of a 13-inch x 9-inch cake. This recipe was tested with Splenda No Calorie Sweetener.

Yield: 1¼ cups.

APRICOT CARAMEL TART

This luscious delight boasts a buttery shortbread crust with a sweet apricot and caramel filling for an appealing finish to any meal. Be sure to chill the dough overnight for easier handling.
—Taste of Home Test Kitchen

PREP: 30 MIN. + CHILLING **BAKE:** 35 MIN. + COOLING

- 1¼ cups slivered almonds
- 2¼ cups all-purpose flour
- 1 cup plus 1 teaspoon sugar, *divided*
- ¼ teaspoon ground cinnamon
- ¼ teaspoon ground coriander
- ⅛ teaspoon salt
- 1 cup cold butter, cubed
- 4 egg yolks
- 2 tablespoons lemon juice
- ½ teaspoon almond extract
- 1 jar (12 ounces) apricot preserves
- ½ cup caramel ice cream topping
- 1 egg, lightly beaten
- ¼ teaspoon water
- 3 tablespoons sliced almonds

- Place slivered almonds in a food processor; cover and process until chopped. Add the flour, 1 cup sugar, cinnamon, coriander and salt; cover and pulse to blend. Add butter; cover and pulse until mixture resembles coarse crumbs. Add the egg yolks, lemon juice and almond extract; cover and process until dough forms a ball.

- Divide dough in half; wrap in plastic wrap. Cover and refrigerate overnight.

- Let dough stand at room temperature for 30 minutes. Press one portion of dough onto the bottom and up the sides of a greased 9-in. fluted tart pan with a removable bottom. Combine preserves with ice cream topping; spread over crust. Roll out remaining pastry; make a lattice crust. Trim and seal edges. Beat egg and water; brush over lattice top. Sprinkle with remaining sugar and sliced almonds. Place on a baking sheet.

- Bake at 400° for 10 minutes. Reduce heat to 325°; bake 25-30 minutes longer or until golden brown. Cool on a wire rack.
Yield: 12 servings.

WINNING APPLE CRISP

I live in apple country, and this delicious crisp is my favorite way to put my abundance to good use. It's a snap to make, too.
—Gertrude Bartnick *Portage, Wisconsin*

PREP: 20 MIN. **BAKE:** 1 HOUR

- 1 cup all-purpose flour
- ¾ cup rolled oats
- 1 cup packed brown sugar
- 1 teaspoon ground cinnamon
- ½ cup butter, softened
- 4 cups chopped peeled apples
- 1 cup sugar
- 2 tablespoons cornstarch
- 1 cup water
- 1 teaspoon vanilla extract

Vanilla ice cream, optional

- In a large bowl, combine first four ingredients. Cut in butter until crumbly. Press half into a greased 2½-qt. baking dish or a 9-in. square baking pan. Cover with apples.

- In a small saucepan, combine the sugar, cornstarch, water and vanilla. Bring to a boil; cook and stir for 2 minutes or until thick and clear. Pour over apples. Sprinkle with remaining crumb mixture.

- Bake at 350° for 60-65 minutes or until apples are tender. Serve warm, with ice cream if desired.

Yield: 8 servings.

MARSHMALLOW-ALMOND KEY LIME PIE

It's great to see that many grocers now carry key limes, which give this pie its distinctive sweet-tart flavor.
—*Judy Castranova* *New Bern, North Carolina*

PREP: 40 MIN. **BAKE:** 15 MIN. + CHILLING

- 1 cup all-purpose flour
- 3 tablespoons brown sugar
- 1 cup slivered almonds, toasted, *divided*
- ¼ cup butter, melted
- 1 tablespoon honey
- 1 can (14 ounces) sweetened condensed milk
- 1 package (8 ounces) cream cheese, softened, *divided*
- ½ cup key lime juice
- 1 tablespoon grated key lime peel

Dash salt

- 1 egg yolk
- 1¾ cups miniature marshmallows
- 4½ teaspoons butter
- ½ cup heavy whipping cream

⦿ Place the flour, brown sugar and ½ cup almonds in a food processor. Cover and process until blended. Add melted butter and honey; cover and process until crumbly. Press onto the bottom and up the sides of a greased 9-in. pie plate. Bake at 350° for 8-10 minutes or until crust is lightly browned. Cool on a wire rack.

⦿ In a large bowl, beat the milk, 5 ounces cream cheese, lime juice, peel and salt until blended. Add egg yolk; beat on low speed just until combined. Pour into crust. Bake for 15-20 minutes or until center is almost set. Cool on a wire rack.

⦿ In a large saucepan, combine marshmallows and butter. Cook and stir over medium-low heat until melted. Remove from the heat and transfer to a bowl. Add cream and remaining cream cheese; beat until smooth. Cover and refrigerate until chilled.

⦿ Beat marshmallow mixture until light and fluffy. Spread over pie; sprinkle with remaining almonds.

Yield: 8 servings.

CHERRY COLA CHOCOLATE CAKE

For a truly different chocolate cake, think outside the box—and inside the slow cooker! This easy dessert comes out warm, moist, fudgy and wonderful.
—*Elaine Sweet* *Dallas, Texas*

PREP: 30 MIN. + STANDING **COOK:** 2 HOURS + STANDING

- ½ cup cola
- ½ cup dried tart cherries
- 1½ cups all-purpose flour
- ½ cup sugar
- 2 ounces semisweet chocolate, chopped
- 2½ teaspoons baking powder
- ½ teaspoon salt
- 1 cup chocolate milk
- ½ cup butter, melted
- 2 teaspoons vanilla extract

TOPPING:

- 1¼ cups cola
- ½ cup sugar
- ½ cup packed brown sugar
- 2 ounces semisweet chocolate, chopped
- ¼ cup dark rum

Vanilla ice cream and maraschino cherries, optional

⦿ In a small saucepan, bring cola and dried cherries to a boil. Remove from the heat; let stand for 30 minutes.

⦿ In a large bowl, combine the flour, sugar, chocolate, baking powder and salt. Combine the chocolate milk, butter and vanilla; stir into dry ingredients just until moistened. Fold in cherry mixture. Pour into a 3-qt. slow cooker coated with cooking spray.

⦿ For topping, in a small saucepan, combine the cola, sugar and brown sugar. Cook and stir until sugar is dissolved. Remove from the heat; stir in chocolate and rum until smooth. Pour over cherry mixture; do not stir.

⦿ Cover and cook on high for 2 to 2½ hours or until set. Turn off heat; let stand, covered, for 30 minutes. Serve warm with ice cream and maraschino cherries if desired.

EDITOR'S NOTE: This recipe does not use eggs.

Yield: 8 servings.

WILLIAM TELL'S NEVER-MISS APPLE CAKE

I bake my famous apple cake to usher in the fall season. It tastes so good that eating just one piece is nearly impossible.
—**Jamie Jones** *Madison, Georgia*

PREP: 40 MIN. **BAKE:** 50 MIN. + COOLING

- 1 package (8 ounces) cream cheese, softened
- 2 cups sugar, *divided*
- 4 eggs
- 1 cup canola oil
- 2 cups all-purpose flour
- 2 teaspoons baking powder
- 2 teaspoons ground cinnamon
- 1 teaspoon salt
- ¼ teaspoon baking soda
- 2 cups chopped peeled tart apples
- 1 cup shredded carrots
- ½ cup chopped pecans

PRALINE ICING:

- ½ cup packed brown sugar
- ¼ cup butter, cubed
- 2 tablespoons 2% milk
- ½ cup confectioners' sugar
- ½ teaspoon vanilla extract
- ¼ cup chopped pecans, toasted

⊙ In a small bowl, beat cream cheese and ¼ cup sugar until smooth. Beat in 1 egg; set aside.

⊙ In a large bowl, beat oil with remaining sugar and eggs until well blended. Combine the flour, baking powder, cinnamon, salt and baking soda; gradually beat into oil mixture until blended. Stir in the apples, carrots and pecans.

⊙ Transfer half of the apple batter to a greased and floured 10-in. fluted tube pan; layer with cream cheese mixture and remaining apple batter.

⊙ Bake at 350° for 50-60 minutes or until a toothpick inserted near the center comes out clean. Cool for 10 minutes before removing from pan to a wire rack to cool completely.

⊙ In a large saucepan, bring the brown sugar, butter and milk to a boil. Cook and stir for 1 minute. Remove from the heat; whisk

in confectioners' sugar and vanilla until smooth. Drizzle over cake. Sprinkle with pecans.

Yield: 12 servings.

CHOCOLATE ZUCCHINI CUPCAKES

My grandkids love these yummy chocolate cupcakes, and I love that they get a little extra nutrition from zucchini. They don't believe us when we tell them there are veggies in them! I'm always asked for this recipe.
—**Carole Fraser** *North York, Ontario*

PREP: 25 MIN. **BAKE:** 20 MIN. + COOLING

- 1¼ cups butter, softened
- 1½ cups sugar
- 2 eggs
- 1 teaspoon vanilla extract
- 2½ cups all-purpose flour
- ¾ cup baking cocoa
- 1 teaspoon baking powder
- 1 teaspoon baking soda
- ½ teaspoon salt
- ½ cup plain yogurt
- 1 cup grated zucchini
- 1 cup grated carrots
- 1 can (16 ounces) chocolate frosting

⊙ In a large bowl, cream butter and sugar until light and fluffy. Add eggs, one at a time, beating well after each addition. Stir in vanilla. Combine the flour, baking cocoa, baking powder, baking soda and salt; add to the creamed mixture alternately with yogurt, beating well after each addition. Fold in zucchini and carrots.

⊙ Fill paper-lined muffin cups two-thirds full. Bake at 350° for 18-22 minutes or until a toothpick inserted near the center comes out clean. Cool for 10 minutes before removing from pans to wire racks to cool completely. Frost cupcakes.

Yield: 21 cupcakes.

LAYERED TURTLE CHEESECAKE

After receiving a request for a special turtle cheesecake and not finding a good recipe, I created my own. Everyone was thrilled with the results and this cheesecake remains a favorite at the coffee shop where I work.
—*Sue Gronholz* *Beaver Dam, Wisconsin*

PREP: 40 MIN. **BAKE:** 1¼ HOURS + CHILLING

    1   cup all-purpose flour
    ⅓   cup packed brown sugar
    ¼   cup finely chopped pecans
    6   tablespoons cold butter, chopped
FILLING:
    4   packages (8 ounces *each*) cream cheese, softened
    1   cup sugar
    ⅓   cup packed brown sugar
    ¼   cup plus 1 teaspoon all-purpose flour, *divided*
    2   tablespoons heavy whipping cream
    1½ teaspoons vanilla extract
    4   eggs, lightly beaten
    ½   cup milk chocolate chips, melted and cooled
    ¼   cup caramel ice cream topping
    ⅓   cup chopped pecans
GANACHE:
    ½   cup milk chocolate chips
    ¼   cup heavy whipping cream
    2   tablespoons chopped pecans
Optional garnish: pecan halves and additional caramel ice cream topping

- Place a greased 9-in. springform pan on a double thickness of heavy-duty foil (about 18 in. square). Securely wrap foil around the pan.

- In a small bowl, combine the flour, brown sugar and pecans; cut in butter until crumbly. Press onto the bottom of prepared pan. Place pan on a baking sheet. Bake at 325° for 12-15 minutes or until set. Cool on a wire rack.

- In a large bowl, beat cream cheese and sugars until smooth. Beat in ¼ cup flour, cream and vanilla. Add eggs; beat on low speed just until combined. Remove 1 cup of batter to a small bowl; stir in melted chocolate until blended. Spread over crust.

- Combine caramel topping and remaining flour; stir in pecans. Drop by tablespoonfuls over chocolate batter. Top with remaining batter. Place springform pan in a large baking pan; add 1 in. of hot water to larger pan.

- Bake at 325° for 1¼ to 1½ hours or until center is just set and top appears dull. Remove springform pan from water bath. Cool on a wire rack for 10 minutes. Carefully run a knife around edge of pan to loosen; cool 1 hour longer. Refrigerate overnight.

- Place chips in a small bowl. In a small saucepan, bring cream just to a boil. Pour over chips; whisk until smooth. Cool slightly, stirring occasionally.

- Spread over cheesecake. Sprinkle with chopped pecans. Refrigerate until set. Remove sides of pan. Garnish with pecan halves and additional caramel topping if desired.

Yield: 12 servings.

COCONUT CREAM ANGEL PIE

Mom used to whip up this wonderful dessert on an impulse, using an ancient whisk and an old skillet. I am still amazed that the pie turned out perfect every time!
—*Ginny Werkmeister* *Tilden, Nebraska*

PREP: 30 MIN. **BAKE:** 20 MIN. + CHILLING

½ cup sugar

¼ cup cornstarch

¼ teaspoon salt

2 cups whole milk

3 egg yolks, lightly beaten

½ cup flaked coconut

1 tablespoon butter

1½ teaspoons vanilla extract

1 pastry shell (9 inches), baked

MERINGUE:

3 egg whites

¼ teaspoon cream of tartar

¼ teaspoon vanilla extract

6 tablespoons sugar

¼ cup flaked coconut

• In a small heavy saucepan, combine the sugar, cornstarch and salt. Add milk; stir until smooth. Cook and stir over medium-high heat until thickened and bubbly. Reduce heat to low; cook and stir for 2 minutes longer.

• Remove from the heat. Stir a small amount of hot filling into egg yolks; return all to the pan, stirring constantly. Bring to a gentle boil; cook and stir 2 minutes longer. Remove from heat; stir in coconut, butter and vanilla. Pour into prepared shell.

• In a small bowl, beat the egg whites, cream of tartar and vanilla on medium speed until soft peaks form. Gradually beat in sugar, 1 tablespoon at a time, on high until stiff peaks form. Spread meringue over hot filling, sealing edges to crust. Sprinkle with coconut.

• Bake at 350° for 17-20 minutes or until golden brown. Cool on a wire rack for 1 hour. Refrigerate for at least 3 hours before serving. Store leftovers in the refrigerator.

Yield: 8 servings.

FRENCH SILK PIE

This creamy, quick chocolate pie not only melts in your mouth, it also melts any and all resistance to dessert! I first prepared French Silk Pie when I was in high school. Years later, I experimented with the recipe until I was happy with it. Now, it's one of my husband's favorites.
—*Lisa Francis* Elba, Alabama

PREP: 40 MIN. **COOK:** 10 MIN. + CHILLING

1 sheet refrigerated pie pastry

⅔ cup sugar

2 eggs

2 ounces unsweetened chocolate, melted

1 teaspoon vanilla extract

⅓ cup butter, softened

⅔ cup heavy whipping cream

2 teaspoons confectioners' sugar

Whipped cream and chocolate curls, optional

• Cut pastry sheet in half. Repackage and refrigerate one half for another use. On a lightly floured surface, roll out remaining half into an 8-in. circle. Transfer to a 7-in. pie plate; flute edges.

• Line shell with a double thickness of heavy-duty foil. Bake at 450° for 4 minutes. Remove foil; bake 2 minutes longer or until crust is golden brown. Cool on a wire rack.

• In a small saucepan, combine sugar and eggs until well blended. Cook over low heat, stirring constantly, until mixture reaches 160° and coats the back of a metal spoon. Remove from the heat. Stir in chocolate and vanilla until smooth. Cool to lukewarm (90°), stirring occasionally.

• In a small bowl, cream butter until light and fluffy. Add cooled chocolate mixture; beat on high speed for 5 minutes or until light and fluffy.

• In another large bowl, beat cream until it begins to thicken. Add confectioners' sugar; beat until stiff peaks form. Fold into chocolate mixture.

• Pour into crust. Chill for at least 6 hours before serving. Garnish with whipped cream and chocolate curls if desired. Refrigerate leftovers.

Yield: 6 servings.

KITCHEN TIP

If you find the cream is starting to break down and get watery as you're whipping, you may be overbeating it, which will cause it to curdle and separate. For best results, start with cold whipping cream. Choose a deep metal bowl, as the cream will double in volume. Place the bowl and beaters in the freezer for at least 15 minutes before using. Beat quickly, scraping the bowl occasionally. Do not overbeat. Beat only until soft or stiff peaks form, depending on what your recipe needs.

BEATERS: BRAND X PICTURES

HOT FUDGE PUDDING CAKE

My mom used to prepare a recipe like this when I was younger. I decided to make some healthy changes, and this version is just as good as the original, if not better. Being a dietitian, I love to come up with creative ways to lighten up recipes.
—*Jackie Termont* *Richmond, Virginia*

PREP: 15 MIN. **BAKE:** 30 MIN.

1	cup all-purpose flour
1	cup sugar, *divided*
3	tablespoons plus ¼ cup baking cocoa, *divided*
2	teaspoons baking powder
¼	teaspoon salt
½	cup fat-free milk
⅓	cup prune baby food
1½	teaspoons vanilla extract
¼	cup plus 2 tablespoons packed brown sugar
1¼	cups boiling water

○ In a large bowl, combine the flour, ¾ cup sugar, 3 tablespoons cocoa, baking powder and salt. In another bowl, combine the milk, baby food and vanilla. Stir into dry ingredients just until moistened. Spread into an 8-in. square baking dish coated with cooking spray.

○ Combine brown sugar with remaining sugar and cocoa; sprinkle over the batter. Carefully pour water over the top (do not stir). Bake, uncovered, at 350° for 28-32 minutes or until top is set and edges pull away from sides of dish. Serve warm.

Yield: 9 servings.

FROZEN BANANA SPLIT PIE

This no-bake dessert is special enough to make even the most casual dinner a meal to remember! Standing tall and pretty, it tastes just like a frozen banana split. Make it a few days before your party to save time for last-minute preparations.
—*Joy Collins* *Birmingham, Alabama*

PREP: 25 MIN. + FREEZING

3	tablespoons chocolate hard-shell ice cream topping
1	graham cracker crust (9 inches)
2	medium bananas, sliced
½	teaspoon lemon juice
½	cup pineapple ice cream topping
1	quart strawberry ice cream, softened
2	cups whipped topping
½	cup chopped walnuts, toasted

Chocolate syrup

8	maraschino cherries with stems

○ Pour chocolate topping into crust; freeze for 5 minutes or until chocolate is firm.

○ Meanwhile, place bananas in a small bowl; toss with lemon juice. Arrange bananas over chocolate topping. Layer with pineapple topping, ice cream, whipped topping and walnuts.

○ Cover and freeze until firm. Remove from the freezer 15 minutes before cutting. Garnish with chocolate syrup and cherries.

Yield: 8 servings.

WHITE CHOCOLATE RASPBERRY CHEESECAKE

I'm happily married to a dairy farmer and am proud to say I have experience making cheesecakes. I rank this white chocolate raspberry sensation as my very best.
—**Wendy Barkman** *Breezewood, Pennsylvania*

PREP: 25 MIN. **BAKE:** 1 HOUR 20 MIN. + CHILLING

- 1½ cups graham cracker crumbs
- ¼ cup sugar
- ⅓ cup butter, melted

FILLING:

- 3 packages (8 ounces *each*) cream cheese, softened
- ¾ cup sugar
- ⅓ cup sour cream
- 3 tablespoons all-purpose flour
- 1 teaspoon vanilla extract
- 3 eggs, lightly beaten
- 1 package (10 to 12 ounces) white baking chips
- ¼ cup seedless raspberry jam

● In a small bowl, combine the graham cracker crumbs, sugar and butter. Press onto the bottom of a greased 9-in. springform pan; set aside.

● In a large bowl, beat cream cheese and sugar until smooth. Beat in the sour cream, flour and vanilla. Add eggs; beat on low speed just until combined. Fold in the chips. Pour over crust.

● In a microwave, melt raspberry jam; stir until smooth. Drop by teaspoonfuls over batter; cut through the batter with a knife to swirl.

● Place pan on a double thickness of heavy-duty foil (about 18 in. square). Securely wrap foil around pan. Place in a large baking pan; add 1 in. of hot water to larger pan.

● Bake at 325° for 80-85 minutes or until center is just set. Cool on a wire rack for 10 minutes. Carefully run a knife around edge of pan to loosen; cool 1 hour longer. Cover and refrigerate overnight. Remove sides of pan.

Yield: 12 servings.

MINT-CHOCOLATE ICE CREAM CAKE

This versatile ice cream cake is pretty enough for company and simple enough for a weeknight treat. Try food coloring to tint the whipped topping, or use different flavors of ice cream, extracts and cookie or candy crumbs to suit different holidays and occasions!
—**Kathy Morrow** *Hubbard, Ohio*

PREP: 15 MIN. + FREEZING

- 1 package (16 ounces) Suzy Q's
- 3 cups mint chocolate chip ice cream, softened
- 12 cream-filled chocolate sandwich cookies, crushed, *divided*
- 2 cups whipped topping
- ½ teaspoon mint extract, optional

● Line an 8-in. x 4-in. loaf pan with plastic wrap. Place four Suzy Q's in pan, completely covering the bottom. Spread ice cream over Suzy Q's; sprinkle with half of the cookie crumbs. Press remaining Suzy Q's on top. Cover and freeze for at least 3 hours.

● Just before serving, remove from the freezer and invert onto a serving plate. Remove pan and plastic wrap.

● Combine whipped topping and extract if desired; frost top and sides of cake. Sprinkle with remaining cookie crumbs.

Yield: 10 servings.

DULCE DE LECHE CHEESECAKE, PAGE 194

201

199

196

EDITORS'
FAVORITES

The Taste of Home Food Editors read, test and taste hundreds of recipes each year. Here we have gathered their top picks—from crowd-pleasing appetizers and sides to must-have main dishes, desserts and every course in between. These are the recipes they've been asked to share time and again...and they're sure you'll get requests for the recipes, too!

The kitchen is the heart of the home. Here at *Taste of Home*, we celebrate the desire to nourish and comfort by bringing together the voices and wisdom of thousands of real family cooks just like you. With all this sharing, it's never been easier to serve up classic heart-warming meals with a big side dish of love.

Here are a few reader specialties I'm proud to include in my own personal recipe box. Wake up tired taste buds with Easy Molasses Sticky Buns. You'll agree that the decadent drizzle is finger-licking good! Lemon-Sage Chicken bakes up moist and tender and boasts a delightful citrus flavor. And if you're craving something luscious and velvety, try a heavenly slice of Dulce de Leche Cheesecake to put the final touch on dinner. —**KAREN BERNER** TASTE OF HOME FOOD EDITOR

DULCE DE LECHE CHEESECAKE

I'm originally from Paraguay, and dulce de leche reminds me of my origins. If you can't find it at your grocery store, try caramel ice cream topping instead. It tastes different, but this decadent dessert will still be amazing!
—**Sonia Lipham** *Ranburne, Alabama*

PREP: 40 MIN. **BAKE:** 1 HOUR + CHILLING

- 1¾ cups crushed gingersnap cookies (about 35 cookies)
- ¼ cup finely chopped walnuts
- 1 tablespoon sugar
- ½ teaspoon ground cinnamon
- 6 tablespoons butter, melted

FILLING:
- 3 packages (8 ounces *each*) cream cheese, softened
- 1 cup plus 2 tablespoons sugar
- ¼ cup 2% milk
- 2 tablespoons all-purpose flour
- 1 teaspoon vanilla extract
- 3 eggs, lightly beaten
- 1 can (13.4 ounces) dulce de leche
- 1 cup (6 ounces) semisweet chocolate chips
- 1½ teaspoons chili powder

- Place a greased 9-in. springform pan on a double thickness of heavy-duty foil (about 18 in. square). Securely wrap foil around pan. In a large bowl, combine the cookie crumbs, walnuts, sugar, cinnamon and butter. Press onto the bottom and 2 in. up the sides of prepared pan.

- In a large bowl, beat cream cheese and sugar until smooth. Beat in the milk, flour and vanilla. Add eggs; beat on low speed just until combined. Pour into crust.

- Pour dulce de leche into a microwave-safe bowl; microwave at 50% power until softened. Drop dulce de leche by tablespoonfuls over batter; cut through the batter with a knife to swirl.

- Place springform pan in a large baking pan; add 1 in. of hot water to larger pan. Bake at 350° for 60-70 minutes or until center is just set and top appears dull.

- Remove springform pan from water bath. Cool on a wire rack for 10 minutes. Carefully run a knife around edge of pan to loosen; cool 1 hour longer.

- In a microwave-safe bowl, melt chips; stir until smooth. Stir in chili powder. Spread over cheesecake. Refrigerate overnight. Remove sides of pan.

EDITOR'S NOTE: This recipe was tested with Nestle dulce de leche. Look for it in the international foods section.

Yield: 16 servings.

LEMON-SAGE CHICKEN

While it's my mom's recipe, I had completely forgotten about this fantastic dish until I recently found a copy of it. The rich sauce and wonderful batter that go on the chicken make this an exquisite entree that's special enough for company.
—**Denise Kleffman** *Gardena, California*

PREP: 30 MIN. **BAKE:** 15 MIN.

- 4 boneless skinless chicken breast halves (6 ounces *each*)
- 3 eggs, lightly beaten
- ¼ cup grated Parmesan and Romano cheese blend
- 1 tablespoon minced fresh parsley
- 1 teaspoon dried basil
- ½ teaspoon salt
- ⅛ teaspoon pepper
- ½ cup all-purpose flour
- 2 tablespoons olive oil

SAUCE:
- 2 tablespoons chopped shallot

3 garlic cloves, minced
¼ cup white wine
4½ teaspoons lemon juice
1 tablespoon minced fresh parsley
1 teaspoon dried sage leaves
1 teaspoon grated lemon peel
½ cup heavy whipping cream
3 tablespoons cold butter

◎ Flatten chicken to ½-in. thickness. In a shallow bowl, combine the eggs, cheese and seasonings. Place flour in another shallow bowl. Coat chicken with flour, then dip in egg mixture.

◎ In a large skillet, brown chicken in oil in batches. Transfer to a greased 15-in. x 10-in. x 1-in. baking pan. Bake, uncovered, at 375° for 15-20 minutes or until a thermometer reads 170°.

◎ In the drippings, saute shallot until tender. Add garlic; cook 1 minute longer. Add the wine, lemon juice, herbs and lemon peel; cook over medium heat until liquid is reduced by half. Add cream; cook until thickened, stirring occasionally. Stir in butter until melted. Serve sauce with chicken.

Yield: 4 servings.

COOL BEANS SALAD

This protein-filled dish could be served as a colorful side or a meatless main entree. When you make it, you might want to double the recipe because it will be gone in a flash! Basmati rice adds a unique flavor and the dressing gives it a bit of tang.
—**Janelle Lee** *Appleton, Wisconsin*

PREP/TOTAL TIME: 20 MIN.

3 cups cooked basmati rice
1 can (16 ounces) kidney beans, rinsed and drained
1 can (15 ounces) black beans, rinsed and drained
1½ cups frozen corn, thawed
4 green onions, sliced
1 small sweet red pepper, chopped
¼ cup minced fresh cilantro
DRESSING:
½ cup olive oil
¼ cup red wine vinegar
1 tablespoon sugar

1 garlic clove, minced
1 teaspoon salt
1 teaspoon ground cumin
1 teaspoon chili powder
¼ teaspoon pepper

◎ In a large bowl, combine the first seven ingredients. In a small bowl, whisk the dressing ingredients; pour over salad and toss to coat. Chill until serving.

Yield: 6 servings.

EASY MOLASSES STICKY BUNS

Your family will jump out of bed when they smell these finger-licking good caramel rolls baking in the oven. The tender treats look just as delicious as they taste!
—**Nancy Foust** *Stoneboro, Pennsylvania*

PREP: 20 MIN. + RISING **BAKE:** 25 MIN.

2 loaves (16 ounces *each*) frozen bread dough, thawed
⅓ cup butter, softened
½ cup sugar
1½ teaspoons ground cinnamon
MOLASSES SAUCE:
1 cup packed brown sugar
½ cup butter, cubed
½ cup water
¼ cup molasses

◎ Roll out each loaf of bread dough into a 10-in. square. Spread with butter to within ½ in. of edges. Combine sugar and cinnamon; sprinkle over butter. Roll up jelly-roll style; pinch seams to seal. Cut each loaf into six slices.

◎ For sauce, in a small saucepan, bring the brown sugar, butter, water and molasses to a boil. Pour into a greased 13-in. x 9-in. baking dish. Place rolls, cut side down, in molasses sauce.

◎ Cover dough and let rise in a warm place until doubled, about 30 minutes. Bake at 350° for 25-30 minutes or until golden brown. Cool in dish for 5 minutes; invert onto a serving platter. Serve warm.

Yield: 1 dozen.

You can have the best of both worlds! With *Taste of Home Healthy Cooking*, readers happily share healthy, light recipes that don't skimp on flavor or fulfillment...recipes that include a full spectrum of nutritionally redeeming foods that are mouthwatering, delicious and still boast the same down-home appeal families know and love.

Want to pack in some extra nutrition with dinner? Loaded with veggies, Gnocchi with White Beans is slimmed-down comfort food at its best. Lightened-Up Pasta Fagioli Soup is a great option if you're watching your sodium intake. Have room for dessert? With sensations like Makeover Peanut Butter Bars, you don't have to give up your favorite sweet treats. So dig right in and see just how delicious eating right can be!

—**PEGGY WOODWARD**, RD, HEALTHY COOKING FOOD EDITOR

MACARONI COLESLAW

My good friend brought this coleslaw to one of our picnics, and everyone liked it so much, we all had to have the recipe.
—**Sandra Matteson** *Westhope, North Dakota*

PREP: 25 MIN. + CHILLING

- 1 package (7 ounces) ring macaroni *or* ditalini
- 1 package (14 ounces) coleslaw mix
- 2 medium onions, finely chopped
- 2 celery ribs, finely chopped
- 1 medium cucumber, finely chopped
- 1 medium green pepper, finely chopped
- 1 can (8 ounces) whole water chestnuts, drained and chopped

DRESSING:
- 1½ cups Miracle Whip Light
- ⅓ cup sugar
- ¼ cup cider vinegar
- ½ teaspoon salt
- ¼ teaspoon pepper

● Cook macaroni according to the package directions; drain and rinse in cold water. Transfer macaroni to a large bowl; add the coleslaw mix, onions, celery, cucumber, green pepper and water chestnuts.

● In a small bowl, whisk the dressing ingredients. Pour over salad; toss to coat. Cover and refrigerate for at least 1 hour.

Yield: 16 servings.

GNOCCHI WITH WHITE BEANS

Warm their hearts on chilly nights with this yummy skillet dish full of veggies, beans, gnocchi, melty cheese and Italian flavors. It makes a fast and easy meal in one.
—**Julianne Meyers** *Hinesville, Georgia*

PREP/TOTAL TIME: 30 MIN.

- 1 medium onion, chopped
- 1 tablespoon olive oil
- 2 garlic cloves, minced
- 1 package (16 ounces) potato gnocchi
- 1 package (6 ounces) fresh baby spinach
- 1 can (15 ounces) white kidney *or* cannellini beans, rinsed and drained
- 1 can (14½ ounces) Italian diced tomatoes, undrained
- ¼ teaspoon pepper
- ½ cup shredded part-skim mozzarella cheese
- 3 tablespoons grated Parmesan cheese

● In a large skillet, saute onion in oil until tender. Add garlic; cook 1 minute longer. Add gnocchi; cook and stir for 5-6 minutes or until golden brown. Stir in spinach; cook until spinach is wilted.

● Add the beans, tomatoes and pepper; heat through. Sprinkle with cheeses; cover and remove from the heat. Let stand for 3-4 minutes or until cheese is melted.

EDITOR'S NOTE: Look for potato gnocchi in the pasta or frozen foods section.

Yield: 6 servings.

EDITORS' FAVORITES

MAKEOVER PEANUT BUTTER BARS

Lighter in calories and fat than most peanut butter bars, this ooey-gooey dessert is a family favorite. Try it and you'll see why!
—**Lori Stevens** *Riverton, Utah*

PREP: 20 MIN. + CHILLING **BAKE:** 20 MIN. + COOLING

- 1¾ cups reduced-fat creamy peanut butter, *divided*
- ⅓ cup butter, softened
- 1 cup packed brown sugar
- ¾ cup sugar
- 2 eggs
- ½ cup unsweetened applesauce
- 1 teaspoon vanilla extract
- 2 cups all-purpose flour
- 2 cups quick-cooking oats
- 1 teaspoon baking soda

FROSTING:

- 4½ cups confectioners' sugar
- ⅓ cup fat-free milk
- ¼ cup baking cocoa
- ¼ cup butter, softened
- 1 teaspoon vanilla extract
- ½ teaspoon salt

● In a large bowl, cream 1 cup peanut butter, butter, brown sugar and sugar until light and fluffy. Add eggs, one at a time, beating well after each addition. Beat in applesauce and vanilla. Combine the flour, oats and baking soda; gradually add to creamed mixture and mix well (batter will be thick).

● Spread into a 15-in. x 10-in. x 1-in. baking pan coated with cooking spray. Bake at 350° for 18-22 minutes or until lightly browned. Cool on a wire rack for 10 minutes; spread with remaining peanut butter. Cool to room temperature, then refrigerate for 30 minutes.

● In a large bowl, beat frosting ingredients until light and fluffy. Spread over the peanut butter layer. Cut into bars.

Yield: 3 dozen.

LIGHTENED-UP PASTA FAGIOLI SOUP

After trying pasta fagioli at a popular restaurant, I was determined to make it at home, only healthier. It turns out mine was a big hit! Loaded with veggies, it is such a simple way to boost nutrition and fiber at mealtime.
—**Cindie Kitchin** *Grants Pass, Oregon*

PREP: 20 MIN. **COOK:** 40 MIN.

- 1 pound lean ground turkey
- 1 large onion, chopped
- 2 celery ribs, chopped
- 2 medium carrots, sliced
- 1 garlic clove, minced
- 3 cups water
- 1 can (16 ounces) kidney beans, rinsed and drained
- 2 cans (8 ounces *each*) no-salt-added tomato sauce
- 1 can (14½ ounces) no-salt-added diced tomatoes, undrained
- 1 tablespoon dried parsley flakes
- 2 teaspoons reduced-sodium beef bouillon granules
- ½ teaspoon dried oregano
- ½ teaspoon dried basil
- ¼ teaspoon pepper
- 2 cups shredded cabbage
- 1 cup fresh *or* frozen cut green beans (1-inch pieces)
- ½ cup uncooked elbow macaroni

● In a Dutch oven coated with cooking spray, cook the turkey, onion, celery and carrots over medium heat until meat is no longer pink. Add garlic; cook 1 minute longer. Add the water, beans, tomato sauce, tomatoes, parsley, bouillon, oregano, basil and pepper. Bring to a boil. Reduce heat; cover and simmer for 20 minutes.

● Add the cabbage, green beans and macaroni; cover and simmer 8-10 minutes longer or until the vegetables and macaroni are tender.

Yield: 6 servings (2¼ quarts).

At *Simple & Delicious* we're all about offering our busy readers quick, easy and fuss-free takes on their favorite comfort food classics. Most of our recipes come from cooks just like you, so you know they've been family-tested and -approved.

Here are a few gems I whip up for my own family. Who doesn't like golden garlic bread straight from the oven? It's guaranteed to enhance any meal, particularly Italian fare such as Make-Ahead Lasagna, which features a wonderful yummy pizza flavor. Cinnamon and maple syrup turn ho-hum chops into something extraordinary with these Maple Glazed Pork Chops. Love s'mores but can't wait for summer to enjoy them? I guarantee these scrumptious S'more Bars will hit the sweet spot.

—AMY WELK-THIEDING, RD, SIMPLE & DELICIOUS FOOD EDITOR

GARLIC-CHEESE CRESCENT ROLLS

Here's a recipe that couldn't be quicker or easier and is sure to add a nice touch to any dinner. The garlic and Parmesan flavors really come through. Enjoy!

—*Lori Abad* East Haven, Connecticut

PREP/TOTAL TIME: 20 MIN.

QUICK & EASY

- 1 tube (8 ounces) refrigerated crescent rolls
- 3 tablespoons butter, melted
- 1½ teaspoons garlic powder
- 1 teaspoon dried oregano
- 2 tablespoons grated Parmesan cheese

● Separate crescent dough into eight triangles. Roll up from the wide end and place point side down 2 in. apart on an ungreased baking sheet. Curve ends to form a crescent.

● Combine the butter, garlic powder and oregano; brush over rolls. Sprinkle with cheese.

● Bake at 375° for 10-12 minutes or until golden brown. Serve warm.

Yield: 8 servings

HOMEMADE MAPLE GLAZED PORK CHOPS

These chops will be an often-requested dinner option at your house. Basic pantry ingredients come together in a wonderful dish the whole family is sure to love. Maple syrup lends a touch of sweetness.

—**Athena Russell** *Florence, South Carolina*

PREP/TOTAL TIME: 30 MIN.

QUICK & EASY

- ½ teaspoon salt
- ½ teaspoon paprika
- ¼ teaspoon ground cumin
- ¼ teaspoon ground cinnamon
- ¼ teaspoon pepper
- 2 bone-in pork loin chops (7 ounces *each*)
- 1 tablespoon maple syrup
- 1½ teaspoons butter, melted
- 1½ teaspoons Dijon mustard

● Combine the first five ingredients; rub over pork chops. Place in a greased 11-in. x 7-in. baking dish. Bake, uncovered, at 425° for 20 minutes. Combine the remaining ingredients; pour over chops. Bake 5 minutes longer or until meat juices run clear.

Yield: 2 servings.

EDITORS' FAVORITES

S'MORE BARS

Once school starts, it can be hard for kids to let go of summer. But these rich, scrumptious bars will surely bring back sweet campfire memories.
—**Lisa Moriarty** *Wilton, New Hampshire*

PREP: 20 MIN. **BAKE:** 25 MIN. + COOLING

- ½ cup butter, softened
- ¾ cup sugar
- 1 egg
- 1 teaspoon vanilla extract
- 1⅓ cups all-purpose flour
- ¾ cup graham cracker crumbs
- 1 teaspoon baking powder
- ⅛ teaspoon salt
- 5 milk chocolate candy bars (1.55 ounces *each*)
- 1 cup marshmallow creme

- In a large bowl, cream butter and sugar until light and fluffy. Beat in egg and vanilla. Combine the flour, cracker crumbs, baking powder and salt; gradually add to creamed mixture. Set aside ½ cup for topping.

- Press remaining mixture into a greased 9-in. square baking pan. Place candy bars over crust; spread with marshmallow creme. Crumble remaining graham cracker mixture over top.

- Bake at 350° for 25-30 minutes or until golden brown. Cool on a wire rack. Cut into bars. Store in an airtight container.

Yield: 1½ dozen.

GLAZED SNAP PEAS

I have to have veggies with every meal, and this recipe is perfect for busy days! I love the natural sweet taste of the sugar snap peas, and this makes a nice side dish for any occasion.
—**Ida Tuey** *South Lyon, Michigan*

QUICK & EASY

PREP/TOTAL TIME: 20 MIN.

- 2 packages (24 ounces *each*) frozen sugar snap peas
- ¼ cup honey
- 2 tablespoons butter
- 1 teaspoon salt
- ¼ teaspoon crushed red pepper flakes
- ¼ cup real bacon bits

- Cook peas according to package directions; drain. Stir in the honey, butter, salt and pepper flakes. Sprinkle with bacon.

Yield: 10 servings.

MAKE-AHEAD LASAGNA

This is a favorite standby when time's limited and guests are expected for dinner. It's a combination of several easy lasagna recipes that I've tried over the years.
—**Mary Grimm** *Williamsburg, Iowa*

PREP: 35 MIN. + CHILLING **BAKE:** 55 MIN. + STANDING

- 1 pound lean ground beef (90% lean)
- 1 pound bulk hot Italian sausage
- 1 can (15 ounces) pizza sauce
- 1 jar (14 ounces) marinara sauce
- 2 eggs, lightly beaten
- 1 carton (15 ounces) ricotta cheese
- ½ cup grated Parmesan cheese
- 1 tablespoon dried parsley flakes
- ½ teaspoon pepper
- 12 no-cook lasagna noodles
- 4 cups (16 ounces) shredded part-skim mozzarella cheese

- In a large skillet, cook the beef and sausage over medium heat until no longer pink; drain. Stir in the pizza and marinara sauces. In a large bowl, combine the eggs, ricotta, Parmesan, parsley and pepper.

- Spread 1 cup meat sauce into a greased 13-in. x 9-in. baking dish. Layer with four noodles, half of the cheese mixture, 1 cup meat sauce and 1 cup mozzarella. Repeat layers. Top with remaining noodles, meat sauce and mozzarella. Cover and refrigerate for 8 hours or overnight.

- Remove from the refrigerator 30 minutes before baking. Bake, covered, at 375° for 45 minutes. Uncover; bake 10-15 minutes longer or until cheese is melted. Let stand for 10 minutes before cutting.

Yield: 12 servings.

People always say that we have great recipes, and I believe *Country Woman* readers are great cooks. That's why we're proud to share a wealth of from-scratch recipes that call for fresh, whole foods as ingredients.

As Food Editor, I have many favorites, but here are a few that stand out. If you're looking for a quick, easy appetizer that makes a beautiful presentation, give this Mediterranean Layered Dip a try. Moroccan Chickpea Stew is a favorite winter soup that my family loves. It's bright, colorful and full of healthy ingredients. Grilled Sweet Potato and Red Pepper Salad is a fresh take on potato salad, making it perfect for company. To end dinner on a sweet note, turn to Lemonade Dessert. It is super easy and so refreshing during those dog days of summer!

—**WENDY STENMAN** COUNTRY WOMAN FOOD EDITOR

MEDITERRANEAN LAYERED DIP

With holiday gatherings to host or attend, it's nice to have a quick and easy appetizer up your sleeve. This Greek-style layered dip uses purchased hummus as the base. It's great with store-bought or homemade pita chips.
—**Patterson Watkins** *Philadelphia, Pennsylvania*

QUICK & EASY

PREP/TOTAL TIME: 15 MIN.

2½ cups roasted garlic hummus
¾ cup chopped roasted sweet red peppers
1 cup fresh baby spinach, coarsely chopped
3 tablespoons lemon juice
2 tablespoons olive oil
2 tablespoons coarsely chopped fresh basil
1 tablespoon coarsely chopped fresh mint
½ cup crumbled feta cheese
½ cup Greek olives, sliced
¼ cup chopped red onion
Assorted fresh vegetables *or* baked pita chips

● Spread hummus onto a 12-in. round serving platter; top with roasted peppers.

● In a small bowl, combine the spinach, lemon juice, oil, basil and mint. Using a slotted spoon, spoon spinach mixture over peppers. Top with cheese, olives and onion. Serve with vegetables or pita chips.

Yield: 20 servings.

LEMONADE DESSERT

Here's a tasty way to finish off your summer barbecue. Adults and kids will be standing in line for this easy-to-make treat.
—**Margaret Linder** *Quincy, Washington*

PREP: 30 MIN. + FREEZING

1½ cups all-purpose flour
¾ cup packed brown sugar
¾ cup cold butter, cubed
¾ cup chopped pecans
½ gallon vanilla ice cream, softened
1 can (12 ounces) frozen pink lemonade concentrate, thawed

● In a small bowl, combine flour and brown sugar; cut in butter until crumbly. Stir in pecans. Spread in a single layer into a greased 15-in. x 10-in. x 1-in. baking pan.

● Bake at 375° for 9-12 minutes or until golden brown, stirring once. Cool on a wire rack for 10 minutes.

● In a large bowl, beat ice cream and lemonade until blended. Sprinkle half of the crumbles into a greased 13-in. x 9-in. dish. Spread with ice cream mixture; sprinkle with remaining crumbles. Cover and freeze overnight. Remove from the freezer 15 minutes before serving.

Yield: 12-15 servings.

EDITORS' FAVORITES

GRILLED SWEET POTATO AND RED PEPPER SALAD

This recipe combines vibrant colors and tastes to create an unusual salad that makes an exciting accompaniment to any entree. Try it at your next cookout or picnic.

—*Irene Eager* Claremont, New Hampshire

PREP: 30 MIN. **GRILL:** 20 MIN.

¼ cup olive oil
2 tablespoons lime juice
1 garlic clove, minced
1 teaspoon chopped seeded jalapeno pepper, optional
1 teaspoon salt
½ teaspoon ground cumin
¼ teaspoon pepper
2 large sweet red peppers
1½ pounds medium sweet potatoes, peeled and cut into ½-inch slices
2 celery ribs, thinly sliced
3 green onions, thinly sliced
⅓ cup minced fresh cilantro

● For dressing, in a small bowl, whisk the first seven ingredients; set aside.

● Using long-handled tongs, moisten a paper towel with cooking oil and lightly coat the grill rack. Grill red peppers over medium heat for 10-15 minutes or until the skins blister, turning frequently. Immediately place peppers in a large bowl; cover and let stand for 15 minutes.

● Meanwhile, in a shallow bowl, drizzle sweet potato slices with 2 tablespoons dressing; toss to coat. Set remaining dressing aside. Arrange potato slices on a grilling grid; place on a grill rack. Grill, covered, over medium heat for 5-6 minutes on each side or until tender. Cut into bite-size pieces.

● Peel off and discard charred skin from peppers; seed and coarsely chop. In a large bowl, combine the potatoes, peppers, celery, onions and cilantro. Whisk the reserved dressing; pour over salad and toss to coat. Serve at room temperature.

EDITOR'S NOTE: We recommend wearing disposable gloves when cutting hot peppers. Avoid touching your face. If you do not have a grilling grid, use a disposable foil pan. Poke the bottom of the pan with a meat fork to make holes.

Yield: 8 servings.

MOROCCAN CHICKPEA STEW

When I served this spicy stew to guests, three of whom were vegetarians, they were thrilled with the bounty of squash, potatoes, tomatoes and zucchini.

—*Cindy Beberman* Orland Park, Illinois

PREP: 20 MIN. **COOK:** 30 MIN.

1 large onion, finely chopped
2 tablespoons olive oil
1 tablespoon butter
2 garlic cloves, minced
2 teaspoons ground cumin
1 cinnamon stick (3 inches)
½ teaspoon chili powder
4 cups vegetable broth
2 cups cubed peeled butternut squash
1 can (15 ounces) chickpeas *or* garbanzo beans, rinsed and drained
1 can (14½ ounces) diced tomatoes, undrained
1 medium red potato, cut into 1-inch cubes
1 medium sweet potato, peeled and cut into 1-inch cubes
1 medium lemon, thinly sliced
¼ teaspoon salt
2 small zucchini, cubed
3 tablespoons minced fresh cilantro

● In a Dutch oven, saute onion in oil and butter until tender. Add the garlic, cumin, cinnamon stick and chili powder; saute 1 minute longer.

● Stir in the broth, squash, chickpeas, tomatoes, potatoes, lemon and salt. Bring to a boil. Reduce the heat; cover and simmer for 15-20 minutes or until potatoes and squash are almost tender.

● Add zucchini; return to a boil. Reduce heat; cover and simmer for 5-8 minutes or until vegetables are tender. Discard cinnamon stick and lemon slices. Stir in cilantro.

Yield: 9 servings (about 2 quarts).

PINK VELVET CUPCAKES, PAGE 204

213

221

212

SEASONAL SPECIALTIES

Christmas, Thanksgiving, Easter, the Fourth of July...special occasions call for special food. Family cooks know that holidays and the changing of the seasons offer an opportunity to experiment with new ingredients and flavors...and to get creative in the kitchen! In this chapter, you'll find some of their most popular recipes sure to impress guests during festive celebrations. From summer's flame-broiled fare to winter's cozy comfort foods, the perfect dish is always at your fingertips.

PINK VELVET CUPCAKES

Pretty in pink, these cupcakes were a big success at my daughter's princess-themed birthday party. They would be perfect for Valentine's Day parties, too!
—**Paulette Smith** *Winston-Salem, North Carolina*

PREP: 30 MIN. + CHILLING **BAKE:** 25 MIN. + COOLING

- 1 cup butter, softened
- 1¼ cups sugar
- ⅛ teaspoon pink paste food coloring
- 3 eggs
- 1 teaspoon vanilla extract
- 2½ cups all-purpose flour
- 1½ teaspoons baking powder
- ¼ teaspoon baking soda
- ¼ teaspoon salt
- 1 cup buttermilk

WHITE CHOCOLATE GANACHE:

- 2 cups white baking chips
- ½ cup heavy whipping cream
- 1 tablespoon butter

Pink coarse sugar and edible glitter

● In a large bowl, cream the butter, sugar and food coloring until light and fluffy. Add eggs, one at a time, beating well after each addition. Beat in vanilla. Combine the flour, baking powder, baking soda and salt; add to creamed mixture alternately with buttermilk, beating well after each addition.

● Fill paper-lined muffin cups two-thirds full. Bake at 350° for 23-27 minutes or until a toothpick inserted near the center comes out clean. Cool for 10 minutes before removing from pans to wire racks to cool completely.

● Meanwhile, place white chips in a small bowl. In a small saucepan, bring cream just to a boil. Pour over chips; whisk until smooth. Stir in butter. Transfer to a large bowl. Chill for 30 minutes, stirring once.

● Beat on high speed for 2-3 minutes or until soft peaks form and frosting is light and fluffy. Cut a small hole in the corner of

a pastry or plastic bag; insert #30 star tip. Fill bag with frosting; frost cupcakes. Sprinkle with coarse sugar and edible glitter. Store in the refrigerator.

EDITOR'S NOTE: Edible glitter is available from Wilton Industries. Call 800-794-5866 or visit *wilton.com*.

Yield: 2 dozen.

HOMEMADE PEANUT BUTTER CUPS

Forget store-bought chocolates! Make a lasting impression on Valentine's Day with this luscious candy featuring a dark chocolate shell and a gooey peanut butter center. Colorful sprinkles add a special touch.
—**Lavonne Hegland** *Saint Michael, Minnesota*

PREP: 20 MIN. + CHILLING

- 1 cup creamy peanut butter, *divided*
- 4½ teaspoons butter, softened
- ½ cup confectioners' sugar
- ½ teaspoon salt
- 2 cups (12 ounces) semisweet chocolate chips
- 4 milk chocolate candy bars (1.55 ounces *each*), coarsely chopped

Colored sprinkles, optional

● In a small bowl, combine ½ cup peanut butter, butter, confectioners' sugar and salt until smooth; set aside.

● In a microwave, melt the chocolate chips, candy bars and remaining peanut butter; stir until smooth.

● Drop teaspoonfuls of the chocolate mixture into paper-lined miniature muffin cups. Top each with a scant teaspoonful of peanut butter mixture; top with another teaspoonful of the chocolate mixture. Decorate with the colored sprinkles if desired. Refrigerate until set. Store peanut butter cups in an airtight container.

Yield: 3 dozen.

STRAWBERRY VALENTINE COOKIES

You'll make your sweetie's heart skip a beat when you set these whimsical cookies on the table. The strawberry flavor is a perfect complement to the chocolate glaze.
—**Marna Heitz** *Farley, Iowa*

PREP: 50 MIN. **BAKE:** 10 MIN./BATCH + COOLING

⅔ cup butter, softened	GLAZE:
⅔ cup sugar	1 cup (6 ounces) semisweet chocolate chips
1 egg	1 teaspoon shortening
1 tablespoon lemon juice	FROSTING:
2 cups all-purpose flour	⅓ cup butter, softened
⅓ cup strawberry drink mix	2 tablespoons strawberry drink mix
2 teaspoons baking powder	⅛ teaspoon salt
½ teaspoon salt	3 cups confectioners' sugar
	3 to 5 tablespoons 2% milk

● In a small bowl, cream butter and sugar until light and fluffy. Beat in egg and lemon juice. Combine the flour, drink mix, baking powder and salt; gradually add to creamed mixture and mix well.

● On a lightly floured surface, roll out dough to ¼-in. thickness. Cut with a floured 2½- to 3-in. heart-shaped cookie cutter. Place 2 in. apart on ungreased baking sheets. Bake at 350° for 8-10 minutes or until set and edges begin to brown. Cool for 2 minutes before removing to wire racks to cool completely.

● In a microwave, melt chocolate chips and shortening; stir until smooth. Spread over cookies; let stand until set.

● In a small bowl, beat the butter, drink mix and salt until blended. Gradually beat in confectioners' sugar. Add enough milk to achieve desired consistency. Decorate cookies.

Yield: about 2 dozen.

IRISH CREME CHOCOLATE TRIFLE

I created this yummy trifle when I was had some leftover peppermint candy and also received a bottle of Irish cream liqueur as a gift. I've made it with Irish creme coffee creamer and candy canes instead, but both ways are rich and delicious!

—Margaret Wilson *Sun City, California*

PREP: 20 MIN. **BAKE:** 30 MIN. + CHILLING

1	package (18¼ ounces) devil's food cake mix	2	packages (3.9 ounces *each*) instant chocolate pudding mix
1	cup refrigerated Irish creme nondairy creamer	3	cups whipped topping
3½	cups cold milk	12	spearmint candies, crushed

● Prepare and bake cake according to package directions, using a greased 13-in. x 9-in. baking pan. Cool on a wire rack for 1 hour.

● With a meat fork or wooden skewer, carefully poke holes in cake about 2 in. apart. Slowly pour creamer over cake; refrigerate for 1 hour.

● In a large bowl, whisk the milk and pudding mixes for 2 minutes. Let stand for 2 minutes or until soft-set.

● Cut cake into 1½-in. cubes; place a third of the cubes in a 3-qt. glass bowl. Top with a third of the pudding, whipped topping and candies; repeat layers twice. Store trifle in the refrigerator.

Yield: 14-16 servings.

EASY CORNED BEEF 'N' CABBAGE

Planning a festive St. Patrick's Day meal this year? You'll have no shortage of good luck with this traditional Irish recipe on hand. It's easy and so delicious, and the corned beef tastes great on sandwiches the next day...if you have any leftovers!
—**Ruth Warner** *Wheat Ridge, Colorado*

PREP: 10 MIN. **COOK:** 45 MIN.

    4   cups water
    1   corned beef brisket with spice packet (2 pounds)
    1   medium head cabbage, cut into 8 wedges
    2   large red potatoes, cut into 2-inch chunks
    1   can (14½ ounces) chicken broth
    4   large carrots, cut into 2-inch chunks
    1   medium onion, cut into 2-inch pieces

○ In a 6-qt. pressure cooker, combine water and contents of corned beef seasoning packet; add beef. Close cover securely; place pressure regulator on vent pipe. Bring cooker to full pressure over high heat. Reduce heat to medium-high and cook for 45 minutes. (Pressure regulator should maintain a slow steady rocking motion; adjust heat if needed.)

○ Meanwhile, in a large saucepan, combine the cabbage, potatoes and broth. Bring to a boil. Reduce the heat; cover and simmer for 10 minutes. Add the carrots and onion. Cover and simmer 20-25 minutes longer or until the vegetables are tender; drain.

○ Remove pressure cooker from the heat; allow pressure to drop on its own. Remove beef to a serving platter. Discard cooking liquid. Serve the beef with cabbage, potatoes, carrots and onion.

Yield: 4-6 servings.

IRISH SODA BREAD

This bread is prepared much like a biscuit. Mix the dough just until moist to keep it tender.
—**Gloria Warczak** *Cedarburg, Wisconsin*

PREP: 15 MIN. **BAKE:** 30 MIN.

    2   cups all-purpose flour
    2   tablespoons brown sugar
    1   teaspoon baking powder
    1   teaspoon baking soda
    ½   teaspoon salt
    3   tablespoons butter
    2   eggs
    ¾   cup buttermilk
    ⅓   cup raisins

○ In a large bowl, combine flour, brown sugar, baking powder, baking soda and salt. Cut in butter until crumbly. In a small bowl, whisk 1 egg and buttermilk. Stir into flour mixture just until moistened. Fold in raisins.

○ Knead on a floured surface for 1 minute. Shape into a round loaf; place on a greased baking sheet. Cut a ¼-in.-deep cross in top of loaf. Beat remaining egg; brush over loaf.

○ Bake at 375° for 30-35 minutes or until golden brown.

CARAWAY IRISH SODA BREAD: Add 1 to 2 tablespoons caraway seeds to the dry ingredients.

Yield: 6-8 servings.

KITCHEN TIP

In the case of light brown vs. dark brown sugar, the choice is yours! But keep in mind that light brown sugar has a subtle, delicate taste. If you like a more intense molasses flavor in baked goods, use dark brown instead.

BROWN SUGAR: RDA-GID

CHOCOLATE-COVERED EGGS

These chocolaty eggs beat store-bought varieties hands down! The smiles you'll see when you serve these adorable candies make them worth the effort.
—**Louise Oberfoell** *Bowman, North Dakota*

PREP: 1 HOUR + CHILLING

- ¼ cup butter, softened
- 1 jar (7 ounces) marshmallow creme
- 1 teaspoon vanilla extract
- 3 cups plus 1 tablespoon confectioners' sugar, *divided*
- 3 to 4 drops yellow food coloring, optional
- 2 cups (12 ounces) white baking chips *or* semisweet chocolate chips
- 2 tablespoons shortening

Icing of your choice

Assorted decorating candies

◦ In a large bowl, beat the butter, marshmallow creme and vanilla until smooth. Gradually beat in 3 cups confectioners' sugar. Place ¼ cup creamed mixture in a bowl; add yellow food coloring if desired and mix well. Shape into 24 small balls; cover and chill for 30 minutes. Wrap plain mixture in plastic wrap; chill for 30 minutes.

◦ Dust work surface with remaining confectioners' sugar. Divide plain dough into 24 pieces. Wrap one piece of plain dough around each yellow ball and form into an egg shape. Place on a waxed paper-lined baking sheet; cover with plastic wrap. Freeze for 15 minutes or until firm.

◦ In a microwave, melt chips and shortening; stir until smooth. Dip eggs in mixture; allow excess to drip off. Return eggs to waxed paper. Refrigerate for 30 minutes or until set. Decorate with icing and decorating candies as desired. Store in an airtight container in the refrigerator.

Yield: 2 dozen.

ASPARAGUS WITH ORANGE-GINGER BUTTER

Zesty orange and earthy ginger are the perfect complement to this veggie that has become a springtime staple at my house.
—**Lisa Feld** *Grafton, Wisconsin*

PREP/TOTAL TIME: 15 MIN.

QUICK & EASY

- 1½ pounds fresh asparagus, trimmed
- ½ cup butter, softened
- ½ cup orange marmalade
- 1 tablespoon minced crystallized ginger
- 1 tablespoon balsamic vinegar
- 2 teaspoons grated orange peel

◦ In a large skillet, bring 1/2 in. of water to a boil. Add asparagus; cover and boil for 3-5 minutes or until crisp-tender. Drain; transfer to a serving platter and keep warm.

◦ In a small bowl, beat the butter, marmalade, ginger, vinegar and orange peel until blended. Spoon over asparagus.

Yield: 6 servings.

CHAMPAGNE BAKED HAM

Champagne, brown sugar and honey combine to make a glossy, elegant glaze. The ham turns out tender and juicy every time.
Linda Foreman *Locust Grove, Oklahoma*

PREP: 10 MIN. **BAKE:** 2 HOURS

- 1 boneless fully cooked ham (9 pounds)
- 1½ cups Champagne
- ¾ cup packed brown sugar
- 4½ teaspoons honey
- ¾ teaspoon ground ginger
- ¾ teaspoon ground mustard

○ Place ham on a rack in a shallow roasting pan. Score the surface of the ham, making diamond shapes ½ in. deep. Bake, uncovered, at 325° for 1½ hours.

○ Meanwhile, in a small saucepan, combine the remaining ingredients. Bring to a boil; cook until glaze is reduced by half. Remove from the heat.

○ Baste ham with glaze; bake 30 minutes longer or until a thermometer reads 140°, basting twice with glaze. Serve with remaining glaze.

Yield: 18 servings.

> "Delicious glaze! I used a sweet Champagne, which worked very well with the ham. And who minds toasting to a delicious dinner with the leftover Champagne?"
>
> —**LSBEE** FROM TASTEOFHOME.COM

SPRINGTIME SALMON SALAD

I use this wonderful main-dish salad as a delicious way to get my family to eat a combination of nutritious foods.
—**Trisha Kruse** *Eagle, Idaho*

QUICK & EASY

PREP/TOTAL TIME: 20 MIN.

- 1 can (11 ounces) mandarin oranges, undrained
- 3 cups cut fresh asparagus (1-inch pieces)
- 1 package (5 ounces) spring mix salad greens
- ½ cup slivered almonds, toasted
- ½ cup frozen peas, thawed
- ¾ pound smoked salmon fillet, flaked

DRESSING:
- ¼ cup olive oil
- 2 tablespoons lemon juice
- 1 teaspoon Dijon mustard
- ½ teaspoon salt
- ¼ teaspoon pepper

○ Drain oranges, reserving 1/4 cup juice. Set oranges aside. In a small saucepan, bring 2 cups water to a boil. Add asparagus; cover and boil for 3 minutes. Drain and immediately place asparagus in ice water. Drain and pat dry.

○ In a large bowl, toss the salad greens, asparagus, oranges, almonds and peas. Divide salad among four serving plates. Top with salmon.

○ In a small bowl, whisk the dressing ingredients and reserved juice; drizzle over salads. Serve immediately.

Yield: 4 servings.

GRADUATION CAPS

Nothing says graduation like a mortarboard with a tassel! If your local grocer doesn't carry After Eight thin mints, try chocolate-covered graham crackers or squares from chocolate candy bars. You can also use fruit roll-ups for the tassels. Select ingredients that match your grad's school colors.
—**Margy Stief** Essington, Pennsylvania

PREP/TOTAL TIME: 25 MIN.

- 24 miniature peanut butter cups
- 1 tube (6 ounces) decorating frosting in color of your choice
- 24 After Eight thin mints
- 24 milk chocolate M&M's in color of your choice *or* 24 semisweet chocolate chips

○ Remove paper liners from peanut butter cups; place upside down on waxed paper. Place a small amount of frosting on each peanut butter cup; center a mint on each. Using frosting, make a loop for each cap's tassel. Place an M&M on top of each loop.

Yield: 2 dozen.

> ❝I made these for my daughter's graduation party and received more positive comments on these cute treats than on the cake!❞

—VALLOONEY FROM TASTEOFHOME.COM

CREAMY PINEAPPLE SALAD

Guests of all ages will gravitate to this traditional "fluff" salad, chock-full of pineapple, marshmallows and cherry bits.
—**Janice Hensley** Owingsville, Kentucky

PREP/TOTAL TIME: 25 MIN.

- 1 package (8 ounces) cream cheese, softened
- 1 can (14 ounces) sweetened condensed milk
- ¼ cup lemon juice
- 2 cans (20 ounces *each*) pineapple tidbits, drained
- 1½ cups multicolored miniature marshmallows, *divided*
- 1 carton (8 ounces) frozen whipped topping, thawed
- ½ cup chopped nuts
- ⅓ cup maraschino cherries, chopped

○ In a large bowl, beat the cream cheese, milk and lemon juice until smooth. Add pineapple and 1 cup marshmallows; fold in whipped topping. Sprinkle with the nuts, cherries and remaining marshmallows. Refrigerate leftovers.

Yield: 16 servings (1/2 cup each).

RASPBERRY ICE TEA

Frozen raspberries lend fruity flavor and lovely color to this refreshing iced tea. The recipe calls for just a few common ingredients and offers make-ahead convenience.
—Lois McGrady *Hillsville, Virginia*

PREP: 10 MIN. + CHILLING

    4 quarts water
 1½ cups sugar
    1 package (12 ounces) frozen unsweetened raspberries
  10 individual tea bags
   ¼ cup lemon juice

○ In a Dutch oven, bring water and sugar to a boil. Remove from the heat; stir until sugar is dissolved. Add the raspberries, tea bags and lemon juice. Cover and steep for 3 minutes. Strain; discard berries and tea bags.

○ Transfer tea to a large container or pitcher. Refrigerate until chilled. Serve over ice.

TOUCH-OF-MINT ICED TEA: Bring 2 quarts of water to a boil. Steep 5 individual tea bags for 5 minutes and discard; cool for 15 minutes. Add 1⅓ cups packed fresh mint and steep for 5 minutes. Strain tea and stir in 1 cup lemonade concentrate. Refrigerate until chilled. Serve over ice.

Yield: 16 servings (4 quarts).

BERRY TOSSED SALAD

Kiwi and feta add interest to this delightful salad that's the perfect medley of sweet, tangy, creamy and tart. It pairs nicely with any grilled entree such as chicken or ribs.
—Krista Smith Kliebenstein *Broomfield, Colorado*

QUICK & EASY

PREP/TOTAL TIME: 30 MIN.

    1 package (10 ounces) ready-to-serve salad greens
    1 cup sliced fresh strawberries

    1 kiwifruit, peeled and sliced
   ¼ cup chopped red onion
   ¼ cup crumbled feta cheese
    2 tablespoons slivered almonds
CREAMY RASPBERRY DRESSING:
   ½ cup mayonnaise
    2 tablespoons plus 2 teaspoons sugar
    1 tablespoon raspberry vinegar
    1 tablespoon 2% milk
 2½ teaspoons poppy seeds
 2½ teaspoons seedless raspberry jam

○ In a large salad bowl, combine the greens, strawberries, kiwi, onion, feta cheese and almonds.

○ In a small bowl, whisk the raspberry dressing ingredients. Drizzle desired amount over salad and toss to coat. Refrigerate any leftover dressing.

Yield: 8 servings.

> "Love this salad! I've made it several times and often get requests for the recipe. I sometimes omit the cheese and almonds and add croutons instead. A definite hit at our table."
>
> **—CHERIANNE** FROM TASTEOFHOME.COM

GRILLED CORN ON THE COB

I'd never had grilled corn until last summer, when my sister-in-law served it to us. What a treat! So simple, yet delicious, it's now a must for my favorite summer menus.

—Angela Leinenbach *Mechanicsvlle, Virginia*

PREP: 20 MIN. + SOAKING **GRILL:** 25 MIN.

8	medium ears sweet corn
½	cup butter, softened
2	tablespoons minced fresh basil
2	tablespoons minced fresh parsley
½	teaspoon salt

○ Soak corn in cold water for 20 minutes. Meanwhile, in a small bowl, combine the butter, basil, parsley and salt. Carefully peel back corn husks to within 1 in. of bottoms; remove silk. Spread butter mixture over corn.

○ Rewrap corn in husks and secure with kitchen string. Grill corn, covered, over medium heat for 25-30 minutes or until tender, turning occasionally. Cut strings and peel back husks.

Yield: 8 servings.

ZUCCHINI BREAD

I like this bread because it's lighter and fluffier than most zucchini breads. Plus, it's a great way to put that abundant vegetable to good use!

—Kevin Bruckerhoff *Columbia, Missouri*

PREP: 15 MIN. **BAKE:** 55 MIN. + COOLING

2	cups sugar
1	cup canola oil
3	eggs
2	teaspoons vanilla extract
3	cups all-purpose flour
1	teaspoon salt
1	teaspoon baking soda
¼	teaspoon baking powder
1	teaspoon ground cinnamon
2	cups shredded zucchini (about 2 medium)
½	cup chopped nuts
1	teaspoon grated lemon peel

○ In a large bowl, beat the sugar, oil, eggs and vanilla until well blended. Combine the flour, salt, baking soda, baking powder and cinnamon; stir into sugar mixture just until moistened. Stir in the zucchini, nuts and lemon peel.

○ Transfer to two greased 8-in. x 4-in. loaf pans. Bake at 350° for 55-65 minutes or until a toothpick inserted near the center comes out clean. Cool for 10 minutes before removing from pans to wire racks to cool completely.

MINI ZUCCHINI LOAVES: Transfer batter to four greased 5¾-in. x 3-in. x 2-in. loaf pans. Bake at 350° for 35-40 minutes or until a toothpick inserted near the center comes out clean. Cool as directed.

CHOCOLATE ZUCCHINI BREAD: Omit lemon peel and nuts. Reduce flour to 2¾ cups. Add ⅓ cup baking cocoa to flour mixture. Stir in 1 cup semisweet chocolate chips with zucchini. Bake as directed.

ZUCCHINI APPLE BREAD: Omit lemon peel. Reduce sugar to 1 cup and add 1 cup brown sugar. Add ¼ teaspoon ground nutmeg with cinnamon. Reduce zucchini to 1½ cups. Add 1 cup grated peeled tart apple with zucchini and nuts. Bake as directed.

Yield: 2 loaves (12 slices each).

TOMATO CORN SALAD

Warm and colorful, this tantalizing side dish bursts with refreshing vegetable flavor. Fresh herbs and Dijon mustard add to the pizzazz.
—**Carrie Componile** *Roselle Park, New Jersey*

PREP/TOTAL TIME: 30 MIN.

QUICK & EASY

  3 large tomatoes, chopped
  1 small red onion, halved and thinly sliced
  ⅓ cup chopped green onions
  ¼ cup balsamic vinegar
  3 tablespoons minced fresh basil
  1 tablespoon minced fresh cilantro
  1 teaspoon salt
  ½ teaspoon pepper
  4 cups fresh corn (about 9 ears of corn)
  2 tablespoons olive oil
  3 garlic cloves, peeled and thinly sliced
  1 tablespoon Dijon mustard

● In a large bowl, combine the first eight ingredients. In a large skillet, saute corn in oil until tender. Add garlic; cook 1 minute longer. Stir in mustard. Add to vegetable mixture; toss to coat. Serve with a slotted spoon.

Yield: 7 servings.

HEAVENLY FILLED STRAWBERRIES

Here comes strawberry season! These luscious stuffed berries are the perfect bite-size dessert for a summer party.
—**Stephen Munro** *Beaverbank, Nova Scotia*

PREP/TOTAL TIME: 20 MIN.

QUICK & EASY

  1 pound fresh strawberries
  2 packages (one 8 ounces, one 3 ounces) cream cheese, softened
  ½ cup confectioners' sugar
  ¼ teaspoon almond extract
Grated chocolate

● Remove stems from strawberries; cut a deep "X" in the tip of each berry. Gently spread berries open.

● In a small bowl, beat the cream cheese, confectioners' sugar and extract until light and fluffy. Pipe or spoon about 2 teaspoons into each berry; sprinkle with chocolate. Chill until serving.

Yield: about 3 dozen.

BERRY CHEESECAKE PIE

Since I don't care for traditional pie crust, I usually eat only the pie filling. But that changed when I discovered this unique recipe. Boasting a creamy cheesecake flavor, it gets creative with a flaky phyllo-dough crust.
—Deanne Causey *Midland, Texas*

PREP: 20 MIN. **BAKE:** 35 MIN. + CHILLING

- 8   sheets phyllo dough (14 inches x 9 inches)
- 6   tablespoons butter, melted
- 2   packages (8 ounces *each*) cream cheese, softened
- ½   cup sugar
- 1   teaspoon vanilla extract
- 2   eggs, lightly beaten
- 2   cups fresh *or* frozen blueberries
- ½   cup strawberry jelly
- 1   cup whipped topping
  Sliced fresh strawberries and additional blueberries, optional

◦ Place one phyllo sheet in a greased 9-in. pie plate; brush with butter. Repeat seven times; trim edges. (Keep remaining phyllo covered with plastic wrap and a damp towel to prevent it from drying out.)

◦ Bake at 425° for 6-8 minutes or until edges are lightly browned (center will puff up). Cool on a wire rack.

◦ For filling, in a large bowl, beat the cream cheese, sugar and vanilla until smooth. Add eggs; beat on low speed just until combined. Fold in blueberries. Spoon into crust.

◦ Bake at 350° for 10 minutes; cover edges with foil to prevent overbrowning. Bake 23-27 minutes longer or until center is almost set. Cool pie on a wire rack for 1 hour. Refrigerate cheesecake until chilled.

◦ In a small bowl, beat jelly until smooth; spread over filling. Spread with whipped topping. Garnish with strawberries and additional blueberries if desired.

EDITOR'S NOTE: If using frozen blueberries, use without thawing to avoid discoloring the batter.

Yield: 6-8 servings.

FLAG CAKE

This festive stars-and-stripes cake is sure to set off some fireworks at your Fourth of July party or other patriotic celebration. It starts with a classic French vanilla cake mix and is topped with luscious berries bursting with fresh summer flavor.
—Taste of Home Test Kitchen

PREP: 1½ HOURS + CHILLING **BAKE:** 35 MIN. + COOLING

- 1   package (18¼ ounces) French vanilla cake mix
- 1   cup buttermilk
- ⅓   cup canola oil
- 4   eggs

FILLING:
- 1   package (3 ounces) berry blue gelatin
- 1½   cups boiling water, *divided*
- 1   cup cold water, *divided*
  Ice cubes
- 1   package (3 ounces) strawberry gelatin
- ⅔   cup finely chopped fresh strawberries
- ¼   cup fresh blueberries

FROSTING:
- ¾   cup butter, softened
- 2   cups confectioners' sugar
- 1   tablespoon 2% milk
- 1   jar (7 ounces) marshmallow creme

◦ Line a 13-in. x 9-in. baking pan with waxed paper and grease the paper; set aside. In a large bowl, combine the first four ingredients; beat on low speed for 30 seconds. Beat on medium for 2 minutes. Pour into prepared pan.

◦ Bake at 350° for 35-40 minutes or until a toothpick inserted near the center comes out clean. Cool for 10 minutes before removing from pan to a wire rack to cool completely.

◦ Transfer cake to a covered cake board. Using a small knife, cut out a 5-in. x 4-in. rectangle (½ in. deep) in the top left corner of cake, leaving a ½-in. border along edges of cake. For red stripes, cut out ½-in. wide rows (½ in. deep), leaving a ½-in. border. Using a fork, carefully remove cut-out cake pieces.

- In a small bowl, dissolve berry blue gelatin in ¾ cup boiling water. Pour ½ cup cold water into a 2-cup measuring cup; add enough ice cubes to measure 1¼ cups. Stir into gelatin until slightly thickened. Scoop out and discard any remaining ice cubes. Repeat, making strawberry gelatin.

- In a small bowl, combine strawberries and 1 cup strawberry gelatin. In another bowl, combine blueberries and 1 cup blue gelatin. Refrigerate for 20 minutes or just until soft-set. (Save remaining gelatin for another use.)

- Stir gelatin mixtures. Slowly pour blueberry mixture into rectangle; spoon strawberry mixture into stripes.

- In a large bowl, beat butter until fluffy; beat in the confectioners' sugar and milk until smooth. Add marshmallow creme; beat well until light and fluffy. Spread 1 cup over sides and top edge of cake. Refrigerate the remaining frosting for 20 minutes.

- Cut a small hole in the corner of pastry or plastic bag; insert a large star tip. Fill the bag with remaining frosting. Pipe frosting in between rows of strawberry gelatin and around edges of cake. Refrigerate for 1-2 hours or until gelatin is set.

Yield: 15 servings.

PATRIOTIC TRIFLE

Everyone will ooh and aah when you bring out this colorful patriotic trifle for your annual Fourth of July festivities. Dress it up with tiny American flags that the kids can keep.
—**Sandra Brown** *Independence, Iowa*

PREP: 30 MIN. + CHILLING

- 1 package (3 ounces) berry blue gelatin
- 1 package (3 ounces) strawberry gelatin
- 2 cups boiling water
- 1 cup cold water
- 2 cups cold milk
- 2 packages (3.4 ounces *each*) instant vanilla pudding mix
- 1 carton (8 ounces) frozen whipped topping, thawed, *divided*
- 1 pint fresh blueberries
- 1 quart fresh strawberries, quartered
- 1 prepared angel food cake (8 to 10 ounces), cut into 1-inch cubes

- In two small bowls, combine each gelatin flavor with 1 cup boiling water. Stir ½ cup cold water into each. Pour each into an ungreased 9-in. square pan. Refrigerate for 1 hour or until set.

- In a large bowl, whisk milk and pudding mixes for 2 minutes. Let stand for 2 minutes or until soft-set. Fold in 2 cups whipped topping.

- Set aside ¼ cup blueberries and ½ cup strawberries for garnish. Cut the gelatin into 1-in. cubes. In a 3-qt. trifle bowl or serving dish, layer the strawberry gelatin, half of the cake cubes, the remaining blueberries and half of the pudding mixture.

- Top with blue gelatin and remaining cake cubes, strawberries and pudding mixture. Garnish with reserved berries and remaining whipped topping. Serve immediately.

Yield: 16-20 servings.

BLACKBERRY COBBLER

I pick fresh blackberries in summer to use in this recipe and other sweet delights. I also freeze the fruit so I can enjoy this warm, comforting cobbler any time of year.
—**Lori Daniels** *Beverly, West Virginia*

PREP: 25 MIN. **BAKE:** 30 MIN.

- 3 cups fresh *or* frozen blackberries
- 1 cup sugar
- ¼ teaspoon ground cinnamon
- 3 tablespoons cornstarch
- 1 cup cold water
- 1 tablespoon butter

BISCUIT TOPPING:
- 1½ cups all-purpose flour
- 1 tablespoon sugar
- 1½ teaspoons baking powder
- ½ teaspoon salt
- ½ cup cold butter, cubed
- ½ cup 2% milk

Whipped topping *or* vanilla ice cream, optional

- In a large saucepan, combine the blackberries, sugar and cinnamon. Cook and stir until mixture comes to a boil. Combine cornstarch and water until smooth; stir into fruit mixture. Bring to a boil; cook and stir for 2 minutes or until thickened. Pour into a greased 8-in. square baking dish. Dot with butter.

- For topping, in a small bowl, combine the flour, sugar, baking powder and salt. Cut in butter until mixture resembles coarse crumbs. Stir in milk just until moistened. Drop by tablespoonfuls onto hot berry mixture.

- Bake, uncovered, at 350° for 30-35 minutes or until filling is bubbly and topping is golden brown. Serve warm with whipped topping or ice cream.

Yield: 9 servings.

RUSTIC AUTUMN FRUIT TART

Your guests are sure to love this impressive dessert featuring rich, buttery pastry with apple and pear. It's surprisingly easy.
—*Jennifer Wickes* *Pine Beach, New Jersey*

PREP: 25 MIN. + CHILLING **BAKE:** 40 MIN. + COOLING

- ½ cup butter, softened
- 4 ounces cream cheese, softened
- 1½ cups all-purpose flour
- 2 large apples, peeled and thinly sliced
- 1 medium pear, peeled and thinly sliced
- 4½ teaspoons cornstarch
- ½ teaspoon ground cinnamon
- ¼ teaspoon ground cardamom
- ¼ teaspoon ground nutmeg
- ¼ cup orange juice
- ⅓ cup packed brown sugar
- ½ cup apricot jam, warmed

● In a small bowl, beat butter and cream cheese until smooth. Gradually add flour, beating just until mixture forms a ball. Cover and refrigerate for 1 hour.

● In a large bowl, combine apples and pear. In a small bowl, combine cornstarch and spices; stir in orange juice until smooth. Stir in brown sugar until blended. Add to apple mixture and stir gently to coat.

● On a lightly floured surface, roll out dough into a 14-in. circle. Transfer to a parchment paper-lined baking sheet. Spoon filling over the pastry to within 2 in. of edges. Fold up edges of pastry over filling, leaving center uncovered.

● Bake at 375° for 40-45 minutes or until crust is golden and filling is bubbly. Spread with apricot jam. Using parchment paper, slide tart onto a wire rack to cool.

Yield: 6 servings.

BUTTER PECAN PUMPKIN PIE

Whenever I serve this delightful frozen pie, everyone thinks I worked all day to make it, but it's actually a cinch to assemble. It's handy to have in the freezer when friends stop over for coffee and dessert.
—*Arletta Slocum* *Venice, Florida*

PREP: 20 MIN. + FREEZING

- 1 quart butter pecan ice cream, softened
- 1 pastry shell (9 inches), baked
- 1 cup canned pumpkin
- ½ cup sugar
- ¼ teaspoon *each* ground cinnamon, ginger and nutmeg
- 1 cup heavy whipping cream, whipped
- ½ cup caramel ice cream topping
- ½ cup chocolate ice cream topping, optional

Additional whipped cream

● Spread ice cream into the crust; freeze for 2 hours or until completely firm.

● In a small bowl, combine the pumpkin, sugar, cinnamon, ginger and nutmeg; fold in whipped cream. Spread over ice cream. Cover and freeze for 2 hours or until firm. May be frozen for up to 2 months.

● Remove from the freezer 15 minutes before slicing. Drizzle with caramel ice cream topping. Drizzle with chocolate ice cream topping if desired. Dollop with whipped cream.

Yield: 8 servings.

KITCHEN TIP

If you don't have any cinnamon, ginger or nutmeg on hand to make the pumpkin layer in Butter Pecan Pumpkin Torte, you can replace the spices with traditional pumpkin pie spice.

PUMPKIN PIE SPICE: RDA-MKE

SPIDERWEB DIP WITH BAT TORTILLA CHIPS

Every year, our daughter and her friends look forward to our annual Halloween party. All the little ghosts and ghouls have a blast dipping these bat-shaped chips into the zesty dip.
—**Sonia Candler** *Edmonton, Alberta*

PREP/TOTAL TIME: 30 MIN.

20	chipotle chili and pepper tortillas *or* flour tortillas (8 inches)

Cooking spray

¾ teaspoon garlic salt

¾ teaspoon ground coriander

¾ teaspoon paprika

⅜ teaspoon pepper

DIP:

1 package (8 ounces) cream cheese, softened

¾ cup salsa

½ cup prepared guacamole

1 to 2 tablespoons sour cream

○ Cut tortillas into bat shapes with a 3¾-in. cookie cutter. Place tortillas on baking sheets coated with cooking spray. Spritz tortillas with cooking spray. Combine the garlic salt, coriander, paprika and pepper; sprinkle over tortillas. Bake at 350° for 5-8 minutes or until edges just begin to brown.

○ In a small bowl, combine cream cheese and salsa. Spread into a 9-in. pie plate. Carefully spread guacamole to within 1 in. of edges.

○ Place sour cream in a small resealable plastic bag; cut a small hole in a corner of bag. Pipe thin concentric circles an inch apart over guacamole. Beginning with the center circle, gently pull a knife through circles toward center edge. Wipe knife clean. Repeat to complete spiderweb pattern. Serve with tortilla bats.

Yield: about 1½ cups dip and about 7 dozen chips.

YUMMY MUMMY CHEESE SPREAD

My annual Halloween bash wouldn't be the same without the now famous Mummy Man. When kids first see him, they wonder if he's actually edible. I assure them he is, and we get the spooky fun started by hacking off a foot or an arm with some crackers.

—Rebecca Eremich *Barberton, Ohio*

PREP/TOTAL TIME: 30 MIN.

QUICK & EASY

2 port wine cheese logs (12 ounces *each*)	1 tablespoon 2% milk
1 package (8 ounces) cream cheese, softened	2 whole peppercorns
	1 pimiento strip

- Cut cheese logs into pieces for mummy's head, body, arms and legs; arrange on a serving plate.

- In small bowl, beat cream cheese and milk. Cut a small hole in the corner of a pastry or plastic bag; insert basket weave tip #47. Pipe rows across the mummy, creating bandages. Add peppercorns for eyes and a pimiento strip for the mouth. Chill until serving.

Yield: 1 cheese log.

"This was so cute and easy!"

—GVO FROM TASTEOFHOME.COM

PUMPKIN SPICE CUPCAKES WITH CREAM CHEESE FROSTING

I love the flavor of pumpkin, especially during fall. And the cream cheese frosting, generously spiced with cinnamon, adds an extra-special touch to these treats.
—**Debbie Wiggins** *Longmont, Colorado*

PREP: 25 MIN. **BAKE:** 20 MIN. + COOLING

- ¾ cup butter, softened
- 2½ cups sugar
- 3 eggs
- 1 can (15 ounces) solid-pack pumpkin
- 2⅓ cups all-purpose flour
- 1 tablespoon pumpkin pie spice
- 1 teaspoon baking powder
- 1 teaspoon ground cinnamon
- ¾ teaspoon salt
- ½ teaspoon baking soda
- ½ teaspoon ground ginger
- 1 cup buttermilk

FROSTING:

- 1 package (8 ounces) cream cheese, softened
- ½ cup butter, softened
- 4 cups confectioners' sugar
- 1 teaspoon vanilla extract
- 2 teaspoons ground cinnamon

◉ In a large bowl, cream butter and sugar until light and fluffy. Add eggs, one at a time, beating well after each addition. Add pumpkin. Combine the flour, pie spice, baking powder, cinnamon, salt, baking soda and ginger; add dry ingredients to the creamed mixture alternately with buttermilk, beating well after each addition.

◉ Fill paper-lined muffin cups three-fourths full. Bake at 350° for 20-25 minutes or until a toothpick inserted in the center comes out clean. Cool for 10 minutes before removing from pans to wire racks to cool completely.

◉ For frosting, in a large bowl, beat cream cheese and butter until fluffy. Add the confectioners' sugar, vanilla and cinnamon; beat until smooth. Frost cupcakes. Refrigerate leftovers.

Yield: 2 dozen.

ROASTED PUMPKIN SEEDS

If you have leftover seeds from your carved pumpkins, simply spice 'em and bake 'em for a fun snack!
—**Dawn Fagerstrom** *Warren, Minnesota*

PREP: 20 MIN. **BAKE:** 50 MIN.

- 2 cups fresh pumpkin seeds
- 3 tablespoons butter, melted
- 1 teaspoon salt
- 1 teaspoon Worcestershire sauce

◉ Line a 15-in. x 10-in. x 1-in. baking pan with foil and grease the foil. In a small bowl, combine all the ingredients; spread into the prepared pan. Bake the pumpkin seeds at 250° for 45-50 minutes, stirring occasionally.

◉ Increase heat to 325°. Bake 5 minutes longer or until seeds are dry and lightly browned. Serve warm, or cool before storing in an airtight container.

Yield: 2 cups.

KITCHEN TIP

Salt is a flavor enhancer in most recipes. You can easily eliminate the salt from Roasted Pumpkin Seeds if you're following a low-sodium diet. Try adding herbs or spices to make up for the missing salt.

SALT: RDA-MKE

GRUYERE MASHED POTATOES

Gruyere cheese and chives take mashed potatoes to a whole new level in this party-special side dish. Don't have chives on hand? Simply use extra green onion instead.
—**Salsarose** *TasteofHome.com*

QUICK & EASY

PREP/TOTAL TIME: 25 MIN.

- 2 pounds potatoes, peeled and cubed
- ½ cup sour cream
- ⅓ cup milk
- ¼ cup butter, cubed
- ¼ cup shredded Gruyere *or* Swiss cheese
- ¼ cup chopped green onions
- ¼ cup minced chives
- 1 teaspoon minced garlic
- ½ teaspoon garlic salt
- ¼ teaspoon pepper

- Place potatoes in a Dutch oven and cover with water. Bring to a boil. Reduce heat; cover and cook for 10-15 minutes or until tender. Drain.

- In a large bowl, mash potatoes with remaining ingredients.

Yield: 8 servings.

PESTO-PEPPER CHEESE SPREAD

I always get tons of recipe requests whenever I bring this zippy spread to a party. Use convenient store-bought pesto or your favorite homemade version.
—**Lara Pennell** *Mauldin, South Carolina*

PREP: 25 MIN. + CHILLING

- 2 packages (8 ounces *each*) cream cheese, softened
- 2 cups crumbled goat cheese
- 2 tablespoons olive oil
- 1 teaspoon dried thyme
- 2 garlic cloves, minced
- 3 tablespoons prepared pesto
- 1/3 cup chopped roasted sweet red peppers

Assorted crackers *or* sliced French bread baguette

- In a large bowl, combine the cream cheese, goat cheese, oil, thyme and garlic.

- Line a 1-qt. bowl with plastic wrap. Place a third of the cheese mixture in bowl; top with pesto, half of the remaining cheese mixture, the peppers and remaining cheese mixture. Cover and refrigerate for at least 3 hours.

- Invert cheese mixture onto a serving plate; discard the plastic wrap. Serve spread with crackers.

Yield: 3 cups.

ROASTED CITRUS & HERB TURKEY

Thanksgiving has never been the same since I tried this recipe. I have made it for the past couple of years, and it never fails to impress both in presentation and taste. This is a true showstopper!
—**Nancy Niemerg** *Dieterich, Illinois*

PREP: 30 MIN. **BAKE:** 2¾ HOURS

1 turkey (14 to 16 pounds)	1 medium orange, quartered
¼ cup butter, softened	3 fresh rosemary sprigs
2 tablespoons Italian seasoning	3 sprigs fresh sage
2 teaspoons salt	3 cups chicken broth, *divided*
2 teaspoons pepper	¼ cup all-purpose flour
1 large onion, quartered	Additional citrus fruits and herb sprigs, optional
1 medium lemon, quartered	

◦ Pat turkey dry. Combine butter and Italian seasoning. With fingers, carefully loosen skin from the turkey breast; rub half of the butter under skin. Rub remaining mixture over the skin. Rub cavity with salt and pepper and fill with onion, lemon, orange, rosemary and sage. Skewer turkey openings; tie drumsticks together. Place breast side up on a rack in a roasting pan. Pour 2 cups broth into pan.

◦ Bake at 325° for 2¾ to 3¼ hours or until a thermometer reads 180°, basting occasionally with pan drippings. Cover loosely with foil if turkey browns too quickly. Cover turkey and let stand for 20 minutes before carving.

◦ Pour drippings into a small saucepan; skim fat. Combine flour and remaining broth until smooth; whisk into the pan. Bring to a boil; cook and stir for 2 minutes or until thickened.

◦ Discard onion, lemon, orange and herbs from the turkey; transfer turkey to a serving platter. Garnish the platter with additional citrus fruits and herb sprigs if desired.

Yield: 14-16 servings (2 cups gravy).

JEWELED FRUITCAKE

I promise this jeweled fruitcake is simply fantastic. Even my friends and family members who don't normally care for fruitcake say they love it!
—**Sharon Hoffman** *Donna, Texas*

PREP: 30 MIN. **BAKE:** 1 HOUR + COOLING

- 2 packages (8 ounces *each*) pitted dates, chopped
- ½ pound pecan halves
- ½ pound Brazil nuts
- 1 jar (10 ounces) red maraschino cherries, well drained
- 1 jar (10 ounces) green maraschino cherries, well drained
- ½ cup flaked coconut
- 1½ cups all-purpose flour
- 1½ cups sugar
- 1 teaspoon baking powder
- 1 teaspoon salt
- 3 eggs
- 2 teaspoons vanilla extract

○ Line four greased and floured 5-3/4-in. x 3-in. x 2-in. loaf pans with waxed paper and grease the paper; set aside.

○ In a large bowl, combine the dates, nuts, cherries and coconut. Combine the flour, sugar, baking powder and salt; stir into fruit mixture until well coated.

○ In a small bowl, beat eggs and vanilla until foamy. Fold into fruit mixture and mix well. Pour into prepared pans.

○ Bake at 300° for 60-70 minutes or until a toothpick inserted near the center comes out clean. Cool for 10 minutes before removing from pans to wire racks to cool completely. Wrap tightly and store in a cool dry place. Cut with a serrated knife.

EDITOR'S NOTE: Fruitcake may be baked in two greased and floured 8-in. x 4-in. loaf pans lined with waxed paper at 300° for 70-80 minutes or until a toothpick inserted near the center comes out clean.

Yield: 4 mini loaves (6 slices each).

CHOCOLATE PEPPERMINT SCONES

Try my decadent scones for breakfast, brunch or as a snack served with coffee. Festively decked out in red and white peppermint candy, these are something to celebrate!
—**Shelly Platten** *Amherst, Wisconsin*

PREP: 25 MIN. **BAKE:** 20 MIN.

- 2 cups all-purpose flour
- ½ cup whole wheat pastry flour
- ½ cup baking cocoa
- ½ cup packed brown sugar
- 2 teaspoons baking powder
- 1 teaspoon baking soda
- ½ cup cold butter, cubed
- ¾ cup (6 ounces) vanilla yogurt
- ½ cup buttermilk
- 1 egg
- 1 teaspoon peppermint extract
- 1 cup 60% cacao bittersweet chocolate baking chips
- 1 tablespoon coarse sugar
- 2 ounces bittersweet chocolate, melted
- ¼ cup crushed peppermint candies

○ In a large bowl, combine the first six ingredients. Cut in butter until mixture resembles coarse crumbs. In a small bowl, whisk the yogurt, buttermilk, egg and extract; add to crumb mixture just until moistened. Stir in chocolate chips.

○ Turn onto a floured surface; knead 10 times. Divide dough in half; transfer each portion to a greased baking sheet. Pat into a 6-in. circle. Cut into six wedges, but do not separate. Sprinkle with sugar.

○ Bake at 400° for 18-20 minutes or until puffed and tops are cracked. Remove to wire racks; cool slightly. Drizzle with melted chocolate and sprinkle with peppermint candies. Serve warm.

Yield: 1 dozen.

ORANGE-CRANBERRY COFFEE CAKES

These wonderful coffee cakes are packed with the zesty flavors of cranberries and orange. They make a pretty addition to a Christmas morning brunch.
—**Loraine E. Meyer** *Bend, Oregon*

PREP: 40 MIN. + RISING **BAKE:** 20 MIN. + COOLING

- ½ cup sugar
- 1 package (1/4 ounce) active dry yeast
- 1¼ teaspoons salt
- 4 to 4½ cups all-purpose flour
- 1 cup 2% milk
- ½ cup butter, cubed
- ¼ cup water
- 1 egg

FILLING:
- 1 cup fresh *or* frozen cranberries, thawed
- ¼ cup sugar
- ¼ cup chopped walnuts
- ¼ cup dark corn syrup
- 1 tablespoon grated orange peel
- ¼ teaspoon ground ginger

ICING:
- 2½ cups confectioners' sugar
- 3 tablespoons plus 1 teaspoon orange juice
- ¼ cup toasted chopped walnuts

⊙ In a large bowl, combine the sugar, yeast, salt and 2-1/2 cups flour. In a small saucepan, heat the milk, butter and water to 120°-130°. Add to dry ingredients; beat just until moistened. Add egg; beat until smooth. Stir in enough remaining flour to form a stiff dough.

⊙ Turn onto a floured surface; knead until smooth and elastic, about 6-8 minutes. Place in a greased bowl, turning once to grease the top. Cover and let rise in a warm place until doubled, about 1 hour.

⊙ Place cranberries in a blender; cover and process until chopped. Drain well; discard liquid from cranberries. In a small bowl, combine cranberries with the remaining filling ingredients. Set aside.

⊙ Punch down dough; turn onto a lightly floured surface. Divide in half. Roll each half into a 16-in. x 10-in. rectangle; spread with filling to within 1 in. of edges. Roll up each jelly-roll style, starting with a long side; seal seams. Place in greased 15-in. x 10-in. x 1-in. baking pans; shape ends to form crescent shapes.

⊙ With kitchen scissors or a small sharp knife, cut a lengthwise slit down the center of each loaf, ½ in. deep and stopping 2 in. from the ends.

⊙ Cover loaves and let rise in a warm place until doubled, about 30 minutes. Bake at 350° for 20-25 minutes or until golden brown. Remove from pans to wire racks to cool.

⊙ Combine confectioners' sugar and orange juice; drizzle over coffee cakes. Top with walnuts; press onto icing to secure.

Yield: 2 coffee cakes (12 servings each).

NO-BAKE COOKIE BALLS

My pop-in-your-mouth bites are just the thing when you're short on time or don't want to turn on the oven. I make them a day or two ahead to let the flavors blend.
—**Carmeletta Dailey** *Winfield, Texas*

QUICK & EASY

PREP: 20 MIN. + STANDING

- 1 cup (6 ounces) semisweet chocolate chips
- 3 cups confectioners' sugar
- 1¾ cups crushed vanilla wafers (about 55 wafers)
- 1 cup chopped walnuts, toasted
- ⅓ cup orange juice
- 3 tablespoons light corn syrup

Additional confectioners' sugar

⊙ In a large microwave-safe bowl, melt chocolate chips; stir until smooth. Stir in the confectioners' sugar, vanilla wafers, walnuts, orange juice and corn syrup.

⊙ Roll into 1-in. balls; roll in additional confectioners' sugar. Let stand until set. Store in an airtight container.

Yield: 5 dozen.

ITALIAN CHRISTMAS COOKIES

A single batch of these mouthwatering cookies is never enough. I usually make at least one to give away and two more to keep at home. Adding ricotta cheese to the batter makes the morsels extra-moist.
—**Doris Marshall** *Strasburg, Pennsylvania*

PREP: 25 MIN. **BAKE:** 10 MIN./BATCH + COOLING

1 cup butter, softened	1 teaspoon baking soda
2 cups sugar	FROSTING:
3 eggs	¼ cup butter, softened
1 carton (15 ounces) ricotta cheese	3 to 4 cups confectioners' sugar
2 teaspoons vanilla extract	½ teaspoon vanilla extract
4 cups all-purpose flour	3 to 4 tablespoons milk
1 teaspoon salt	Colored sprinkles

○ In a bowl, cream butter and sugar. Add the eggs, one at a time, beating well after each addition. Beat in ricotta and vanilla. Combine flour, salt and baking soda; gradually add to creamed mixture.

○ Drop by rounded teaspoonfuls 2 in. apart onto greased baking sheets. Bake at 350° for 10-12 minutes or until lightly browned. Remove to wire racks to cool.

○ In a bowl, cream butter, sugar and vanilla. Add enough milk until frosting reaches spreading consistency. Frost cooled cookies and immediately decorate with sprinkles. Store in the refrigerator.

Yield: 8½ dozen.

❝These cookies have become a huge tradition in our family. My dad doesn't even wait for them to cool—he just starts poppin' them in!❞

—**BECKIBOO** FROM TASTEOFHOME.COM

WHITE CHOCOLATE PEPPERMINT FUDGE

I make several batches of my white chocolate fudge to give as Christmas gifts. It's not too sweet, and the peppermint candies are colorful, crunchy and festive.
—Sue Schindler *Barnesville, Minnesota*

PREP: 10 MIN. **COOK:** 10 MIN. + CHILLING

- 1½ teaspoons plus ¼ cup butter, softened, *divided*
- 2 cups sugar
- ½ cup sour cream
- 12 squares (1 ounce *each*) white baking chocolate, chopped
- 1 jar (7 ounces) marshmallow cream
- ½ cup crushed peppermint candy
- ½ teaspoon peppermint extract

○ Line a 9-in. square pan with foil. Grease the foil with 1½ teaspoons butter; set aside.

○ In a large heavy saucepan, combine the sugar, sour cream and remaining butter. Cook and stir over medium heat until sugar is dissolved. Bring to a rapid boil; cook and stir until a candy thermometer reads 234° (soft-ball stage), about 5 minutes.

○ Remove from the heat; stir in white chocolate and marshmallow creme until melted. Fold in peppermint candy and extract. Pour into prepared pan. Chill until firm.

○ Using foil, lift fudge out of pan. Gently peel off foil; cut fudge into 1-in. squares. Store in the refrigerator.

EDITOR'S NOTE: We recommend that you test your candy thermometer before each use by bringing water to a boil; the thermometer should read 212°. Adjust your recipe temperature up or down based on your test.

Yield: 2 pounds.

PEPPERMINT MELTAWAYS

These minty little bites are so pretty and Christmasy on a holiday cookie platter—or sitting on a plate covered with red or green plastic wrap with a bright bow in one corner. And, yes, they really do melt in your mouth!
—Denise Wheeler *Newaygo, Michigan*

PREP: 30 MIN. **BAKE:** 10 MIN./BATCH + COOLING

- 1 cup butter, softened
- ½ cup confectioners' sugar
- ½ teaspoon peppermint extract
- 1¼ cups all-purpose flour
- ½ cup cornstarch

FROSTING:
- 2 tablespoons butter, softened
- 1½ cups confectioners' sugar
- 2 tablespoons 2% milk
- ¼ teaspoon peppermint extract
- 2 to 3 drops red food coloring, optional
- ½ cup crushed peppermint candies

○ In a small bowl, cream butter and confectioners' sugar until light and fluffy. Beat in extract. Combine flour and cornstarch; gradually add to creamed mixture and mix well.

○ Shape into 1-in. balls. Place 2 in. apart on ungreased baking sheets. Bake at 350° for 10-12 minutes or until bottoms are lightly browned. Remove to wire racks to cool.

○ In a small bowl, beat butter until fluffy. Add the confectioners' sugar, milk, extract and food coloring if desired; beat until smooth. Spread over cooled cookies; sprinkle with crushed candies. Store in an airtight container.

Yield: 3½ dozen.

GENERAL INDEX

This handy index lists every recipe by food category, major ingredient and/or cooking method, so you can easily locate recipes to suit your needs.

p. 162

p. 29

p. 133

p. 76

p. 59

CHEESECAKES

CHERRIES

CHICKEN

CHOCOLATE

p. 204

p. 172

p. 111

p. 78

p. 112

p. 213

p. 59

This handy index lists every recipe in alphabetical order so you can easily find your favorite recipes.

p. 163

p. 99

p. 153

p. 71

p. 115

p. 31

p. 201

p. 79

p. 209

GET COOKING WITH A WELL-STOCKED KITCHEN

In a perfect world you would plan out weekly or even monthly menus and have all the ingredients on hand to make each night's dinner. The reality, however, is you likely haven't thought about dinner until you've walked through the door.

With a reasonably stocked pantry, refrigerator and freezer, you'll still be able to serve a satisfying meal in short order. Consider these tips:

QUICK-COOKING MEATS like boneless chicken breasts, chicken thighs, pork tenderloin, pork chops, ground meats, Italian sausage, sirloin and flank steaks, fish fillets and shrimp should be stocked in the freezer. Wrap them individually (except shrimp), so you can remove only the amount you need. For the quickest defrosting, wrap meats for freezing in small, thin packages.

FROZEN VEGETABLES prepackaged in plastic bags are a real time-saver. Simply pour out the amount needed. No preparation is required!

PASTAS, RICE, RICE MIXES AND COUSCOUS are great staples to have in the pantry—and they generally have a long shelf life. Remember, thinner pastas, such as angel hair, cook faster than thicker pastas. Fresh (refrigerated) pasta cooks faster than dried.

DAIRY PRODUCTS like milk, sour cream, cheeses (shredded, cubed or crumbled), eggs, yogurt and butter or margarine are more perishable, so check the use-by date on the packages and replace as needed.

CONDIMENTS such as ketchup, mustard, mayonnaise, salad dressings, salsa, taco sauce, soy sauce, stir-fry sauce, lemon juice, etc. add flavor to many dishes. Personalize the list to suit your family's needs.

FRESH FRUIT AND VEGETABLES can make a satisfying predinner snack. Oranges and apples are not as perishable as bananas. Ready-to-use salad greens are great for an instant salad.

DRIED HERBS, SPICES, VINEGARS and seasoning mixes add lots of flavor and keep for months.

PASTA SAUCES, OLIVES, BEANS, broths, canned tomatoes, canned vegetables, and canned or dried soups are great to have on hand for a quick meal...and many of these items are common recipe ingredients.

GET YOUR FAMILY INTO THE HABIT of posting a grocery list. When an item is used up or is almost gone, just add it to your list for the next shopping trip. This way you won't completely run out of an item, and you'll also save time when writing your grocery list.

MAKE THE MOST OF YOUR TIME EVERY NIGHT

With recipes in hand and your kitchen stocked, you're well on your way to a relaxing family meal. Here are some pointers to help you get dinner on the table fast:

WHEN USING AN OVEN OR GRILL, preheat it before starting on the recipe.

PULL OUT ALL THE INGREDIENTS, mixing tools and cooking tools before beginning any prep work.

WHENEVER POSSIBLE, use convenience items, such as prechopped garlic, onion and peppers, shredded or cubed cheese, seasoning mixes, jarred sauces, etc.

MULTI-TASK! While the meat is simmering for a main dish, toss a salad, cook a side dish or start on dessert.

ENCOURAGE HELPERS. Have younger children set the table. Older ones can help with ingredient preparation or even assemble simple recipes themselves.

TAKE CARE OF TWO MEALS IN ONE NIGHT by planning main dish leftovers or making a double batch of favorite sides.

TRICKS TO TAME HUNGER WHEN IT STRIKES

Are the kids begging for a presupper snack? Calm rumbling tummies with some nutritious, yet not too filling noshes.

START WITH A SMALL TOSSED SALAD. Try a ready-to-serve salad mix and add their favorite salad dressing and a little protein like cubed cheese or julienned slices of deli meat.

CUT UP AN APPLE and smear a little peanut butter on each slice. Or offer other fruits such as seedless grapes, cantaloupe, oranges or bananas. For variety, give kids a vanilla yogurt or reduced-fat ranch dressing as a dipper for the fruit or combine a little reduced-fat sour cream with a sprinkling of brown sugar. Too tired to cut up the fruit? A fruit snack cup will do the trick, too.

DURING THE COLD MONTHS, a small mug of soup with a few oyster crackers will hit the spot.

RAW VEGGIES, such as carrots, cucumbers, mushrooms, broccoli and cauliflower, are tasty treats, especially when served with a little reduced-fat dressing for dipping. Plus, many of these vegetables can be purchased precut.

GIVE KIDS A SMALL SERVING of cheese and crackers. Look for presliced cheese and cut the slices into smaller squares to fit the crackers. Choose a cracker that is made from whole wheat, such as an all-natural, 7-grain cracker.

INGREDIENT SUBSTITUTIONS

WHEN YOU NEED:	IN THIS AMOUNT:	SUBSTITUTE:
Baking Powder	1 teaspoon	½ teaspoon cream of tartar plus ¼ teaspoon baking soda
Broth	1 cup	1 cup hot water plus 1 teaspoon bouillon granules *or* 1 bouillon cube
Buttermilk	1 cup	1 tablespoon lemon juice *or* white vinegar plus enough milk to measure 1 cup; let stand 5 minutes. *Or* 1 cup plain yogurt.
Cajun Seasoning	1 teaspoon	¼ teaspoon cayenne pepper, ½ teaspoon dried thyme, ¼ teaspoon dried basil and 1 minced garlic clove
Chocolate, Semisweet	1 square (1 ounce)	1 square (1 ounce) unsweetened chocolate plus 1 tablespoon sugar *or* 3 tablespoons semisweet chocolate chips
Chocolate	1 square (1 ounce)	3 tablespoons baking cocoa plus 1 tablespoon shortening *or* canola oil
Cornstarch	1 tablespoon	2 tablespoons all-purpose flour (for thickening)
Corn Syrup, Dark	1 cup	¾ cup light corn syrup plus ¼ cup molasses
Corn Syrup, Light	1 cup	1 cup sugar plus ¼ cup water
Cracker Crumbs	1 cup	1 cup dry bread crumbs
Cream, Half-and-Half	1 cup	1 tablespoon melted butter plus enough whole milk to measure 1 cup
Egg	1 whole	2 egg whites *or* 2 egg yolks *or* ¼ cup egg substitute
Flour, Cake	1 cup	1 cup minus 2 tablespoons (⅞ cup) all-purpose flour
Flour, Self-Rising	1 cup	1-½ teaspoons baking powder, ½ teaspoon salt and enough all-purpose flour to measure 1 cup
Garlic, Fresh	1 clove	⅛ teaspoon garlic powder
Gingerroot, Fresh	1 teaspoon	¼ teaspoon ground ginger
Honey	1 cup	1-¼ cups sugar plus ¼ cup water
Lemon Juice	1 teaspoon	¼ teaspoon cider vinegar
Lemon Peel	1 teaspoon	½ teaspoon lemon extract
Milk, Whole	1 cup	½ cup evaporated milk plus ½ cup water *or* 1 cup water plus ⅓ cup nonfat dry milk powder
Molasses	1 cup	1 cup honey
Mustard, Prepared	1 tablespoon	½ teaspoon ground mustard plus 2 teaspoons cider *or* white vinegar
Onion	1 small onion	1 teaspoon onion powder *or* 1 tablespoon dried minced onion (⅓ cup chopped)
Poultry Seasoning	1 teaspoon	¾ teaspoon rubbed sage plus ¼ teaspoon dried thyme
Sour Cream	1 cup	1 cup plain yogurt
Sugar	1 cup	1 cup packed brown sugar *or* 2 cups sifted confectioners' sugar
Tomato Juice	1 cup	½ cup tomato sauce plus ½ cup water
Tomato Sauce	2 cups	¾ cup tomato paste plus 1 cup water
Yeast	1 package (¼ ounce) active dry	1 cake (⅝ ounce) compressed yeast